A Residence in Tasmania

Eb4

Allport, Esq delt Smith, Elder & Co London

WATER-FALL ON THE GORDON.

A

RESIDENCE IN TASMANIA :

WITH

A DESCRIPTIVE TOUR

THROUGH THE ISLAND,

FROM

MACQUARIE HARBOUR TO CIRCULAR HEAD.

BY

CAPT. H. BUTLER STONEY,

99TH REGIMENT. AUTHOR OF "FIVE YEARS IN THE LEVANT," ETC. ETC.

"Comme je trouve."

LONDON :

SMITH, ELDER, & CO., 65, CORNHILL.

1856.

LONDON:
Printed by SMITH, ELDER, & CO., 15, Old Bailey.

TO THE RIGHT HONORABLE

HENRY LABOUCHERE, M.P.,

SECRETARY OF STATE FOR THE COLONIES;

WHOSE EXTENSIVE ACQUIREMENTS

AND DEVOTION TO HIS COUNTRY'S WELFARE

HAVE BEEN CONSPICUOUSLY SHEWN

IN HIS EARNEST EFFORTS TO PROMOTE

THE ADVANCEMENT OF THE BRITISH COLONIES,

NOW RISING INTO GREATNESS;

THIS WORK

IS (WITH PERMISSION)

RESPECTFULLY DEDICATED,

BY HIS OBLIGED AND HUMBLE SERVANT,

THE AUTHOR.

PREFACE.

In the Mother Country, Van Diemen's Land bears a very bad name, on account of its having been for many years a penal settlement: its very name is associated with chains and crime. It was therefore wise and politic to change its name for the more euphonious one of Tasmania.

The author of this work (a simple narrative of facts, having no pretensions and aiming only at truth) has undertaken the task of laying before the British public the present condition and state of the Island, in the earnest hope that some of those prejudices now so common against Van Diemen's Land may be lessened, if not removed.

Little is known of Tasmania beyond its repute as a convict settlement; but five years have now elapsed since it ceased to be one; and as the traces of its former state are fast disappearing, it is to be hoped that the recollection of it will also vanish. The free-born sons of Britain have flocked to its shores, carrying with them the noble characteristics of the mother country, and by their unceasing perseverance and industry adding to the lustre of their race.

The author has spared no pains to render this edition worthy of the objects he had in view; namely, to call attention to those daring pioneers in the far South whose indomitable energies have earned for them an imperishable reputation, and to make known the advantages offered by this colony as a field for emigration: and every care has been taken to make it a safe book of reference on all matters appertaining to Tasmania.

CORK, *July*, 1856.

CONTENTS.

LIST OF ILLUSTRATIONS.

ERRATUM.

Page 266, line 3, *for* "sassafracor, *Athnosperma moschata*," *read* "sassafras, or *Atherosperma moschata*."

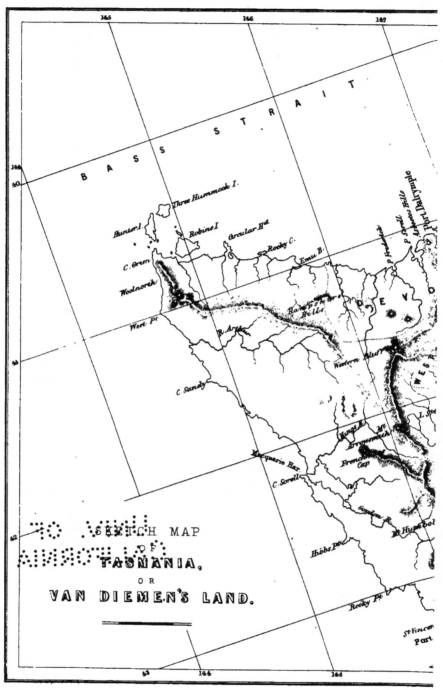

SKETCH MAP
OF
TASMANIA,
OR
VAN DIEMEN'S LAND.

London Smith, E.

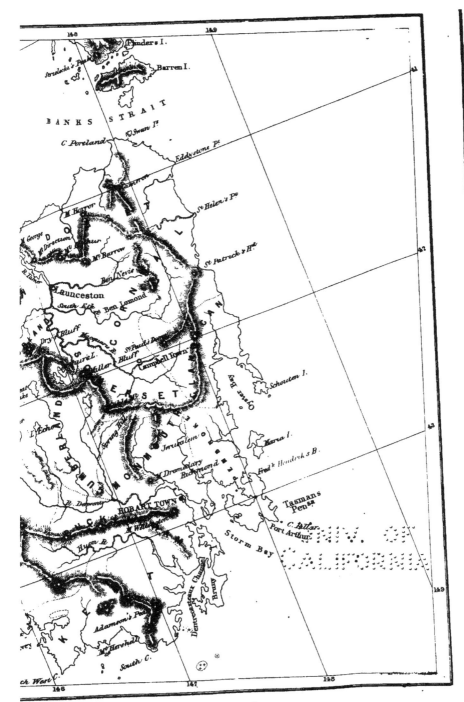

r & Cº 65, Cornhill

A

RESIDENCE IN TASMANIA.

CHAPTER I.

O'er the glad waters of the dark blue sea,
Our thoughts as boundless and our souls as free,
Far as the breeze can bear, the billows roam,
Survey our empire, and behold our home !

THE CORSAIR.

THERE are few delights so entrancing as the blue outline of land to the sea-tossed landsman. After having passed weary months, the sport of every storm, upon that long and tedious way from the chalk cliffs of " merry England " to the green hills of Tasmania ; with what feelings of pleasure does he watch the rising mountain tops, as the gallant ship flies onward, and each headland grows more and more distinct as she approaches the long-looked for shore ! The step of the voyager becomes freer and firmer, his spirits more buoyant and elastic, and

1

he feels an impatient eagerness to set foot on that land which now appears one large and picturesque domain to his longing eyes.

There is no land in the world that appears more lovely than this Island,—whether it be from the length of time during which voyagers have nothing but the wild waste of waters before them; or from the very bold and romantic formation of the high lands above Macquarie Harbour (which are often those first made) and the peculiar vegetation and aspect of the long line of country extending along D'Entrecasteaux Channel and round the entrance to Storm Bay; or from the contrast of the impressions now felt, with those formerly produced by the hated words a 'penal settlement,' one cannot decide : such, however, is the case. It invariably happens that the stranger is at once captivated by the first glance of this—in very truth—most beautiful island.

Macquarie Harbour, famous as the principal source of the Huon Pine, and which is often the first point the outward bound makes, was in former years a settlement; but it is now no longer inhabited, save by a few hardy sawyers, who face the hardships of a bush life, and earn no trifling amount by the cutting of timber, which the tough-built coasting vessels carry to market, at Hobarton or Launceston — not at all times without risk and danger; the swell on this side of the island being very heavy, even in fine weather. The harbour itself is, however, safe and commodious, and of great extent; being, in fact, a land-locked arm of the sea.

The heads of Macquarie Harbour are in latitude 42·14 S. and longitude 145·10 E. From the heads an estuary extends for a distance of about six and twenty miles in a south-easterly direction. It is here terminated by the Gordon River meeting it; although it branches off to the southward into Birch's Inlet, and to the northward into Kelly's Basin. On the south head from the entrance were formerly a signal station and a pilot station, which are now dismantled. The settlement was formed on a small island twenty-five miles from the 'Gates,' or entrance, and continued to be the double or most severe convict station, from the 2nd January, 1822, (the day the first party landed under Lieut. Cuthbertson, of the 48th Regiment,) until November, 1833, when it was partly abandoned: it finally ceased to be a settlement on the 11th January, 1834.*

A gold digging expedition was sent from Hobarton through Macquarie Harbour, in the 'Gem,' on the 12th December, 1854. It was fitted out by a number of merchants in Hobarton, who had

---

* Were it not the object of this work to speak only of the present, there are several interesting anecdotes relative to this settlement still unpublished, and which the author discovered amongst a pile of papers placed in his possession, and intended for the press by the late lamented Assistant Commissary-General Lempriere. However, as from those papers he intends to lay before the public a work of much interest at some early date, he must now return to the subject matter in hand.

received a report that gold was to be found in that locality. The party took up their residence in the deserted buildings of the settlement on the island, from whence they made exploring excursions all through the neighbourhood. On first landing they found a piece of gold on the shore, but were not so fortunate in their subsequent researches: in short, the expedition returned to Hobarton a failure.

Although the high range of hills behind Macquarie Harbour is often the first land made by the outward bound, still it is by no means a favourite course; the better one being far more to the southward, so as to make South Cape or Tasman's Head the first land, by which a clear run is obtained into Storm Bay, and the baffling winds prevalent along the western shore are avoided. The most common object, however, to glad the longing gaze of the mariner is Pedro Blanco, a rock some twenty miles to sea, southward of South Cape, and bearing the exact resemblance to a ship: indeed, so perfect is the illusion that it is quite impossible to decide whether it be really a ship or a rock, till coming quite close; for, if made early in the day, the sunbeams on the white rock give it the appearance of a vessel shifting sail. Above this, nearer in shore to the westward, are several dangerous rocks and some shoal water; so that in all cases the more offing there is to the southward the better.

After rounding the South Cape, the very magnificent estuary of D'Entrecasteaux Channel opens, and scenery unequalled in the world is spread before your gaze : for, extending far away before you, this arm of the sea runs into the defiles; a beautifully undulating land stretches far to the westward; and, in the background, Mount Wellington rises majestic over all, with its snow-capped peak. Again, to the eastward, is the thickly timbered and verdant island of Bruni, and the entrance round its point to Storm Bay, which your barque is hastening to with a fresh and favourable breeze,—for during nine months out of the twelve, fair breezes welcome the stranger to these shores.

There are numerous fine harbours in D'Entre-casteaux Channel, and good anchorage all round. A very good lighthouse, on the eastern cape of the inlet called Bruni Head, may be seen at a great distance, and is a sure mark by which the Acteon Reef may be avoided.

In the channel the soundings are regular, and the shores bold; and there are three harbours, often used for refitting, watering, etc.,—Recherche, Muscle, and Esperance Bays. The shores are extremely beautiful, and the vegetation luxuriant; the dingy green colour of the foliage, which so much surprises at first, the stranger soon gets accustomed to, so as to forget the rich and varied verdure of our own forests. The general outline is most picturesque; and the first impression on seeing this lovely land

stretching out before you is,—pity that thousands in
England, who have hardly sufficient to subsist upon
from day to day, should not come to a land where
their labour would soon raise them to independence
and comfort—to a land whose scenery and climate
are equal to, if they do not surpass, the most
healthy and admired parts of Great Britain.

The scenery of the Huon is still of a richer
character. Its banks are clothed with the loftiest
and most valuable timber of the colony: some of
the trees measure from 180 to 200 feet in height,
and 28 to 30 in circumference. It is gratifying,
also, to know that the land which bears such
splendid timber has equally rich and productive
soil, and that it fully repays the settler, by the
abundance it yields under moderately good management, for the great labour required in clearing at
the outset.

Rounding the Friars you enter Storm Bay, so
called from its exposure to the stormy gales of the
wide ocean to the south; yet it is by no means
dangerous, as you soon make the Iron Pot Light,
and, rounding the point of the island, pass the
lower entrance of D'Entrecasteaux Channel, and
sail up the romantic and splendid river Derwent.
The distance from the Iron Pot to Hobarton is
twelve miles; and to the bay over which the city
hangs, the Derwent can scarcely be called a river,
but rather a succession of deep indented bays, until

you round Sandy Point, when a view unequalled in the world presents itself.

Tasmania was first discovered by Tasman, the Dutch navigator, who called it Van Diemen's Land in honour of his father-in-law, Van Diemen; it is, therefore, but a just tribute to its first discoverer for it to bear the name of Tasmania, which by a late Act of the British Government has been duly authorized. Tasman hove in sight of the bold shores of Storm Bay on the 24th November, 1642, and cast anchor the 1st December; remaining there a few days, he landed and made a short excursion in the interior, but was not prepossessed with its appearance. It was afterwards visited by Cook in 1777, who remained some time in Recherche Bay, and spoke more favourably of it than his predecessor. It did not become a British Colony till 1804, when, Governor Collins finding the settlement of Port Philip a failure, removed in the February of that year, and made the first settlement at Risdonferry, so called from Rest-Down.

The Governor-General from Sydney (General Lackland Macquarie) made a visit to Tasmania on the 23rd November, 1811. He landed in Sullivan's Cove, and caused a regular plan to be made of a proposed town; giving it the name of Hobart Town, after the name of Lord Hobart, then Secretary to the Colonies. He also established a signal-post on Mount Nelson. He next crossed the country to Port

Dalrymple, as Launceston was then called, taking fifteen days to get there. A camp had been formed here, but he disapproved of the site, and ordered it to be removed to York Town, at the right bank of the entrance to the Tamar; this locality he describes in glowing terms, and assimilates the scenery to that of Mount Edgecombe in Cornwall. He also established military posts through the island, and then returned to Sydney.

These settlements were under the New South Wales Government until 1825. Colonel Davey succeeded Colonel Colling in 1813; Colonel Sorell, in 1817; Colonel Arthur, in 1824; Sir John Franklin, in 1837; Sir J. Eardley Wilmot, in 1843; Sir W. T. Denison, in 1847; and Sir H. Fox Young, in 1855.

The country is 250 miles in extreme length, and 200 in width; it contains 24,000 square miles, or 15,000,000 acres, of which 150,000 are under cultivation. The population is 100,000 : there are about a dozen of the aborigines still alive at Osyter Cove; which we shall describe hereafter. The climate is considered one of the healthiest in the world.

The early history of Van Diemen's Land is one of crime and misery. The destruction of crops in New South Wales by the flood of Hawkesbury left the new settlement without succour, and nothing was issued from the public stores for some months. The country districts were ravaged by troops of

armed bush-rangers: in vain were the terrors of
the law employed. Governor Davey then placed the
colony under martial law. The stern discipline and
good example of Colonel Arthur checked the evil,
and made the island the abode of peace and safety.
After this the commercial interest received attention,
for we find that the exports, which only amounted in
1819 to £20,000, in the following year amounted
to £33,000. From the earliest records we find
some attempt at literature by the issue of a paper
called the 'Derwent Star' in 1810, and 'Bent's
Hobart Gazette' in 1816.

In 1840 the probation system was introduced,
whereby the prisoners served a certain portion of
their time in working gangs, apart from the ordinary
population. At the earnest appeal of the settlers
for the cessation of transportation, Tasmania ceased
to be a penal settlement in the early part of 1853 ;
from which period the convict establishment has
been gradually reduced. Port Arthur is still kept
complete for the punishment of criminals transported
for life ; and it is the intention of the Government
to retain that station alone, whither the criminals
of the colony can in future be sent. As the transported felons are daily diminishing in numbers, in a
few years the remnants of the system will have
disappeared.

CHAPTER II.

Time has but touch'd, not seal'd in gloom,
The turrets of almighty Rome:
The same deep stream which toss'd of yore
The infants in their ark ashore,
Whose power, since deified, has piled,
This seven-hill'd city in the wild.

. . . . . . ROGERS.

WE should not wish to prognosticate for the seven-hilled city of Hobarton, a fate similar to that of Rome, either in reference to its grandeur or its fall; indeed the comparison ceases with its seven hills; yet there are few cities in the world that look more imposing than the capital of Tasmania. Beholding it, at early morn, from the vessel which has been your home for weary months, and just as the autumn sun gilds the summit of that most peculiarly cut hill on the Richmond side (which seems as if sliced perpendicularly from its summit), throwing its shadow over the city and the tran-

quil waters at its base, while a deep belt of fleecy
cloud fondly lingers round "Knocklofty," or, driven from its rest, and warmed with the rosy tints
of morning, it wends its way to the still more
lofty peak of Mount Wellington; impressed by the
effulgent beauty of the fair scene, you stand en-
tranced with the view, and pronounce the panorama
perfect.

For a city of but fifty years' growth, none
ever equalled Hobarton in beauty, on a first view.
Yet, on a nearer inspection, it is found to have
many defects: the very irregularity of its streets,
which adds so much to its beauty, is a sad drawback
to the convenience of trade, to the cleanliness of
the city, and to the general comfort of its inhabitants; and we must in truth own, that though, as
regards general appearance and situation, Hobarton
stands pre-eminent in beauty as a city, yet the
stranger who enters its streets has reason to be disappointed, and cannot fail to remark a lack of order
and cleanliness. When one considers the means
which during fifty years were at the command of the
rulers of Tasmania, and the immense amount of convict labour ever at their disposal, it was matter
of surprise that the sideways remained so long
unflagged,—that there was no sewerage of the
town,—and that an open creek, still in its original
state, (fortunately, however, a running stream at all
seasons), should have been allowed to remain as

a receptacle for every nuisance, with imperfect bridges over it, and likely every season, after heavy rains, to threaten the city with an inundation most destructive to life and property. These evils, however, will soon vanish; and when we look at the large amount of capital in the city, and the daily increasing importance and general wealth of the community, we have a sufficient guarantee that, ere many seasons glide over, the interior of the city will correspond to the extreme beauty of the bird's-eye view.

Our prognostications relative to the interior of the city have been indeed already realized; for it has assumed a new appearance :—flagged side paths have been made through every street,—a general sewerage is in progress,—a gasometer partly built, and gas pipes laid down through the city. During the last session of Parliament, additional powers and money were granted to the Corporation, and also a bill brought in for the purpose of surveying a suitable line for a railroad to Launceston. Considering the wealth of the inhabitants of Hobarton, and the vast internal resources of the country, with such a spirit of improvement abroad, we may venture to assert that Hobarton will eventually rival any city in the south.

Sensible that, however true a description may be, and however correct in style and language, it

must, in most instances, fall short of reality, and
fail to convey to the mind the exact ideas the
author desires to convey—having vividly before him
the memory of what his eye so oft looked upon,—
we proceed in our description. From whatever
point you view Hobarton, it is fair to look upon:
it is situated, as before stated, on seven hills, within
an amphitheatre, as it were, formed by a higher
range rising above them, and terminating on its
north-west side in the lofty cone of Mount Wellington, full four thousand feet high. At its base, the
clear water of the Derwent glides gracefully away
round the public plaisance called the Domain, and
then, stretching away in sinuous bays, flows on to
the sea.

The bay above which the town is built forms a
splendid harbour; and, as there are quays and
docks built on three sides of it, ships of the largest
size can be warped alongside: commodious cranes
and deep wharves afford every facility to lading
and unlading merchandize. At the southern end
is the Signal-staff, on a gentle eminence, which
has communication with another higher up; and
this again communicates with one on Nelson-hill,
which commands the entrance to the town and
D'Entrecasteaux Channel.

From Mount Nelson, three miles from the city,
you have a commanding view of the two channels,
the Iron Pot Lighthouse, and Brown's River Station

(now in ruins), where formerly part of a regiment was quartered as a guard for a large depôt of convicts. Along the side of the river are several pretty farms and private residences, with well-cultivated fields around; and, on the distant bank, the same fertile and undulating land appears. A beautiful beach stretches towards the town, and the suburban villas of Sandy bay appear nestling under the hill-side, amid flowering gardens and rich shrubberies, with thickly-wooded ridges of high land behind, which gradually ascend, until they merge in the subordinate ranges of Mount Wellington. The view from the entrance into Davey-street, at early day, presents one of the most charming prospects in the world.

The approach from Brown's River is by a very fine road skirting along the bay, sometimes touching the beach and again crossing over some jutting headland, which forms the favourite drive and ride for the idle and gay of the city: it is also the principal, as well as the most healthy, promenade for the pedestrian. This road branches into two at the foot of a hill, one leading up the hill to the left into Davey and Macquarie-streets, and the other, skirting the Military Barracks, leads to the quays.

The pedestrian can still stroll along the beach, and, on ascending an uncultivated hill, and leaving St. George's Church on the left hand, he will pass the very pretty house and gardens of Mr. Perry, under whose residence are to be seen the dock-yards and ship-building establishments of Messrs. De Graves and others. This part is almost shut out from the other side of the town; yet it boasts of several well-built and comfortable houses, with neat gardens and a fine prospect of the sea. From St. George's Church

the road leads by Stowell, the residence of the Butler family—a fine house, with a splendid garden and green fields around, and well worthy of the title, "*rus in urbe.*"

Passing the charming residence of Mr. M'Naughten, you ascend the hill to the Military Barracks, which are commodious and well laid out: they embrace some twenty acres of land, enclosed with a timber paling. The buildings run along the brow and crown of the hill, leaving clear the eastern point,

on which stands a Signal-staff. Here is also
erected a neat Column built to commemorate the
officers and men who nobly fell in action against
the New Zealand insurgents in 1844. Around the
Signal-staff and Column is a promenade and exer-
cising ground, facing the Barrack-square; the men's
barracks forming the base, and the officers' quarters
the sides, of a parallelogram. Here the Band of
the Regiment often plays of an afternoon, when the
beauty and fashion of the city seldom fail to appear,
and in agreeable converse beguile the hours away;
making the exiled soldier fancy, with but little
stretch of the imagination, that he is still in his
own dear native land, beneath British skies, and
with Britain's brightest eyes around him.

From the Signal-staff you have perhaps the
finest view of Hobarton; and, as the setting sun
dips behind the lofty ridge of Mount Wellington,
it casts a deeper shade on the range of hills
around it, throwing out, in fine relief, the city
beneath. The most remarkable features are the
luxuriant gardens and vine-covered trellises, which
are universal appendages to all the houses not in the
half-dozen streets that form the centre of the town;
and, as the eye wanders from one hill to another, it
gladly rests on each pretty villa thus beautified by
flowering shrubs and fine gardens. In the centre of
the town, some few houses still have rich gardens

attached to them; but the increasing value of town land is fast covering them with wood and stone.

Government House is situated midway between the Domain and Barracks. It is in part a wooden building and of no architectural pretensions, but is surrounded with a fine shrubbery and good gardens.

The Custom House is the finest building in Hobarton : it stands on an esplanade, facing the bay and shipping, and is well situate and imposing, though of plain and simple architecture. It contains the Legislative Assembly Rooms, etc. Above it, on the hill, adjoining Government House and facing the Gaol in Murray Street, are the Court Houses, the Government Offices, Police Court, etc., which are still unfinished. Opposite to it is the Diocesan Church, which certainly does not look much like a Cathedral, and deserves to rank little, if at all, above a country church in England.

By a great mistake in the laying out of the town, the streets run at right angles and parallel to each other; and they are, in consequence of the hills over which they run, so steep in some places as to cause great drawbacks to speedy traffic—a matter of essential service in a trading town : if they had been laid out in terraces and crescents, it would have greatly added to the beauty of the city, and would have been of infinite advantage to trade, tending also to equalize the value of sites, now so exorbitant in one locality and moderate in another.

Within the past year, the New Market Place has been opened, and with much *éclat*. It is really a very fine building and well finished, having two large side entrances with elaborately worked iron gates, and a fine internal covered area, lined with side stalls, leaving a large space in the centre for moveable stalls, etc. There is also a centre gate, which opens upon a court intended for a Fish Market, in which there is a *jet-d'eau* which has a pleasing effect as you approach. This court is now used for the periodical Floral and Horticultural Shows, which are always well attended; and every encouragement is given by the Society to florists and gardeners, by award of considerable prizes. The only defect of the Market Place is its situation, being rather at the end of the town, near the Domain and facing the Commissariat Offices and Stores; it is, however, an object of much interest to the townsfolk; and they may be well proud of it.

There has been erected in the rear of the Market Place, on an open site granted by the Government for the purpose, a very elegant Temperance Hall, called St. Patrick's. It is built of hewn granite of light brown color, and has a very pleasing appearance, the style being Gothic. There are scarcely any public buildings of note except the Custom-house; the difficulty of procuring labour and the high price of building materials preventing additions to the number at the present time.

The funds of the town are scarcely adequate to
support its rising greatness; and the Corporation,
being but in its infancy, have not the means, or dare
not advance with the times.   Unfortunately, this
body is crippled in its power as well as its resources;
and can only raise. funds or levy taxes under the
authority of an act of the Legislative Council;
which, up to the present time, seems to be more
anxious to restrict its movements than to give it
free scope, in conformity with the views of the more
liberal and enlightened portion of the community.
These are, however, but evils of a day; and, as we
before remarked, are now rectified.   With increased
powers and funds at disposal, much improvement is
being made in the city.   Cabal may for awhile oc-
cupy the attention of the legislators, but it is to be
hoped, that, having amongst them men of talent,
wealth, and experience, the public good will in due
time outweigh every other consideration, and that
measures of a sound and liberal policy will be adopted, both in reference to the capital and the landed
interests of the Colony.

When we view dispassionately the difficulties
that have beset this Colony, through the baneful
effects of criminals for so many years introduced
from the Parent Country, it is a matter of unfeigned
surprise and admiration to see how the respectable
colonists have struggled on; and how, with all the
drawbacks incident to a penal settlement, they

have manfully conquered. Indeed, the society of Tasmania can at this hour be held up a bright example of correctness and purity even to the boasted society of " Father Land."

CHAPTER III.

Each side the midway path there lay
Small broken crags of granite grey,
By time or mountain lightning riven,
From summits clad in mists of heaven.

GIAOUR.

SUCH is oft the aspect of the giant hill that o'erlooks
the Tasmanian capital; and summer and winter
alike see it frequently clad with clouds. Sometimes
they hang over it, extending low along its wooded
sides — anon they sweep majestically across its
highest top and reveal its summit to your view, four
thousand two hundred feet above the level of the

sea. Though snow is very rarely seen in the plain,
yet for more than six months in the year, the summit of Mount Wellington, as shown in the preceding
sketch, is covered with it : an icehouse, built under
the crest, furnishes a sufficient supply during the
summer of this most grateful luxury. The labour
of ascending this mighty guardian of the city seems
almost too difficult to be overcome, still not a season
passes that parties do not ascend to its summit; and,
ever and anon, the more gentle sex, sustained by
spirit more than physical strength, conquer the difficulties of the way, and, having reached the table
land on the top, gaze with rapture on the rich
valley, the capacious bay, and the lordly city at
their feet.

Leaving the city by Macquarie or Davey-street,
you pass the " west end," where, on either side, are
embowered villas of much beauty, and gardens ever
filled with flowers ; for few cities can boast of finer
flower gardens or a longer continuance of their bloom
through every season than Hobarton. As you issue
from the head of these streets you skirt along the
valley by the Town Rivulet, and at the Cascades pass
the Female Penitentiary, which is worth inspecting,
from the extreme regularity and order with which it
is kept. Several mills are built over this mountain
stream, and a suburban village is growing up by
the road-side.

The last establishment on this road is the extensive brewery, house, and grounds of Mr. De Graves one of the wealthiest gentlemen in the Colony. Thence, you soon begin to wind up the hill-side, which seems at first sight almost perpendicular. Surmounting the first ascent, you come on a level, platform; and, again crossing it, ascend another; but a dense wood conceals all around from your view, till, after three or four ascents, you reach the first spur of the hill called the Springs. The way runs here along a cool and gushing streamlet for some distance, and you are gladly refreshed by its sweet water : this is the stream that supplies the city.

From this resting-place you have a very fine view of the windings of the Derwent into Storm Bay.

We fear that the skill of our artist fails, as indeed would that of any artist, in giving a just idea of this most magnificent view, which equals any we have seen in other parts of the world.

To ascend this hill is the favorite trip of the stranger; and, though the toil is great, it is more than repaid by the sublimity of the scene,—D'Entre-casteaux Channel, Brown's River, and the Huon seeming like silver threads amid the dense mass of foliage around. But you are only now half-way, and the ascent higher up is still more laborious; yet the view from this is so very grand that you gain fresh courage and hurry up the towering hill above you. Some level places afford rest to the weary feet; and, as you approach the top, the air becomes more rarefied, cool, and refreshing; at length you throw your exhausted frame on the highest rock, and rejoice that your difficult task is completed. The view from hence is transcendently beautiful; and though from the extreme height the city seems but small, yet the distant sea and all its sinuous bays and inlets, now easily scanned, are spread out like a living panorama before the eye, imposing and grand in the extreme.

On returning from the mountain-top, another excursion awaits you—a stroll to Fern Tree Valley, which the stranger will visit with much pleasure and interest. You reach it by branching off near Mr.

De Graves', from the main pathway up the Mount.

The curious formation of the fern-tree, its umbrella-like fronds, and its pretty grouping, give a very pleasing effect to the valley ; which is a favorite resort during the season for pic-nic parties and merry-makings.

On the opposite side of Hobarton is the Government Domain : there are two entrances to it from the town. A little above the upper entrance, on a rising ground, stands the High School, a building of some pretensions to architectural beauty, built in the Gothic style, and well-placed on the hill-side. At the lower entrance are the Royal Engineer's offices and stores ; and above them is an open grassy space of some extent, where the equestrian, while he breathes his steed, may survey the city spreading o'er hill and dale, from

the foot of the mountain to the very edge of the
bay, with the shipping at anchor in the harbour,
and laying quietly along the well-filled quays.

The Cricket Club have a very fine ground kept
in good order for them in the Domain.

Joining the Cricket Ground, on the bank of the
Derwent, is a piece of land leased to Mr. Goldsmith
by the Colonial Government, for the erection of a
patent Slip, which was brought to the Colony by
him in the year 1848, but was not erected until
1856, in consequence of delay in getting a proper
lease of the ground: it is now erected, and capable
of taking up sailing vessels or steamers of 1,000 tons
at high water, and one of 500 to 600 at low water,
with every capability of repairing any description of
vessel. The Slip is worked by steam power.

In 1848 the Twin Ferry Boat was laid down by
Mr. Goldsmith, of 480 tons, capable of taking four
loaded drays on her deck, besides her passengers.
It was, we believe, the intention of the late Lieut.-
Governor, Sir William Denison, to have cut a road
from Kangaroo Point through Jerusalem, to join the
Launceston main road; and the ferry boat was
intended to convey the traffic across the Derwent to
and from Hobarton.

The Twin Ferry Boat was completed about
twelve months since, but not delivered to the
Government until January last;—the reason of this
the Government is fully aware of. We believe it

arose from the non-fulfilment of the contract on their part.

Proceeding onward, you pass another dockyard, where the Government vessels undergo repair, and where the present Governor, with much skill, laid out the plan for a dry dock; but it is to be regretted it has not met with the support which it merited from the Legislature.

A good road leads you past the Governor's farm by a large quarry, where stone is now being hewn for the building of a Government House, on a gentle eminence to the right of the road—a spot well chosen, as commanding a charming prospect of the city, the bay, and the windings of the Derwent. The foundations are now in progress; and, ere long, it is to be hoped a creditable mansion will be erected for the representative of Her Majesty; which the present edifice, half of timber, certainly is not. The building is still progressing, the basement story being completed; but, in consequence of some demur, by the Parliament, about granting the full sum originally estimated for, the works have been retarded, and the hired labour for the time discontinued.

Some years ago, in this locality, an Observatory* was built, at no trifling expense; but is now

---

* Sir James Ross thus speaks of its erection:—"Anxious to get the permanent Observatory at work as soon as possible, I was rejoiced to learn from the Lieutenant-Governor, Sir John Franklin, that the materials of which it was to be constructed had been prepared several months, according

allowed to go into disuse. A pretty cottage and garden are still kept in good order, and occupied by the officer of engineers; making the old saying true—" The Ordnance seldom forget themselves."

Beyond this pretty cottage you descend to the Royal Society's Botanical Gardens, which stretch along the hill-side down to the winding margin of the river. They are very tastefully laid out and kept in the highest order by the skilful and talented horticulturist, the Superintendent, Mr. Newman; who, upon the means allowed him by the Society, keeps the gardens in beautiful order, making them one of the greatest attractions the city affords—a charming lounge and lovely retreat. During the summer months, the Band of the Regiment stationed in the city plays there once every week, giving another opportunity for the brilliant, gay, and fair, to beguile a quiet hour away, amidst flowers no less fair than themselves. A large plot of ground has been granted to the Society, and it is purposed to extend the gardens: this will add much to their beauty.

to a plan sent from England, and ready to be put together as soon as a site should be determined on. I therefore accompanied Sir John Franklin the next morning to examine several places which he thought likely; and, having selected that which appeared to me the most unexceptionable for the purpose, a party of two hundred convicts were the same afternoon set to work to dig the foundation, prepare the blocks of free-stone which were to form its base, and the solid pillars of the same material, which were to be the supports for the instruments, and to bring prepared timber from the Government store."

Beyond the Botanical Gardens, to the right, is the garden of Government House, always kept in the highest state of cultivation. Leaving the gardens, a winding road conducts you round the Domain till you reach the third entrance. Some hundred yards ere you do so, however, as you emerge from the forest with which the Domain is thickly covered, you will pause and admire one of the prettiest landscapes in the world. The eye is enchanted with the scene bursting before you. Away on the right, the majestic Derwent winds through a lovely valley, now forming a wide and sinuous bay, anon half-concealed by some forest headland; then, stretching far toward some distant hill, it is all but lost to the view, and yet again it reappears, lingering in its meanderings, as if it wooed the sunny slopes and warm picturesque vales through which it glides, and which it caressingly interlaces.

Before you, is the beautiful valley of New Town, thickly covered with pretty cottages, gardens, and grounds; whilst the foreground is charmingly relieved by the very handsome mansion of Mr. Chapman, the member for the city: the grounds are neatly laid out, and kept in good order. The house itself is of simple architecture, but elegant. The author can state that the interior may vie with many a more noble house in the parent country; and it is but a just tribute to the worthy proprietor and his lady to say that none can excel them in the courtesy and hospitality to be met with within those walls.

Below this is Bishopstowe, a very handsome place, enlarged and beautified under the immediate eye of the present Bishop of Tasmania ; a gentleman of fine taste, and of the highest acquirements, and well fitted for the lofty post he adorns.

Close to Bishopstowe is the very pretty place and magnificent gardens of Mr. Roope, a wealthy merchant of the city, who has laid out a fortune in the formation and beautifying of his gardens— subsoiling the ground and trellising the fruit trees : it now, however, by its annual yield, pays good interest for the large amount expended. To the right of the gardens, we pass the fine mansion which Mr. Roope has already built with considerable taste and elegance. From thence, returning by the New Town road, we pass by the handsome residence of Mr. Brewer, one of the most eminent of the Tasmanian barristers. The road by his house leads to Newlands, passing the villa of Mr. Nairn, Deputy Comptroller General, and Sheriff of the Colony.

. The house and grounds of Newlands have recently been purchased by Mr. Stephenson, from the executors of the original proprietor, the late Mr. Charles McLachlan ; a gentleman who will long be regretted in Hobarton, as one of the highest probity and virtue. He had, as an eminent merchant,

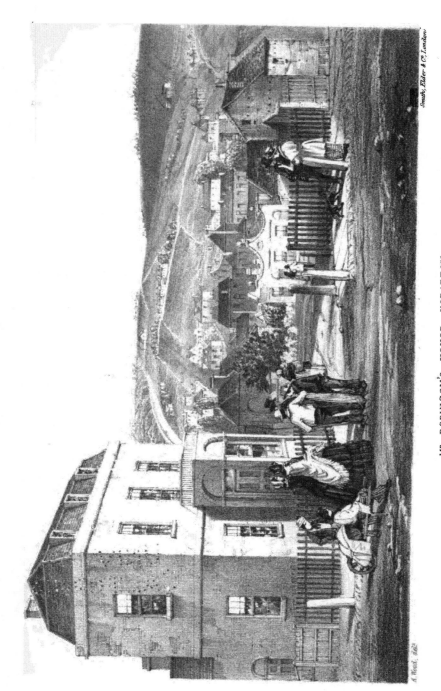

A. Veitch, delt.

Smith, Elder & Co. London.

Mʀ. ROBINSON'S HOUSE, HOBARTON.

accumulated a large fortune, and retired with his amiable family to enjoy the fruit of many years' toil and labour in the financial world. Providence, however, willed it otherwise; and, to the irreparable loss of his family, friends, and country, he was taken to a better world, after a few days' illness.

From hence we retrace our steps by numerous villas, over the New Town Hill, passing the fine mansion of the enterprising landed proprietor, Mr. J. Lord; and leaving to the right the pretty residence of Mr. Swan, we again enter the city by its northern and principal outlet, the high road to Launceston. On a hill to the left is Trinity church; and below it, further to the left, is the Penitentiary, which is well worth a visit from the stranger.

Returning to Hobarton by this road, we pass the house formerly inhabited by Mr. Robinson, well-known as the friend and pacificator of the Aborigines, and who succeeded in collecting the scattered remnants of the tribes whose depredations and murders had become alarming. To conquer them, the whole country had been in arms, forming a grand battue for several weeks, without success; yet, by kindness and persuasion, Mr. Robinson allured them to quit their hiding places, and submit to the Government.

The above circumstance is thus described in a record before us:—" One of the most singular incidents in colonial history was the removal of savages from Van Diemen's Land by a single man, after twenty-seven thousand pounds had been spent to no purpose in a war against them.   A person named Robinson, a bricklayer by trade, but an active and intelligent man, undertook and performed the singular service of bringing every aboriginal man, woman, and child quietly, peaceably, and willingly into Hobart Town ; whence they were shipped to Flinder's Island.   This island is between forty and fifty miles in length, and from twelve to eighteen in width.   It abounds with the smaller species of kangaroo, etc. ; the coasts are plentifully supplied with fish ; and, in addition to this abundance of their natural food, the natives were provided, at the expense of the colony, with dwellings, ample rations of flour and meat, bedding, clothes, garden implements, seeds, fishing-tackle, and all things which could be necessary for their present or improved condition ; besides medical attendance, and the means of careful and judicious instruction in all things fitting or possible for them to learn.

From the time of Mr. Robinson's capture, or rather persuasion of the natives to follow him, a complete change took place in the island ; the remote stock stations were again resorted to, and guns were no longer carried between the handles of the plough.   The means of persuasion employed by

Mr. Robinson to induce the natives to submit to his guidance have ever been a mystery to me. He went into the bush unarmed, and, accompanied by an aboriginal woman, his sole companion, met the different tribes; he used such arguments with them as sufficed at length to achieve his object, after having occupied many months in its pursuit. He received some reward from the local government, although not nearly adequate to the merits of his services. He alone, unassisted in any way, accomplished what Colonel Arthur, with the aid of the military, and all the male population of the island, with an expenditure of £27,000, had failed to do."

A very fine suburban mansion, with beautifully kept grounds, strikes your attention as you turn towards the wooded hill of the demesne before you; it is the seat of the Comptroller-General, and has lately been purchased by Mr. Moses, a wealthy merchant of Hobarton. Passing the Colonial Hospital, a large and imposing building, we once more enter the city, which now seems as if it were being rebuilt; for, not long since, a destructive fire burnt down a great portion of one of the principal streets; and, a few weeks after, an inundation levelled all before it, and swept away two of the principal bridges. From these two unforeseen calamities it is now rapidly rising; and though labour is most difficult to obtain, yet it is

3

surprising how quickly matters are progressing—
we trust with better fortune for the future.

Would it were in our power now, having
taken the stranger so long a ramble, to conduct
his weary steps to some hotel corresponding to
the city. But, alas! Hobarton boasts of nothing
of the kind; we can only conduct him therefore to Broadland house; where, though we cannot
promise him all the luxuries of the season, or
the attendance of " Véry " yet we can assure him
of cleanliness and comfort. We trust that this
want will also soon be rectified, and that another
" Astor House" may arise in this city, to consign
to oblivion the inns not worthy of notice.

CHAPTER IV.

The shallop of a trusty Moor
Convey'd me from this idle shore;
I long'd to see the Isles that gem
Old Ocean's purple diadem:
I sought by turns, and saw them all.
                    BRIDE OF ABYDOS.

ONCE a week the Government steamer leaves the
Commissariat wharf for the stations on the Peninsula. Leaving the Market House behind and the
Commissariat offices on your left, you pass on the
right the stores of that department; and proceeding
along a small but very commodious dock, where
the busy toil of the shipping with which it is
always filled gives you a favourable idea of the
advance of trade, you reach the wharf side, along
which the little steamer is easing off steam ready
for her cruise. Prompt to the hour of half-past
seven, the commander takes his station on the
paddle-wheel; the hawser is slacked off, the word
given, and through the crowd of shipping at anchor,
the Derwent holds on her way, slow, but we regret

to say, not always sure : for a break-down in
the machinery is of such frequent occurrence, that
truth compels us to say, though never was a vessel
better or more ably commanded, there seldom ever
was one kept in worse order—so far as machinery
goes.   However, the kind urbanity of the jovial
skipper, and the splendid scenery around, as you
move over the tranquil water, are in themselves
sufficient to compensate for the chance of a stoppage
on the way, and the stranger will gladly avail himself of a free passage,—always granted for visiting
the Peninsula and the Neck.

After you pass the lighthouse, you steer to the
left.   Passing the base of Storm Bay you enter
Norfolk Bay, an inland sea of some thirty miles in
length by ten to twelve in breadth; though, from
the numerous jutting headlands and deep bays, as
well as several islands, it is not an open expanse
of waters.   Few scenes are more magnificent than
those opening each moment to your view, coasting
along Frederick-Henry Bay; and the stranger immediately exclaims, "What a paradise this might
be, were all those romantic looking hills and undulating lands inhabited!"   But, alas! save at the
Government stations, built solely for the repression
and punishment of crime, no human dwelling meets
the eye.   While thousands crowd the overgrown
cities of the Old World, and street after street is
filled with the abodes of poverty and destitution,

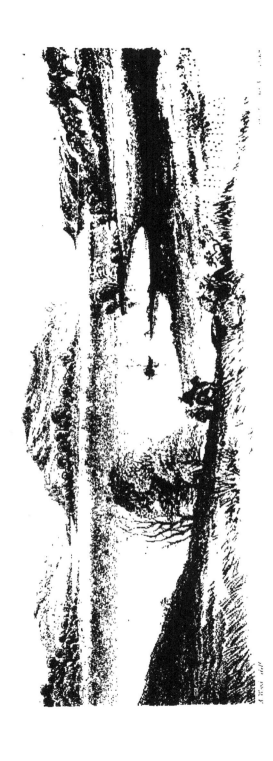

a land richer than the sun ever shone upon now lies a neglected waste; or worse, is prostituted to be the abode of a chain-gang, expurgated from the dregs of that very community which might be so much more happy and comfortable here. Still these are necessary evils; for who can control the unruly wills of sinful men? The poor will never cease from the land, and crime and evil deeds must be punished. Yet there is no place where such feelings are brought nearer to your mind than when sailing along this beautiful shore; for no place seems better adapted for the formation of thriving colonies.

The Peninsula is, however, peculiarly well fitted for the use now made of it; and though we may look forward to its becoming on some future day a free settlement of no mean value and importance, yet we cannot but admire the perfect state in which the establishment is kept, as a convict depôt and prison-house. On entering the bay, you pass a small island (Betsy's Island), where the sportsman finds abundance of the silver-haired rabbit and quail; the former were placed there originally by Lady Franklin, whose property the island is. It is uninhabited and uncultivated.

The next, Slopen Island, is larger, and is rented by one of the magistrates of the Peninsula for a nominal sum: it has one farm house on it and a good farm. This farm was originally a penal settle-

ment; but the great want of water, which could
never be kept good in tanks, made Government
abandon it.   Along the opposite side extends Seven
Mile Beach, a very beautiful sandy shore, running
along for seven miles without a check.   The first
station you reach in the bay is called the "Mines,"
where a coal mine exists and is worked with considerable profit and advantage; but, as the aspect
of this part of the shore is uninviting, few strangers visit it.   The land in the neighbourhood was
formerly granted to Joseph Tice Gellibrand, Esq.,
then the Attorney-General of the Colony.   When
Tasman's Peninsula was fixed upon for a penal
settlement, Mr. Gellibrand was induced to exchange
his claims on the Peninsula for a compensation from
Government.

The soil around the coal-mines is sandy and
unfit for cultivation.   There is a long jetty running
out to sea, on which is a tram-road for bringing
down the coal, the water being very shallow in
shore.   There are some very comfortable houses
here for the Resident Magistrate, Superintendent
Overseer, etc., a chapel and school-house; and to
the visitor it appears like a small village in the coal
districts of England.   The coal is of an inferior
kind, and, when ignited, cracks and sends out
small particles rather injurious to carpets, dresses,
etc.; a wire guard is therefore generally required
in front of the grate.

Near the magistrate's house on Mount Lepus is a miniature Semaphore, which communicates with Mount Stuart. This point forms the post of communication between the Coal Mines and Port Arthur through Mount Communication, or with Eagle Hawk Neck through the Half-way Bluff and Woody Island.

The system was instituted by Captain Booth, who was Commandant of the Peninsula many years, and is of great use in case of convicts escaping, stores required, etc. The Semaphore has not been so much used of late years; but Mr. Boyd, the present Commandant, is about restoring it to its pristine state of action.

The Derwent steamer does not often call at this jetty, but proceeds a mile and a half further on, to the jetty of Salt Water River Station; which, although so near, presents a considerable contrast in its beautifully cultivated fields and rich pasture land: this is the farm of the Peninsula. The cottages of the superintendents are neat and comfortable, with pretty gardens. There is a large store belonging to the Commissariat Depôt; and, although the place is but a prison after all, it has every appearance of a very comfortable village. The Doctor's house is on the side of a hill—a neat cottage with verandah and good garden around it. The farm consists of about three hundred acres under cultivation, and is kept in very good order, producing very fine crops. There is not good water at this station : it is often procured from the Mines, where it is excellent.

Leaving this, you touch at Impression Bay, the invalid station, where is a very good hospital and some fine gardens. The scenery here is of a different description, the country around being densely wooded. The view of the bay from this is very imposing. Away to the north, you see East Bay Neck, which divides Forrestier's Peninsula from the main land ; and, out to sea, in clear weather, you can see Maria Island, of which we will speak hereafter.

From Salt Water River you can proceed on foot and be in time for the steamer at the Cascades, passing Impression Bay *en route*. Sometimes you can borrow a horse, as the magistrates, superintendents, and other gentlemen over the stations, are exceedingly obliging, and always anxious to show every attention to the tourist. The whole distance is eight miles, and rather a smart walk, but repays, by the fine scenery it affords, the labour of surmounting the different ascents of the road. There is also a large sheep station some five miles distant in the other direction, but scarcely worth visiting : it is fenced in, and extends over forty miles of ground. The wool is sent to the different factories for carding, etc.

Leaving Salt Water River, as a pedestrian, you

pass over a causeway worth seeing; it was erected during the time Mr. Pringle was superintendent, partly over the bay, and is five hundred yards in length. The land is very undulating and in some parts very steep until you come over Impression Bay station. This is under the management of a Captain in the Navy, by whom everything is kept in a high state of order and regularity. There are many useful matters manufactured here, such as hand-carts, wheelbarrows, etc., etc. The water is not very good, though a great deal of pains has been taken to bring it from a distance. There is a clergyman and a doctor also stationed here.

Passing along the beach for half-a-mile, you strike into the woods again for about two miles and a half, which brings you to the Cascade Station; it is the prettiest on the Peninsula, and under the superintendence of Mr. Ballantine, whose kindness and urbanity the stranger is ever charmed with: the station is in first-rate order.

Behind the buildings is another Fern-tree Valley and a very pretty cascade: a beautiful stream of good water running from it supplies the station. The principal occupation here is felling timber for shipping purposes, etc., as it is here of the ᵔbest quality on the Peninsula. There is a tram-road which brings it down to the water's edge, where is a store-house and a good jetty for shipment.

The residence of the superintendent is very prettily situated in the midst of most tastefully laid out grounds, with very fine gardens, and on a gentle rise of the hill, which commands a good view of the surrounding scenery.

CHAPTER V.

Yet strange to tell !
In quiet we had learned to dwell :
My very chains and I grew friends,—
So much a long communion tends
To make us what we are ; ———."
PRISONER OF CHILLON.

TASMAN'S Peninsula, the present head quarters of the convicts, is the south-eastern extremity of Van Diemen's Land, and contains about 300,000 acres. The face of the country is hilly and covered with timber, presenting few open spots for tillage, though there are several localities where the soil is rich and good. It remained unnoticed for many years, and was at last selected as a good place to confine the aborigines, who were doing much mischief. Measures were taken in 1830 to drive them by a grand "Battue" through Forrestier's Peninsula. The expedition, however, failed: other plans were adopted, and they were at last all got together in Flinders' Island, where they gradually became extinct.

Port Arthur was next selected as a sawing establishment to supply the Engineering Department with timber: however, the advantages the place afforded for the formation of a penal settlement becoming more apparent, the convicts were removed to it from Macquarie Harbour and Maria Island. It remained strictly a double convict station; no communication being allowed, except through the Government, until 1841, when the agricultural farm was established at Salt Water River: soon afterwards the probation system came in vogue, and the other stations were established.

The steamer, on leaving the Cascades, rounds a point opening the entrance to Norfolk Bay, called by the Captain's kind and most hospitable lady, Expectation Point. Passing Woody Island, once covered with very fine timber, but now nearly bare, you steam to the halting-place of the Derwent. A long jetty forms the landing-place, and the only object of interest is the very pretty cottage of the Captain, always well stocked with flowers, fruit, and vegetables. Here, a most hearty welcome awaits the stranger, if he is disposed to stop; and few can vie with the lady of the cottage in urbanity and attention to a guest.

Norfolk Bay extends some twelve miles across, forming on one side a long low swamp to the right of the jetty, and on the other side a long narrow reach of five miles in extent, running up to Eagle

Hawk Neck, and having Woody Island at its entrance.

From Norfolk Bay to Long Bay, five miles across a neck of land, is a tram-road of a very primitive construction, first built by Captain Booth; the sleepers being of rough timber as felled, and the rail narrow pieces of sawn timber, squared and pegged down. The rail carriages, if so they can be called, are also of a very rude construction; very low, double seated, with four very small cast iron wheels, the same as used in quarries, etc., in England. On either side project two long handles, which the prisoners lean against and thus propel the carriage. The road being not exactly level, but having many inclines and ascents, the transit is very amusing to the stranger; for as you rise up the incline, the prisoners puff and blow, pushing against the carriage, but when descending, up they jump alongside of you, and away you go, dashing, crashing, tearing on. Half-way there is a rest station, where you sometimes get a relief; as there is a considerable ascent for near a mile, and then a like descent down to the jetty, which is really quite a nervous affair: the speed increases as you move along, till each moment you expect to be dashed over into some precipice or deep jungle alongside of the tram. An upset sometimes does happen, but it is seldom attended with any serious consequences. There is always a director with the train, who can check the wheels with a drag as he pleases.

At Long Bay a low jetty runs out into the water, and the Port Arthur boats wait to row you to the station—three miles round Garden Point, by Steward's Bay and Sloping Point into the harbour, passing the dock-yards on the right as you go up to the landing. As you open the entrance round Garden Point, you pass Dead Island, the cemetery of the station; Opossum Bay extends along before you, terminating in a long sandy beach to the left of the settlement, the landing being on an arm of the bay to the right.

The appearance of Port Arthur is exceedingly pretty. The first object that meets the eye is the house and grounds of the Commandant, which (under the active care of Mr. Boyd, who now fills that post), are in very beautiful order; the house having undergone a complete repair, and the grounds and gardens, which had been suffered to fall into partial decay from neglect, now appearing perfect.

The house of the officer commanding the troops next greets the eye. It is a pretty cottage with a long line of steps leading to it; but its best attractions are the extreme kindness and profuse hospitality that greet the stranger within its walls, from its worthy master and most amiable lady.

The next building is in a very quaint sort of architecture in the style of the mediæval ages, with fronting towers and battlements, and is no less than a Barrack. The Lunatic Asylum, a fine building, rises behind it, and a large hospital, besides a barrack not occupied. A neat street leads you to the prisoners' quarters, which are built of timber, and in rather a shaky state.

Next to these, you pass the Court House, where the Commandant administers justice, assisted by the Officer of the Troops, who is also a paid magistrate. To the right, by the water's edge, is a very fine store belonging to the Commissariat Department, but now undergoing the change to a prisoners' barracks—not before it was required. This, at the present time, gives the place rather an untidy appearance, which a few months under the able administration of Mr. Boyd will soon alter.

You next pass the work-shops, cook-house, lavatory, etc.; and passing out of a gate, where is a guard and a semaphore, you enter a shady grove along some lovely gardens. The change is so great from the yellow dress, the clank of chains, and formidable guard with gates and bars, that you can at first scarcely believe your eyes.

Before you stretches a short road with beautiful over-hanging English lime trees; and as you proceed, you fancy you are about to enter the suburban retreat of some London banker. A lovely shrubbery bursts on your view, a pretty iron gate invites you to enter; and before you, peeping through a long vista of English and native trees, appears the neatest church in the Colony, of correct architecture, built of the brown granite. To the left, two or three pretty cottages appear with trellised fronts; and as you proceed and turn through a sweet embowering arch of the multiflora rose in full bloom, a beautiful cottage *ornée* opens to your view.

This is the residence for the Comptroller-General when he visits the station, and is built in very good taste. Here you can wander along walks bordered with the rarest shrubs and flowers of our native land. Anon you find yourself beneath the shady foliage of the weeping willows, known as Buonaparte's; under the largest of which is a very neat summer-house. A sweet little stream runs through the garden, and with very many trees of dear old England around you, it is easy to forget, wandering through this beautiful garden, that seven hundred fellow-creatures, who have lost home and liberty through crime, are in chains so near you.

Passing the church, which is partly overgrown with ivy, giving it a charming appearance, you leave the parson's house on the right, and issue from the gardens by the upper gate, which conducts you to fruit and vegetable gardens of the Government, kept also in the best of order. To the right are three comfortable cottages with grounds and gardens for the doctor, the Roman

Catholic clergyman, and the superintendent (now removed to Salt Water River).

Proceeding along a good road, you have a fine view of the entire settlement; a rich glade presents itself to you of well tilled land, stretching up the hill; also numerous gardens. On a gentle ascent you come to the Penitentiary, built for the silent system; and truly it is a punishment of the severest kind. The plan of the building is a circle within a circle; the inner circle forming the guard and point of direction, from which branch angles and corridors: along these are the cells. Between each line of cells is an iron gate, with two or three yards, forming radii to the centre: all the floors are heavily matted. A bell is gently touched, a cell is quietly opened, and a prisoner appears with a cloth mask over his face. Two small eyelet holes serve to show him a guard pointing to one of the yards: this he enters, and faces a black mark on the wall. The doors are shut and a bell is touched; the mask is turned up over his head, and he walks up and down for one hour; then he returns in the same manner to his cell; it has a trap-door, on which his meals are issued to him. A chapel is in one angle, and the seats are so contrived that each prisoner can see the clergyman, but no one else. Under the pulpit is an indicator to tell each prisoner when he can leave.

4

Above the Penitentiary is the cottage cell of
Smith O'Brien; leaving which, you pass over the
hill-side round Opossum Bay, and skirting its
margin, ramble on about a mile to Point Puer, now
in ruins. Formerly it was the grand depôt for the
boys, but the building is now a heap of rubbish.

Passing round this point, you have a fine view
of the open sea; and under you are some very fine
specimens of the basaltic rock, and several caves.
Cape Raoul, with its high columns of the same
rock, occupies the southernmost point, and is
situated about nine miles from Cape Pillar, between
which is the entrance to Port Arthur, called
Maingon Bay. The exterior coast of the Peninsula
is lined with high perpendicular rocks, occasionally
interrupted with small sandy beaches. On the
west side are Wedge Bay and Fortescue Bay. On
the east, from Maingon, a current sets inward,
which makes it very unsafe to anchor: however,
the entrance to Port Arthur is perfectly safe, and
forms a sufficient rendezvous for a fleet.

Although a visit to the Prisoners' Barracks is
not one of much interest, yet the stranger could
not well leave Port Arthur without such a visit;
for, as the principal feature of the place is gang
after gang of chained convicts, he would naturally like to see where and how they are
located. The system is perfect, and admirably
carried out: it is surprising to see the regularity

of every detail, and how all the arrangements work together so well.

Going over the building, the only thing that strikes you as extraordinary is the dormitory, built after ship-board fashion, with tier upon tier of berths, all in perfect order, comfort, and cleanliness. There is also a separate apartment for every trade and calling, and every one is compelled to work, so as to turn his labour to the best profit. And yet, with all this, the annual expense of the convict establishment in Van Diemen's Land, has exceeded two hundred thousand pounds.

If the stranger be a disciple of Lavater, and a physiognomist, there is no place where he would be more struck than by visiting the church during divine service. The interior appears like an amphitheatre embracing living examples of every kind and grade of crime. To the philanthropist the sight of so many criminals congregated around is most melancholy; yet one cannot help considering that all —though the very dregs of society, the offscouring of the earth—were born in a land where truth prevails; and that, perchance, many who were educated with care and diligence, have been driven by crime to work out a miserable existence in chains and slavery.

CHAPTER VI.

The valley lay smiling before me,
Where lately I left her behind;
Yet I trembled, and something hung o'er me
That saddened the joy of my mind.

MOORE.

AND thus it is ever with the stranger leaving Port Arthur; for it is, in very truth, a smiling valley: and well may we say with another bard,—

"All save the spirit of man is divine."

As the equestrian gains the hill above the settlement and takes a last look over the tranquil bay, the clang of the chain is no longer heard, and the beautiful little church peeps from amid the foliage with a lovely shrubbery surrounding it. The villas seem as gems in the view, with their rich gardens and verdant fields. The sad scene and remembrance of the prison-house is forgotten, and the hope rises that ere long this sweet spot may be in all respects what it now seems to be— the happy abode of the thriving and industious settler. But a yellow-jacketed gang is even now appearing from yonder quarry; so we must turn our horses' heads and resume our way over the hills to the Neck.

The track is a very good one and leads through the woods, so that little of the country is seen till you open on Norfolk Bay. Here, as before stated, is a police station, and the residence of the commander of the steamer; at which, having rested awhile, a *deoch in dorrish*, with a *cead mille failthe* given, you proceed along a narrow path skirting the sea to Eagle Hawk Neck. You pass three constable stations on the way; for the bay is not very wide and has been attempted to be crossed by daring convicts; though, generally speaking, owing to the extreme vigilance of the police, without success.

The distance from Port Arthur to the Neck is ten miles; but as the path-way (for you cannot call it a road) is of hard marly clay, you can canter nearly all the way. As you turn and round the point where the bay runs up towards the Neck, the sea opens to your view, over a small low bar of sand two hundred feet long by sixty wide: this is the Neck. As you approach the sea, you are surprised to see two or three stages built out in the water; on each of which a ferocious dog is chained.

You now come on a level sandy beach, and have just spurred on your steed, when suddenly, as you open the Neck, your ears are assailed by the fierce barking of twelve or fourteen huge dogs chained across the Bar, and presenting a most terrific barrier to further advance. Each dog is of a different breed, but all are ferocious looking brutes; and they are so ranged as to complete the cordon across the Neck: barrels inverted form their kennels, and lamps are fixed on posts in the sand in front of their line. Two sentries are posted in front of this formidable array, and two more in the rear, so that to escape here is impossible; still it has often been attempted.

Once, four absconders faced the rolling surf, (three English, one a negro); the white swimmers were seized by a no less formidable guardian of the waters than the rapacious shark. The darkey got safe to land, but was taken by the outlying piquet.

The guard house is situated in front of the canine phalanx. The dogs are treated somewhat like soldiers, receiving their regular rations of one pound of bread and one pound of meat each day.

On the rise of the hill, some five hundred yards from the Neck, are the barracks for about thirty men; to the right of which are the officer's quarters, surrounded with a neat garden. Lately this cottage has been considerably added to, as the governor and family spent the summer there for the benefit of sea-bathing, the officer moving to Port Arthur during his Excellency's visit. There are several patches of tilled land around, which the industrious soldier is allowed to labour at for his own benefit, and which repays the labour well. A pathway conducts you through a few yards of scrub to the beach.

On the left is a very extraordinary natural curiosity—a long line of tesselated pavement, cut in exact squares and parallelograms, as if the plummet and line directed their formation. It is of considerable extent, and could the corporation of the good city of Hobarton but remove it to their streets, there is abundance to flag it twice over. On the right extends for three miles a very beautiful sandy beach of semicircular form, called Pirate's Cove. Proceeding along this, you pass the before-described Cerberus guard; and leaving the sands, scramble over rocks on to sands again. Then, entering a few yards of jungle, you arrive at the Blow Hole; the deep sound of the waves warning you of its vicinity. This is a perfect tunnel, opening inland some hundred and twenty yards; and as the rolling swell of the ocean rushes through this chasm, the sound is like the booming of distant ordnance. On the sea side it appears only as a deep cave; the rocks around its mouth being deep and precipitous.

Retracing your steps to the beach, you turn back to a pathway leading through a thick scrub, which with difficulty you scramble through, for nearly a mile. Issuing from it, with the thick forest still around you, suddenly you almost stumble into a chasm, which in no small degree startles the stranger. The chasm is about forty feet by two hundred, and is one of the rarest freaks of nature ever met with ; for, as it is inland some fifty to one hundred paces, and the sea is not visible through the thick forest around, coming suddenly on it, you can scarcely credit your senses. Pushing your way from the brushwood, you see the ocean as through a telescope, spread out to your view under a most majestic arch of about two hundred feet in height and width. And to hear the rolling wave thundering in this mighty causeway, sending its spray almost to the top, has a very splendid effect indeed. This spot is a favourite locale for pic-nic parties ; and certainly, after the weary walk and struggle through the bush, the creature comforts of life are not despicable, however impressed one may be by the sublime and beautiful, on beholding the wondrous works of nature and her fantasies.

The scenery in the neighbourhood of Eagle Hawk Neck cannot fail to arrest the attention of the stranger. The beautiful semicircular line of beach, extending some four or five miles in Pirate's Bay, presents a most pleasing effect, being flanked with precipitous rocks whose summits are covered with beautiful trees and shrubs. These rocks are principally "greywacke," and afford to the naturalist much interest, as they contain several specimens of fossil remains and imbedded quartz. Within the point of rock on the south side is the only safe anchorage, as there is generally a heavy rolling surf along the shore, and shoal water around. There are some good fish here, both in the bay opening to the sea and the inner one leading from Frederick Henry Bay.

A remarkable bird of the petrel tribe, called the mutton bird, frequents this coast. At one season of the year they come in innumerable flocks, so as to darken the horizon when they alight and cover the sea for miles. They burrow in holes on the islands round the coast, forming their nests underground. The body, when skinned and salted, is eaten by sealers and whalers. Their feathers are also much used for beds; but they give out a strong heavy smell unless they have first been carefully purified.

There are also some animals on the two peninsulas which afford some pastime to the indefatigable hunter and trapper. First comes the kangaroo, of which so much has been written that it would be needless to speak of it. No animal can be more easily tamed; and it has been known, when tamed, to follow with hounds after its own species: it is worthy of remark, that be the hounds ever so eager in the chase, they never molest the tame kangaroo hopping along with them.

The large hyæna opossum is sometimes caught here; its colour is a dark yellow with transverse black stripes. The wombat is very common; it is

a curious animal, has very coarse hairy fur, and is
easily tamed. The wallaby is of the same kind, and
seems to be of the same habits as the kangaroo,
though it is of a much smaller description. It hops
on its hind legs and has very fine fur, which is made
into superb rugs and overcoats. It is sometimes
caught like the kangaroo, in a noose fastened to a
tree—sometimes in a pit-fall—but is usually hunted
with dogs, and shot down as it emerges from the
thick cover which it frequents.

The *Dasyurus Ursinus*, or, as it is commonly
called, the "Devil," is found in the woods; it is a
small black animal—having invariably, however, one
or two white spots, and is extremely fierce and un-
tameable. Of the native cat, the great plague of the
poultry yard, there are two species; the one of a
light grey colour; the other of a spotted dark
yellow and black colour: it is something between
a weasel and a cat in size and appearance, and has
very good fur. Then come the black, grey, and
ring-tailed opossums: they are easily caught, and
have beautiful fur. There are also found in various
parts of the island those curious animals the *Orni-
thorhynchus* and the *Echidna*.

Yet nothing strikes the stranger, in wending his
way over the wide waste of land, and wandering
over hill and dale or through the trackless forest, so
much as the great absence of animal life; for those
animals above spoken of, though they are to be found

(and great quantities are annually taken by the trappers), are seldom seen or met with in the day : you may wander for miles, alone in the woods, without meeting a single living thing.

As to birds, the quail, the pigeon, and the snipe are abundant; and of other game for the sportsman, there are the bittern, the plover, the coot of several kinds and varieties, not to mention the black swan, the Cape Barwon goose, etc., and the wild duck, on the marshes and lakes. There are some specimens of pretty birds for the ornithologist's collection, but they are seldom met with, unless sought for in the peculiar localities and districts which they affect, and at their proper season; for many of them are migratory.

CHAPTER VII.

Night came, but with it came no hope—no rest
To Conrad's stern and agitated breast:
His thoughts— like lightning o'er some lonely tomb—
Flash'd but to leave behind a darker gloom.
                                                GULNARE.

THERE is some good land on Forrestier's Peninsula;
the most part is thickly wooded and intersected by
high tiers or mountains, in many parts covered
with close underwood interlaced with parasitic vines,
which render them almost impassable.

In attempting to cross one of these tiers, to visit
on duty a whale fishery in Wilmot Harbour, Captain Booth, late 21st Fusileers, and Commandant
of the Peninsulas, lost his way and nearly his life.
The Author obtained an account of his providential
escape from the papers of Assistant-Commissary-
General Lempriere, who was in some measure instru-
mental in saving him, and was honoured with the
public thanks of the Lieutenant-Governor, Sir John
Franklin, on the occasion. Although it is in a

measure foreign from this undertaking, yet as it may give the reader some idea of the difficulties attending a trip through the woods of Tasmania, we here insert the narrative of this officer's mishaps; premising that he had much experience in bush life, and was accompanied by men who understood its difficulties. The story is as follows :—

"On Sunday morning, the 3rd of June, 1838, on my return home after attending divine service, I was met by Power, the Commandant's servant; he stated that he was in great apprehension about his master, who had gone to the Sounds on Forrestier's Peninsula on Thursday, on his way to visit the constable's post at Doctor Imlay's fishery, and was to have returned next day. I ordered a signal to be made to Eagle Hawk Neck to learn whether the Commandant had been heard of. The answer was, that the postman had arrived from Sorell, and stated that Captain Booth had been lost since Friday; also, that two soldiers had been sent from the Neck to search for him.

"The consternation at this intelligence was general on the settlement : civil officers, soldiers, and even convicts, expressed and looked the concern they felt. I determined to set off myself and to leave no stone unturned to find him. I took my bugle, procured from the serjeant, two soldiers named Clark and Watt, manned a boat with the Commandant's crew, took it across the railroad, and in four hours and a half was at the head of the Sounds, a distance of twenty miles. I found there the Woody Island boat and its crew, who had been waiting since Friday. They had no rations left. I learnt that Captain Booth had started on Friday morning, taking with him the coxwain Turner and three kangaroo dogs; that they had lost each other in the bush, and that Turner had returned to give the alarm; and further, that he had now gone with the two soldiers from Eagle Hawk Neck.

"In the course of the night I was joined by Mr. Francis Desailly, a constable named Arnold, and Dr. Desailly's servants (ticket-of-leave men); they informed me that Mr. George Spottswood and Mr. Gilpin were out as well, but in another direction.

"Although distressed in mind on account of Captain Booth, it afforded me much satisfaction to find his worth so much appreciated by the respectable settlers nearest to his command. It was impossible to do anything that night, so we laid down in a bark hut till dawn. I then ordered my boat's crew to give their rations to the Woody Island crew, despatching the former back to Port Arthur for a supply of provisions for the use of the different parties which might join me. The whole party started together for a certain distance. I then continued with my two soldiers and one of the Woody Island crew (who carried my kangaroo rug) straight on towards

Blackman's river, whilst the remainder took to the right in extended orders. I continued sounding my bugle, and they a tin horn, firing shots occasionally.

"After going some distance, I heard shots on the left; and on going in that direction, met private Mooney, of the 21st Regiment, and constable Gill, who, with another soldier, had pulled themselves over in a dingy from the coal mines. I directed them to join me, and we met the remainder of the parties at a bark hut at the head of Blackman's river.

"We found an accession to our strength in Mr. Crocker, the two gentlemen mentioned before, and Turner, with the two soldiers. I interrogated Turner, whose conduct appeared open to suspicion. He had recently received fifty lashes for misconduct by sentence of Captain Booth, and was considered to be of a vindictive disposition. The answer he gave to the first question I put to him was not calculated to remove the unfavourable impression which existed against him; for, on my enquiring as to the facts, instead of expressing any sorrow, he merely said, 'Worse accidents have happened at sea.' I think, if they had had the power, the soldiers would have shot the poor fellow on the spot; so convinced were they that he had made away with their beloved officer. He at first appeared unwilling to answer any more questions; but at length stated that they had lost themselves in a scrub about three miles off; that he stopped to take a thorn out of his boot, Captain Booth

still going on. Turner 'cooeed'* after him, was
answered once or twice, and then no more. He
wandered about the bush the most part of the night,
and then laid down by the foot of a tree, near a
burnt hut. On Saturday morning, finding himself
near Blackman's river, he made the best of his way
to 'Coolabah,' (Captain Spottswood's seat,) to give the
alarm.

I directed Turner to lead the whole party to
the marshy scrub, secretly putting him in charge of
private Mooney.; for I suspected his account to be
incorrect. When near the spot I thought I heard a
' cooee' on the left, and therefore desired the parties
to divide into four and scour around the tier, whilst
I went with my party straight up. The fatigue was
distressing : we heard no sounds on our way up,
although I was almost confident that my ears had
not deceived me.

" On the top we met one of the parties—Messrs.
Gilpin, George Spottswood, and a man of Dr. Imlay's.
I requested them to take to the right, and we would
march to the left, where I still thought I heard a
faint ' cooee '. Our exertions were of no avail, and
we returned to the bark hut at Blackman's river
about three oclock.

" The ground we had gone over was very rough
and fatiguing. Quite exhausted, I threw myself on

* A *Cooee* is a lengthened call used by the natives and adopted by the
settlers.

my rug : however, after a short nap and a warm cup
of tea, I felt myself quite refreshed, and determined
to return to the Sounds to meet the boat and prepare
rations for the whole party, whom I had directed to
rendezvous there the next morning. We had about
eight miles to walk through the bush after night-
fall ; but it being moonlight, and the soldier Clarke,
who had often hunted the grounds, proving a good
guide, we reached the Sounds in safety.

" Here I found Mr. Peter Barrow, who had come
in the boat, and Mr. Crocker, who had taken the
tiers towards the Neck, after scouring the scrubby
marsh in which Captain Booth and Turner had been
separated. Of his party he brought one soldier,
having missed in the tiers the other, with some
volunteers. I found also that some more constables
had joined and had gone into the bush, with the
exception of Reardon, who waited for me.

" The Eagle Hawk Neck boat had also been
despatched to search the coast on the sea-side and
round to Blackman's bay. It began to rain, and my
apprehensions for my poor friend were at their height.
The next morning I despatched Mr. Crocker across
the tiers with three soldiers, and Bailey the Commandant's coxwain, with Captain Booth's terrier 'Tartar:'
this faithful animal, I was sure, would scent his
poor master, dead or alive. Lieutenant Andrews,
the second in command, happening to be in Hobarton,
I thought it best to despatch Constable Reardon

5

with a letter to him, stating the situation we were placed in, and requesting an accession of force and more bugles. About an hour after he had left, whilst expecting the parties in for rations, constable Wetherell came running to the hut: he brought the joyful intelligence that Captain Booth had been found alive, and was to be at Captain Spottswood's that morning. I despatched the only soldier left with me to Eagle Hawk Neck to signalize the event to the settlement. I had but three of the boat's crew left, and the constable, who could not pull. However, I took the steer-oar, and, with the three men, managed to get the boat to East Bay Neck, just half-an-hour after Captain Booth had arrived. I found him in a most emaciated state, without the use of his lower extremities and scarcely of his hands. He had, however, met with the kindest attention from Captain Spottswood's amiable family; and Dr. Desailly, although in ill-health himself, had made a point of meeting him there to tender his professional aid.

"After partaking of some refreshments under Captain Spottswood's hospitable roof, we deposited Captain Booth safely on kangaroo rugs in the bottom of the boat, and mustering another hand to pull, I steered him to the railroad, Norfolk Bay, where we met the other officers of the settlement, all happy to see the Commandant alive. After a safe trip across the railroad, I happily delivered my charge safely at his own quarters.

"I was naturally much disappointed at not having been with the party who found Captain Booth, as I was at the time at Blackman's River, not more than three miles off, when returning to the Sounds. I was vexed also that it was not reported to me till next morning, for it would have avoided some trouble; as, in consequence of my letter to Lieutenant Andrews, which reached him at a ball given to the officers of Her Majesty's ship 'Conway,' the Commanding officer sent down, the next morning, by the 'Eliza,' three officers, thirty soldiers, and bugles.

"The particulars of Captain Booth's recovery were as follows:—Mr. Desailly's party, (with whom were Mooney, Gill, and Turner,) had rounded the tier on which I had been. Mr. Desailly thought he heard a sound, and at the same moment Mooney saw 'Sandy,' one of Captain Booth's kangaroo dogs, come out of the bush. The dog ran back to the spot where his master laid almost insensible. The shout given on account of his being found, and the quick discharging of their fire-arms, showed the feeling of joy which pervaded every breast. A fire was immediately kindled and a party despatched to Dr. Imlay's for blankets, etc. Captain Booth was incautiously brought too near the fire for his frost-bitten feet, and suffered much in consequence.

"He said, that after parting with Turner, (who, aware that much suspicion had attached to him, was greatly rejoiced at his commander's rescue), he had passed the night in a damp swamp, and suffered much from cold. The next morning he with difficulty ascended the tier, and felt quite exhausted. He passed the night on the summit, and found in the morning that he could hardly use his limbs; having no covering except his clothes, nor anything to eat. He tried to descend to what appeared to his eyes a clear place; but when he got there, found, to his mortification, that it was a cascade. He could hardly manage to crawl up again. He resigned himself to his fate, and passed another miserable night. On Monday morning he heard my bugle and shots, and knew a friend was near; he attempted to draw himself nearer towards the sounds, but found it impossible. He heard a shot fired within about one hundred and fifty yards from him. Faint and weak, he could not raise his voice to ' cooee ; ' he tried one of his pistols, the trigger broke, the other had got wet through. The sound of fire-arms appeared to recede, the bugle was no longer heard; all was over: no chance left.

"A few minutes after these melancholy thoughts had assailed him, when he had resigned every idea of being rescued from a miserable and lingering death, kind Providence ordained that his deliverers should be at his side. He could only express his thankfulness by a look."

CHAPTER VIII.

To sit on rocks; to muse o'er flood and fell;
To slowly trace the forest's shady scene,
Where things that own not man's dominion dwell,
And mortal foot hath ne'er or rarely been.

BYRON.

IN the preceding story the danger of losing one's way in the trackless forests of Tasmania is depicted; nevertheless, to the lover of the grand and beautiful, there is a ramble of much interest over those very tiers of Forrestier's Peninsula; and if you are well provided with an intelligent guide, some needful refreshment, and a blanket, in case of extending your stroll beyond the day, you need not fear an accident such as befel Captain Booth. There is one path used by the trapper that leads you over a very fine range of hills, and brings you out to the sea-side, where a range of magnificent rocks of pillar-like formation line the shore, and where the swelling roll of the wave rushing between, dashes the spray all around: the hollow sound reverberates along the aisles thus curiously grouped by nature.

Returning inland, you pass a fine piece of tilled land, and strike into the more traversed path leading from the Neck to King George's Sound. But to the lover of the picturesque and beautiful, there is no greater treat than cruising round this peninsula. On a calm summer's eve, as the sun-set rays glance along the waters of the bay, all the headlands are thrown into bold relief, and the eye, charmed by the sublime beauty of the inland sea with towering hills surrounding and hemming in its pretty bays, finds rest on the long line of the Seven Mile Beach; and as the gentle breeze wafts you onward, the several stations along the shore appear and disappear, like smiling villages in a rich and beautiful country. The chain-gang and its associations are forgotten, and you are in Tasmania —a land of peace and plenty.

Passing the pretty islands of Green and George, you enter the Sounds and pass two small bays, where sweet thoughts cannot fail to spring to your mind. Then rounding a point, you come on the jetty of the Sound, where, strange contrast! are piled baskets of meat from the slaughter-house; this place being the depôt for the contractor. Perhaps, as you approach, they are landing cattle from a small vessel; the animals, in spite of the cooling they receive from a swim ashore, looking exceed-

ingly belligerent and seeming very much inclined
to play all sorts of pranks. Two or three horsemen
are all alive and active amongst them : a service of
considerable danger, requiring wonderful presence
of mind and great equestrian skill; for sometimes
the ox will suddenly turn on the driver, and then
the only chance is the horseman's dexterity and
speed in getting out of the way of the beast, turning and outflanking him, and by a well aimed cut
of a large whip checking the impetuosity of his
career.

The settlers in the counties, when in the interior collecting cattle, which they allow to graze at
large over the wilds, enjoy above all things a good
cattle-hunt, and the owner is sure to have several
young hunters in his train on an expedition of the
kind. From the danger attending the hunt, greater
excitement is produced. The leaps the cattle take are
prodigious;—they gallop along a frowning precipice,
then through a dense forest, leaping over the fallen
trees, and pushing their way with headlong speed
through the jungle, over the mountain's side, or
across the open plain. The cattle will take their
way right a-head through everything : nothing
seems to stop them; and if the hunter once loses
the chase, farewell to its recovery, perhaps, for
days again. The colonists, therefore, are splendid
horsemen, cool and daring; and the generality of
their horses are of wonderful powers of endurance,

and seem to enjoy the hunt even more than the hunter.

From the jetty there is a road to East Bay Neck of four miles, partly over a difficult path through the forest, which intercepts your view; then over a fine level beach which leads you to the Neck. On this beach is sometimes seen the redbill or great oyster catcher, which is often shot by the sportsman, and is not unlike the wild duck in flavour; also the sandpiper. Over the Neck is a tram-road for the conveyance of boats. There used to be a sergeant's guard here, but three or four constables now do the duty. From the Neck, a long, deep, narrow, and tortuous bay with a narrow entrance leads to the open sea; Maria Island being distinctly seen to the left.

Some months ago it was proposed in the legislative council to open a ship canal across the Neck, in order to save the navigation around Cape Raoul, *viâ* Storm Bay; thus lessening the distance to the eastward by two hundred miles, besides avoiding a dangerous shore, and always across heavy sea. After that suggestion it was resolved to visit the place, and a steamer being placed at the disposal of the House, they made a party, inviting naval and mercantile friends, the military, etc. The day was propitious; and, having stopped at the Punt some time, and spent two or three hours examining and hearing the several opinions, they returned to Hobarton. The

prevailing opinion was that, the Neck being two
miles of sand across, and allowing half-a-mile on
either side, it would require three and a half miles
of canal to be regularly faced and built, after sinking; and even then it would be subject to a return
of the sand at high tides. The undertaking therefore was considered not feasible, especially as the
outlay would be enormous; the proposition was
consequently adjourned *sine die*.

The adventurous tourist, however, can still cruise
up this outer bay, and, entering the broad mouth of
Blackman's River, enjoy some of the wildest scenery
imaginable. The river comes up between high hills
covered with fine timber, and a bushman's track
leads over a very magnificent ravine. Scrambling
up a lofty hill, you gain a fine view of the open
sea over Cape Frederick, a high cliff running out
from North Bay; in the bight of which is the
entrance to a large lagoon, where wild duck abound.
Over some towering cliffs of this iron-bound coast,
a driver's path conducts back to the entrance of
Blackman's River.

Maria Island is separated from the main land
by a channel varying from four to eight miles wide,
and navigable for large vessels; though its soundings
have never been properly laid down, as there is
a small island, called Lachlan's Midway, in the
channel, westward of which there is shoal water.
On the east side the island presents a mass of

perpendicular basaltic rock, except in Half-Moon Bay; but the west or inner shore has a very delightful and picturesque appearance, gradually sloping to a sandy beach. The island is nearly divided by a low sandy isthmus, separating Half-Moon from Oyster Bay, the bays running in within a few yards on either side.

From a lofty mountain forming the north-east extremity, the land inclines to the settlement, which was named Darlington. The part of this mountain which faces the sea presents a high wall of turretted rock; and the projecting point, called Cape Boulanger, is distinguished by two immense rocks, one jutting above the other, named (from their appearance) the Bishop and Clerk. The hill itself is called Mount Pedder. A river of excellent water runs by the settlement, where there were several fine buildings; but this very beautiful island is no longer a penal settlement. This is a matter of much gratification, as it is, in very truth, a charming place, having some thousand acres of land capable of cultivation, and some very fine timber: in many parts the soil is excellent, and altogether, a more fertile spot is not in Tasmania. There are several lagoons and running streams; the shores abound with capital fish; and the best oysters are found in the neighbourhood, at Oyster Bay. Several animals, whose fur is valuable, are trapped in the woods, and many birds of variegated plumage. The climate is mild and warm, and whilst the Government settlement was maintained there were several most productive gardens. The island ceased to be a penal settlement in 1851, and is now rented from the Government. Still looking cheerily forward, we prognosticate that a few years will see a thriving city here; adapted, as the site seems to be, for a sea-port town of some importance.

Returning to East Bay Neck, you proceed along the coast for some way, and again enter the forest. Some farm-houses are met with along the road, which is merely a track-way cut through the woods. Passing Carlton River and Plain, where there are two or three very good farms, you again strike into the forest till you come to Dodge's Ferry, the entrance on Seven Mile Beach on the left, and the road to Sorell on the right. Leaving the latter, you skirt along this beach (spoken of before), and coming to Ralph Ferry, where a railroad conveys boats over a narrow neck of land, you take to your boat again in Ralph Bay, a fine reach of considerable extent.

Entering once more on the Derwent, you pass along the left shore some clearings and some fine scenery, till, rounding the outer point, the metropolitan city bursts on your view, nestling like a confiding child under the shade and shelter of its guardian, the mountain range that overhangs it. From this spot, as, in truth, from whatever

point you view it, Hobarton looks a queen of
cities.

The road to Sorell leads along the shore of a still
more inland bay, called Pittwater, till you come
to a small fordable stream; when, entering the
woods, you come on the so-called town of Sorell,—
though only a town in name at present,—situated
in a valley, with a fine ridge of high lands encircling it, commanding a very interesting view
of Pittwater Bay, close to which the township runs.

The district of Sorell is an extensive one,
and contains within its range a vast amount of
very valuable land. There are many settlers, with
good farms, and a great deal of cleared land.
Several coasters ply over the bay to Hobarton.
There are two churches built here—one of the
established religion, and one of the Independent
persuasion; but there are no houses in the town
as yet, save the magistrate's, the doctor's, the
parson's, and the inn. It is proposed to have a
good road from Kangaroo Point, and, by cutting
a causeway through the Bluff Hill, to open a
direct line of communication to Hobarton. The
road, at present, leads round by Richmond, nine
miles; but there is a way for the tourist—a track
to the Bluff, and a ferry-boat, four miles to Sorell.

Kangaroo Point commands an extensive view
up and down the Derwent, a long reach of which
forms an estuary, between the city and Sandy Bay,

of some fifteen miles in circumference. Kangaroo Point Regatta is held here annually, when crowds from the good city visit the bay. This locality is remarkable for its extensive freestone quarries, large quantities of which are constantly being shipped to Port Philip. Latterly, a contract has been entered into with the Victoria Government to supply stone for the building of the new college, and other public buildings at Melbourne.

The township is situated in a plain, at the head of a small and pretty bay within the point; it is called Ivanhoe: at present it contains a neat episcopalian church, three inns, some good stores, and several comfortable cottages. A small steamer, the Venus, plies, half-hourly, every day to Hobarton; and from the fertility of the neighbouring plains and salubrity of its situation, it will, ere long, form one of the most favoured villages for summer residence.

On the opposite shore, where the demesne runs out to Pavilion Point, is held the Grand Tasmanian Regatta, founded by Sir John Franklin, in 1839; it annually comes off on the 24th November, in commemoration of the day of Tasman's discovery of the island. Its principal object is to encourage whalers: the prize of the day being allotted to the whale-boat most completely fitted with all the gear used in the fishing; and if any deficiency in this respect is discovered by the judges of the first boat, the prize is awarded to the first one found complete. The second prize is for watermen, to induce them to keep good ferry-boats.

During the regatta the shops are closed, and a holiday given at all the public offices. It continues two days, and is kept up with much spirit; the races being well contested. Considerable prizes are given besides the above, and everything is done to promote an amusement so beneficial in its results to an island colony. Every species of boat has its peculiar race prizes.

CHAPTER IX.

Yet wanted not the eye far scope to muse,
Nor vistas open'd by the wand'ring stream,
Both where at evening Alleghany views,
Through ridges burning in her western beam,
Lake after lake interminably gleam,
And past those settlers' haunts the eye might roam.

CAMPBELL.

AGAIN must the tourist leave the city, and embark on board the Culloden, a little steamer that plies twice a week to the Huon (remaining one night in the river), and twice to New Norfolk, returning each day. By the former trip you proceed down the Derwent to the entrance of D'Entrecasteaux Channel, and, skirting by the northern extremity of Bruni Island, strike across the bay to the river Huon. We cannot, however, pass Bruni Island without a description.

It is situated between Storm Bay and D'Entre-casteaux Channel, and consists of two parts, North and South Bruni, connected by a narrow neck of land which forms the shore of Adventure Bay, on

the outside. A very fine sandy beach of seven
miles in extent runs round this bay, which is very
beautiful. It is remarkable also as being the place
where Captain Cook first landed: there is a tree
here bearing the marks cut by him and his crew
during their visit. On the southern extremity is
a lighthouse, on Cape Bruni, to the west of Bad
Bay; but though this division of the island is better watered and of good soil, it is not as yet much
settled upon; the northern part possessing better soil
and more pasturage for stock, besides being more
conveniently situated, from its proximity to the
main land and distance from Hobarton. It contains from one hundred and fifty to two hundred
inhabitants. There are several nice farms, though
the settlers suffer much from the want of good
water. There are also many sawyers and splitters
scattered over the island, who earn a comfortable
livelihood by sending firewood to the city, where
it fetches very high prices, averaging from £2 to
£3 per ton.

There are two churches in North Bruni; one
at Variety Bay, built and endowed with ten acres
of land by Mr. William Lawrence, the pilot; the
other at Barnes' Bay, built by subscriptions and
a grant from the Society for the Propagation of the
Gospel in Foreign Parts. The site was given by
Mr. Richard Pybus. There are several lagoons of
fresh water in both islands; one of very peculiarly

attractive appearance in North Bruni, near Adventure Bay, within twenty yards of high water mark, is the property of Mr. Dean. These lagoons are frequented by numerous flocks of wild ducks. There is also an abundance of the wild pigeon tribe found in the island. At Denis Point, North Bruni, there is a ferry-boat, and also a guard-boat well manned. In the winter season great quantities of the kingfish are driven into the different bays and left on the beach; on the receding of the tide, they are collected by the inhabitants, dried, and salted for market.

Barnes' Bay is very handsome, with beautiful scenery around. There is one pretty clearance here belonging to Captain Fayle, and several others are now being commenced. The steamer passes close by, and there is also easy communication to the main land and the Brown's River road to town. On the other side, where there are some settlers, are the safe bays Patrick and Trumpeter; and there is good anchorage in all the inlets of the two islands.

Leaving Kelly's Point on Bruni Island and Tinderbox Bay on the main land, you pass Northwest Bay, a fine open one, with a pretty sandy beach; the shore is dotted here and there with some snug abodes of the settlers, and a field now and then well cultivated. On making the southern point of this bay, you bear a little away to the

right for six or seven miles, the line of coast still
presenting the same appearance, with a back-ground
of high land thickly timbered.   Opening on Birch's
Bay you see the saw-mills of Mr. Taylor, in shore,
and some good houses, with gardens and patches
of cultivated land scattered about.

Leaving this bay, you sight Huon Island at
the mouth of the river; it is about a mile in
circumference. There is a safe passage on both
sides · of this island, though further up the river
are some rocks called the Oil Butts; but, by keeping Huon Island in line with an outer island in
the Channel (called Woody Isle), you steer clear
of all danger.

Garden Island appears from those rocks; and
though from its name one would suppose it was
a fertile spot, it is, on the contrary, rocky and
barren. The shores on both sides of the Huon
are precipitous for a considerable way up, having
very high land in the back-ground, covered with
large timber. About five miles distant, you turn
into a deep bay leading to Port Cygnet, and pass
the first clearing or township of Leamington, situated on the shore of an inner bay, having some
four or five houses and some small patches of cultivation; the principal trade being from the sawyers
and splitters in the interior. It is, however, a
very pretty spot, and the fine range of hill behind
enhances its beauty.

Three miles from it and up the outer bay is the larger township of Port Cygnet, where there are some twenty to thirty houses. It is evidently soon about to become a place of much importance; for, although there is but little cultivated land as yet, still, as the timber is cleared away, agriculture advances; and, the soil being of excellent quality, and settlers thronging to the locality, a very few years will see a large and thriving town here. Up Nicholas Rivulet are also several clearings.

Leaving Port Cygnet Bay, you again enter the river, and passing on the opposite side of Police Point, you proceed by Desolation Bay, where there are some clearings. Flowerpot Bay has a peculiar rock at its entrance, which, from its formation and the brushwood growing on the top, gives it this name. You next pass Bullock Point, where there is a good place for loading timber.

In Flight's Bay are the saw-mills of Mr. Arthur, and in Hospital Bay those of Mr. Hill. Above the Egg Islands the river forms into two channels, leaving a long swamp between; which destroys the navigation in a great measure. Still, the steamer can go up to Franklin Settlement, now in a forward state. This was originally purchased by Lady Franklin, and let out on clearing leases, to encourage settlers. The highest navigable point, at present, is Victoria, where a town has lately been commenced and a church built.

One mile and a half above this are the Falls; and above this the river is deep and navigable for small craft. There are a great many settlements up this river, and the timber, being of excellent quality, affords occupation to hundreds. For the most part the land is of a fine description, and in a short time will form some of the best farms in Tasmania. Altogether, the river trip is one of much interest, and of such diversity of scene and beauty, that it well repays two days' wandering.

To the southward of the entrance of the river is the deep Bay of Esperance and Adamson's River; entering which, from the point, you have a fine view of Adamson's Peak, a high hill overtopping the range. A deep lagoon extends a long way inland, and nearer to the sea is the safe and commodious anchorage of Recherche Bay and Ramsgate township.

We next must take a ramble to Bruni Island, overland, and visit the station where the remains of the former inhabitants of Tasmania dwell. Leaving Hobarton by the Sandy Bay road, you gain Kingston, or, as it is commonly called, Brown's River.

The village of Kingston, ten miles from Hobarton, is an irregular and straggling country township, situate near Brown's River: only an assemblage of scattered cottages, several of which, indeed, are mere huts; there are, however, a few good brick resi-

THE DERWENT AND SANDY BAY ROAD

A. Wood del.

dences. The stranger visiting this little settlement will, however, be gratified: comfort is always obtainable at Fisher's Hotel, the internal economy being exactly what the traveller looks for.

At Kingborough some excellent farms are to be found, the best soils of which are not inferior to those of Pittwater. Mr. Baynton's farm is very prolific, and his house and homestead excellent. Farmers, like others, must consult their own tastes, and not those of passers by; but it has certainly often surprised me to see the indifference with which they cut down every tree in the neighbourhood of their dwellings: many of the trees are eminently handsome; then having thus, in a few days, destroyed what a century could not replace, they commence planting. Mr. Baynton, however, has not fallen into this last error.

A short walk from Baynton's, places you on the shores of North-West Bay, along which the road leads for a short distance. This is a large arm of the sea, but, being shut in on all sides by gloomy and unpicturesque hills, it is not prepossessing. Approaching North-West Bay River, the soil sensibly improves in character, and the coarse, hungry sands we have passed give place to a rich red loam of great fertility. The farms here are small and strictly agricultural, the breeding of stock not being attended to. At this part the stream flows through a rich alluvium, second to nothing in Tasmania. The principal proprietors of this fine tract are the Messrs. Lucas and Fisher.

Falling into the head of North-West Bay is a fine little stream, probably six times the size of the Hobarton rivulet. Its earlier waters are collected from the first flat encountered on the summit of Mount Wellington, a spot familiar enough to Hobartonians ; but ere reaching the sea its channel is of considerable width, and the volume of water it discharges in time of flood is considerable. This rapid little river was spanned by an excellent wooden bridge, which was destroyed by the flood of 1854 : another, however, has been erected in its place. A short distance beyond it is an inn, called "The Half-way House," kept by a person named Groombridge ; and at the same spot are several dwellings, possibly the nucleus of a future town. Two or three of these already assume the name, if not the reality, of "General Stores."

At two miles from North-West Bay River, we cross a small clear brook, called the "Snug River," which discharges its scanty stream into an inlet, whose quiet and agreeable seclusion has given a name, not only to this little stream, but also to the neighbouring country. A short distance from here are the remains of a once excellent edifice, built originally by Mr. Tomkins, but which the desolating bush-fires of January, 1854, utterly destroyed, excepting the mere brick walls. At that time it was used for an hotel; it is now renewed, and its present landlord is a Mr. Hainey.

The next four miles you cross a succession of hills, called "Snug Tier," from the summit of which you catch occasional glimpses of exceedingly fine scenery. Stretching along the horizon there is the mountain tier of South Bruni; to the southeast are the bold and beautiful cliffs of Fluted Cape, about 1000 feet above the level of the sea.

Adventure Bay, on the east coast of Bruni, may also be seen, separated by the long and thread-like isthmus uniting the two peninsulas of Bruni Island. This singular strip of sand looks like an artificial embankment. Its length is several miles, and its average height above high-water mark is under four feet. Within the view, further on, are comprehended Bruni Island, Tasman's and Forrestier's Peninsulas.

The hills about Carlton and Pittwater, as well as the Wellington range, including Storm Bay and D'Entrecasteaux Channel, form a vast and perfect picture. A bend in the road places you in view of the establishment where the few remaining descendants of the ancient inhabitants of Tasmania are now located.

Occupying comparatively low ground, the valley is beautiful; but if this spot were a hundred-fold more prepossessing than nature has already made it, its attractions would scarcely be observed, the

attention being forcibly drawn to an object which,
on account of its inmates, is peculiarly interesting.
How, indeed, should it be otherwise, when we
reflect that within the walls of that low cottage
beneath us are all that now remains of a once
formidable nation; who, in a thirty years' war
with our countrymen, were either sent into captivity, or the grave—they are but now sixteen in
number. The glen in which they live is called,
from the little inlet adjacent, Oyster Cove, a small
arm of D'Entrecasteaux's Channel; a few acres of
which land has been cleared for them along the
banks of a small river that passes by their dwelling. Dr. Milligan is the inspector of the station,
and constantly visits them. All their wants are
supplied from Government funds, which annually
averages £1000, including the salaries of storekeeper, medical officer, and chaplain.

The Culloden steamer starts at eight o'clock
every Monday and Thursday for New Norfolk; to
this place there is also a daily coach, which
leaves the city at six o'clock, a.m. By the steamer
you cruise over the prettiest portion of the Derwent. Rounding the Domain past the Government
dockyard, you have a capital view of the Botanical
Gardens. The river still seems but a succession
of lakes: on either side are rich farms or finely
wooded hills, sloping to the water's edge, thickly
timbered, and giving a degree of richness and

beauty to the scene as you glide over its placid waters; for the stream is exceedingly sluggish and the current scarcely perceptible, more particularly when the tide is coming in.

Passing a wide reach of water, or lake, called Newtown Bay, you come in view of Risdon Ferry, the road to Richmond. A large punt, capable of carrying over carriages and horses, is always in waiting to convey you across an arm of the river,—about three-quarters of a mile over. One mile and a half from the ferry is the extensive property of T. G. Gregson, Esq., M.L.C., situated on an eminence, and almost surrounded by a high range of hills, of which Mount Direction is the principal.

Risdon (originally called Restdown), was the site selected as a resting-place for the first settlers, and the foundations of a town were actually laid here, part of which are still to be seen. The tree where the first camp was pitched by Colonel Geils is also pointed out. It is a very fine place; and the beauty and order of the locality harmonize with the courteous hospitality, good cheer, and kind urbanity of its worthy proprietor, which leave in the stranger's heart feelings of gratitude not easily forgotten.

Beyond this range of hills, at the back of Risdon, the river winds past O'Brien's Bridge, forming a lake which bears a striking similarity to one of the smaller lakes of Killarney; Mount Wellington presenting the appearance of the reeks of Macgillicuddy. The little village is one of the neatest in the island; and a fine rich background of a deep valley running into the mountain gorge adds much to its picturesque beauty. Proceeding on, you pass a fine island and some pretty places, which look most imposing along the sides of the long tier of mountain range that extends from Mount Wellington into the heart of the island.

Passing through the portcullis at Bridgewater, you enter on narrower waters, but not less beautiful; the shores on either side still presenting a most pleasing and picturesque appearance, till, as the river grows narrow with high ridges of forest-covered hills on either side, there opens a splendid view of the valley in which is the town, or rather village, of New Norfolk: a charming resting-place, with a capital hotel and many a delightful walk or ride in every direction. Indeed, there could not be found a more pleasing trip by either land or water than the visit to this pretty place, which affords to the lover of the pencil an opportunity to indulge his taste in every variety of scene and view.

A very fine building, the Lunatic Asylum, a Government Institution, is also to be inspected with interest, and is worthy of note: also, the Governor's country place, although it is now rented, and appears no more than a comfortable cottage, with pretty shrubberies and grounds. A capital road conducts you to Bridgewater and back to the city by the Launceston or main road.

For the following description of the country above New Norfolk the Author is indebted to the extreme kindness of a friend who has resided in its neighbourhood; and, as any addition or change in its style would lessen its beauty, he copies it verbatim, giving it, as it well deserves, a chapter to itself.

CHAPTER X.

The golden sun has colour'd all the woods;
Fresh views succeed, each brighter than the last.
There, barren rocks are channell'd by the floods—
Here, Flora's beauties cannot be surpass'd.

LEIGH.

THE road from New Norfolk to Marlborough, which
it is now our intention to describe, is characterised
by much beauty of scenery; the river Derwent
majestically winding on the left, and the monotony
being lessened by inlets, small islands thickly
covered with shrubs of every description, and
diminutive cataracts, which in time past have been
even dangerous to the venturesome traveller, rushing as they do with velocity over the rocky ridges
which impede the turbulent stream in its headlong
course.

It is also worthy of remark, that the whole
of this part of the river is embedded with solid
rock. The road does but little credit to either
the inhabitants or the Government; it being in

some parts—and more especially in the rainy season of the year—all but impassable: indeed, along the banks of the noble Derwent, as they jut more prominently outward, the traveller, in pursuing his way, runs no inconsiderable risk. The road being destitute of a fence for some considerable distance, and elevated from eighty to a hundred feet above the level of the river, does not decrease its peril; added to which, a high escarpment on the right leaves it scarcely possible, with a restive horse or negligent driver, to escape scatheless, or perchance with life.

The only mode of conveyance in this part of the country, with the exception of the saddle-horse, is a kind of omnibus, or as it is here designated, a van.; it contains six inside, and, by dint of great manœuvring, two with the driver, and being entirely without covering in no way increases its comforts. For some miles to drive tandem is thought preferable.

Many pretty country residences attract the eye on the road to the Woolpack, the place of changing horses; but want of time and space prevent our enumerating them. After passing some short distance by Shooter's Hill, formerly occupied by Josiah Spode, Esq., we bid adieu for a few brief hours to the pure waters of the Derwent; and, as we proceed, the beautiful Macquarie Plains next call forth our admiration. We pause to say a few

words of its inhabitants. We first recognise a
sweet cottage and verdant garden, surrounded by
English meadows, the residence of the Rev. Mr.
Hesketh, officiating clergyman of the Woolpack.
Mr. Barker, an old colonist, has also here his
country seat, and is noted for kindness and hospitality to the stranger. Here again the Derwent
greets our admiring eye, riveting the attention by
new features of sportive form and picturesque
beauty.

Nothing of note occurs until we reach the
Woolpack; which being the half-way house on
the road to Hamilton, is invariably greeted by
the van-traveller with feelings of joy. A pretty
church forms one of its principal objects of attrac-
tion; if we except the beautiful sweetbriar and
hawthorn hedges which line and adorn the entrance
to the inn—a low-roofed, weather-boarded way-
side resting-place. A blacksmith's shop is the
only other habitation there. And now again we
find ourselves proceeding on our journey; and
for some little distance enjoy the comfort of a
good road, passing through the estates of the
very extensive landed proprietor, W. J. T. Clarke,
Esq. Soon again, we are rolling over a vast quantity of sand and loose stone, and find how vain
our anticipations have been of a good road all the
way. After rambling over them for some time,
we arrive at a long and tedious hill, well known

by the name of White's Hill; the steepness of
which obliges our van-travellers to trust to their
personal resources. At its foot, after descending
a rocky declivity, we perceive a small neat cottage.
The extreme civility evinced by its inhabitants,
in rendering all the assistance in their power to
the weary traveller and jaded horse, is worthy
of remark and commendation.

Having, with some difficulty, obtained the summit of this fatiguing height, we look with pleasure
on the lovely plain stretching before us; and, in
glancing around the face of the country, perceive
its aspect is somewhat different, there being but
few trees; whereas that which we have but some
time passed was thickly covered with them—the
gum and wattle prevailing.

And now we hasten on to the township of
Hamilton, the entrance of which strikes the
stranger as being most beautiful. Standing on
the Clyde Hill, we gaze from the quiet little
hamlet lying so prettily in the valley, seemingly
beneath our feet, to the blue ridges of the distant
mountains, as they rise stretching miles away. And
then, as our eye rests more steadily upon each,
we recognise the Wild Crag, or Peak of Teneriffe;
the Snowy Range, over which no foot has trod,
glittering in the sun's bright rays; and Mount
Olympus, in the distance almost as far as the eye
can reach, and only distinguishable by its broad flat

top, adds another charm to excite our admiration,
tempting the traveller to stay his steed and gaze
long and doatingly upon nature's beautiful handi-
work. On descending the Clyde Hill, we pass by
Dr. Sharland's, whose door is never closed to the
stranger, and whose ready hand and warm welcome
bespeak his kindly heart.

But in place of passing through the township,
we turn slightly to the left, that being on our way
to the new country; then for full ten miles we pass
through the most beautiful park-like scenery, Law-
renny, the estate of Edward Lord, Esq. When
about a mile and a half from the Ouse Bridge, we
catch a glimpse through the clustering trees of
Dunrobin, the property of W. A. Bethune, Esq.
Close to this pretty country seat is the bridge now
building across the river Derwent—a noble structure of solid stone. Government labour has been
employed in its erection for the last three years;
and although it has been an immense expense, it
will eventually prove worthy of its cost. There
is also now being cut close by, a road leading to
the western country, discovered and described by
Major Cotton. Would we could also think that
the time, trouble, and expense lavished upon it,
could be repaid by its usefulness. All roads, however, have their uses, and they are particularly
valuable in new countries.

After passing some time in these reflections,

we proceed to the Ouse Bridge, which is rather more than ten miles from Hamilton. It has a small but pretty chapel, post-office, police-station, blacksmith's shop, school-house (which is very well attended), one or two small shops, and—last in our remarks, though not in a traveller's thoughts—a comfortable country inn. Four miles through a pretty country, on the Marlborough road, we catch a last peep of the river Ouse; and having passed through the properties of W. Jamieson and Pringle Whyte, Esqrs., we arrive at the boundary line of Rotherwood, the estate of J. T. Pogson, Esq., whose energies are all directed to following the good old English system of the cottier tenant; and instinctively the eye rests upon the numerous cottages with feelings of pleasure, recalling to memory, as they do, the industry of the English labourer.

About half-a-mile before entering Victoria Valley, a distance of twelve miles from the Ouse Bridge, our attention is attracted to a magnificent waterfall, which, being but a short distance inland, is visible from the road. It is estimated that it falls one hundred feet from an almost perpendicular height, and flows from the Kenmere Rivulet or Native Hut Creek. The appearance of the country is that of a marsh, prettily interspersed with trees: the only thing for which it is remarkable, is that of having once been a probation station.

The folly of the Government, in expending be-

tween £50,000 and £60,000 upon drainage only, is
not to be forgotten; the marsh being now a confused
mass of drains from twenty-two feet wide, with
others smaller, presenting the appearance of diminutive canals: and so far from any benefit being derived
from all this waste, it is universally admitted that
the marsh is of less value than it formerly was.
The houses are in thick clusters, and strike you
as being somewhat similar in appearance to military barracks; and, in the distance, surrounded by
gently rising ground, the face of the country looks
singularly picturesque. It is now rented from the
Government by T. F. Marzetti, Esq., at a mere
nominal rent.

Passing through the stations of Mr. Edolls and
W. J. T. Clarke, Esq., we come to the Dee Scrub—
a dense jungle, some two or three miles in extent.
Gigantic trees of every description here spread
forth their broad and noble boughs, not only ob-
scuring the sun's bright rays, but imparting a feeling of loneliness by enfolding all within a mantle
of darkness.

After pausing to admire this extensive forest, we
again take our onward course; and, some distance
beyond, arrive at the river Dee, which takes its
rise from Lake Echo. Having crossed over a nice
little bridge, we wend our way through the stations of W. Synnott and W. Sharland, Esqs. Low,
marshy land is the chief feature in these properties.

Another probation station next arrests our glance, known as the Seven Mile Creek : but here Desolation reigns supreme, giving it the appearance of some old ruin ; for, with the exception of some shepherds of Mr. Sharland's, it is wholly uninhabited.

The entire road from the Ouse Bridge is a gradual ascent, so that, as we now stand upon the extremity of the rise, the valley, similar to the township of Hamilton, opens almost beneath our feet, suddenly bringing to our view the vast estate of Bronté and the district of Marlborough. The view is most grand—Mount Olympus appearing on a more extended scale, whilst crowds of hills range far back ; not omitting to mention the celebrated Brady's Sugar Loaf, which, as well as Mount Olympus and the Scraggy Peak, is one of the sites for the trigonometrical survey.

We now commence the descent — an almost perpendicular distance of between two and three hundred feet ; and, having gained the bottom of this stupendous height, look around upon the police station and a few shepherds' huts, comprising the only inhabitable part of Marlborough ; except the small cottages on the Bronté estate, now the property of W. J. T. Clarke, Esq.

With astonishment we now observe that the whole of the trees are without foliage, and stand forth like huge gaunt spectres—spreading out their

immense bare arms, and creating such a feeling
of horror in the uninitiated traveller that he
almost shrinks from traversing this solitary path
in the gloom and haze of night. The reason assigned for this strange phenomenon by the inhabitants of the district is, that a most severe frost
in the year 1836 killed, with very few exceptions,
every tree and shrub around: for, save those growing on the range of hills, the eye meets nought
but desolation. It may not be amiss to mention that, notwithstanding its barren appearance,
this is a very heavily timbered country; and it is
the opinion of some that the thick forest, now
withered, dead, and bleached, owed its extinction
to a tremendous fire, which, sweeping like the
doom of Fate over the country, left not a leaf
or twig along its desolating course.

The next object we notice is a beautiful bridge
across the river. The police station, a glimpse of
which we caught when on the rise before entering Marlborough, is now sufficiently near for our
inspection; it consists of a very pretty and substantial stone cottage, which affords excellent accommodation for the traveller. After having passed
by this, and crossed the Nive, the eye rests upon
immense plains with but few trees, whilst innumerable herds of cattle bring to mind the vast
prairies of America. Several small rivers intersect
the land, the two principal being the Clarence

and Travellers' Rest, over which temporary bridges are erected for the purpose of passing stock. The owners of the stations by which we are surrounded are Henric Nicholas, W. J. T. Clarke, and T. Standfield, Esqs. Nothing worthy of remark occurs till we arrive at Lake St. Clair, the entrance to which does not partake of the general beauty of the scenery around, and its monotony causes a feeling of disappointment to arise in the mind of the traveller.

But soon these fancies are dispelled, when, having unmoored the beautiful gig placed there by private subscription, and pulling far out into the centre of the lake, the hands unconsciously relax their grasp of the oars, and the tourist gazes around on the beautiful scenery that meets his enraptured eye. The snow-white beach lining the borders of the lake is adorned by native shrubs, and strewn with shells and pebbles of every description : the "waratah," mingling the brilliant red of its blossoms with a thousand different shades of foliage, is more entrancing to the eye than words can well express. Flowing into the lake on the upper side, is the river Narcissus, which, sweeping again outward from the other extremity, forms the source of the Derwent. The myrtle, cabbage-palm, fern-tree, tea-tree, and pepper-tree, are but a few of those which grow so luxuriantly in this soil ; these, together with the numerous spurs

of the mountain that jut out on the lake, covered
with every description of native shrubs, lay reflected in the crystal mirror; the lofty ranges of
Mount Ida, Mount Olympus, and the Seven Apostles,
at whose immediate base the lake is situated, looking
grand in their towering majesty. The numerous attempts which have been made to sound the depth of
Lake St. Clair have, as yet, ever proved fruitless.
Its length is generally estimated at fifteen miles, and
it extends from two to four miles in breadth. The
desolate aspect of the country for the last eighteen
miles renders the lovely appearance of this noble
sheet of water, surrounded by every beauty the
hand of nature can plant, still more enthralling;
and the stranger feels amply repaid for all the
discomforts of his journey, when in the midst
of a scene upon which he cannot but gaze in
ecstacy.

Before we close our description of this part
of the country we would observe that there is
another road, besides that we have just passed
over, leading to Lake St. Clair—one cut by private
enterprise, and possessing the advantage of being
ten miles shorter; but as it commences from, and
runs the whole way through, the large estates
of T. L. Gellibrand, Esq., it is not generally used,
being thought private. Compared with the large
sums expended upon that made by Government,
its cost has been but some few pounds; which

its usefulness has many times repaid. Mr. Gellibrand's estate of Cleveland is about five miles from the Ouse Bridge, along a fatiguing sandy soil. The house is prettily situated on an eminence overlooking the river Dee, which flows along the bottom of the extensive fruit-garden adjoining.

Here, again, we find a great number of tenants, whose chief characteristics are industry and firm attachment to the small portion of ground forming their only home. And as our eye glances over the sweetly pretty view from the house, of the river winding gracefully through the little shrubs which grow near the water-side, we cannot fail to notice that great attention is paid to irrigation — all the meadows looking as though covered with green velvet: so truly refreshing to the eye is the beautiful English grass.

About two miles from here, we approach the beautiful cataract of the Derwent; which, after dashing and tossing into a thousand different streamlets, unites into one body of water, and flows precipitously between the vast mass of solid rock which, for some considerable distance, lines its course. The force with which it falls, more especially in winter, is very great—greeting the ear some time before this truly pleasing scene meets the eye; and not only rendering the voice perfectly inaudible when standing on the rocks, but filling the heart with a feeling almost amounting

to awe, as the gazer watches with intense interest
the waters bursting in their sparkling grandeur.

A waterfall is also another pretty object of
observation on this estate, known by the name
of Black Bob's Falls. Standing beneath on a small
green spot, we look upwards, a distance of between
forty and fifty feet, upon the water roaring down
the perpendicular precipice; and its dashing course
so rivets and fascinates the attention of the gazer
as to render it difficult to turn away and ramble
again by the still flowing waters of the Dee, or
gaze upon the humble contented tenant, as he toils
at the plough or vigorously thrashes out the grain.

But we must now bid adieu to this scenery,
content if our readers have with us, in fancy,
rambled over the wild country which we have
sought to depict for their amusement and information.

CHAPTER XI.

'Tis education forms the common mind:
Just as the twig is bent, the tree's inclined.
    *   *   *   *
Bid harbours open—public ways extend;
Bid temples worthier of the gods ascend;
Bid the broad arch the dangerous flood contain,
The mole projected break the roaring main;
Back to his bounds the subject sea command,
And roll obedient rivers through the land.

POPE.

HOBART TOWN, or, as it is now more elegantly designated, the City of Hobarton, described as to its general appearance in a former chapter, needs now some note of its progress in the arts and sciences, in which it is rapidly advancing; and it deserves a more worthy account than our humble pen can give.

As we treat only of the present, and write from the experience of one short year, we will not fatigue the reader by any review of the past, but rather, from notes received from individuals well conversant in the matter, compile this chapter of the present state of advancement in the intellectual pursuits.

First in importance are the means of education afforded to youth; in treating of which, we must leave Hobarton awhile to speak of Christ's College, Bishopsbourne, established in 1846 for the

promoting sound and useful learning according to the principles of the Church of England. The College has been set on foot and endowed entirely by private subscriptions here and in England. It possesses 3,200 acres of land at Bishopsbourne, 400 acres at New Town, 100 acres at New Norfolk, and 50 acres at the Huon; with a promise of 500 acres at Tunbridge, provided the College buildings

should be erected on that township.   The annual
rental of the College estates amounts to £1,065.

The Foundation at present consists of a warden,
sub-warden, two honorary fellows, the Gell fellow,
three divinity fellows, and the master of the junior
school.   There are, besides, several scholarships,
founded either by private individuals or by the
various professions collectively.   The present Society consists of Visitor — The Right Reverend
Francis Russel, Lord Bishop of Tasmania.   Warden—Rev. P. V. A. Filleul, M.A.   Sub-warden—
Rev. W. Brooke, B.A.   Honorary Fellows—1, Ven.
Archdeacon Marriott, M.A.; 2, Ven. Archdeacon
Davies, B.A.   Gell Fellow and Bursar—Rev. C.
F. Garnsey.   Divinity Fellows—1, P. P. Fogg;
2, E. P. Adams.   Scholarships—Clerical, £25 per
annum each; Archdeacon's, £20 per annum, A.
Sharland; Magistrate's, A. N. Mason; Medical,
H. A. Brock; Dry's, R. Richardson.   There are
also other Scholarships, viz.: Dumaresq's, Reibey's,
Brown's, Franklin's.

The College terms are £60 per annum, payable
half-yearly in advance.   This sum includes tuition
fees, and board and lodging.   Extras, which consist of washing, drawing, stationery, etc., are
charged at the end of each half year.   The age
of admission is not limited, and no religious test
is exacted.   All members of the College in residence are, however, expected to conform to its

rules, which are adapted to the principles of the Church of England. There is a well-chosen library, consisting of nearly 4000 volumes. Librarian— Rev. C. F. Garnsey. Extracts from the Seventh Annual Commemoration Report will be seen in Appendix [A], and read with interest.

We now return to the city: and first we meet with *The Hutchins School*, founded in memory of the late Archdeacon Hutchins; it is a very neat and elegant building in the Gothic style, covering, with its gardens, play-grounds, etc., nearly two acres, situated in a very central locality in Mac-quarie-street. The following account was furnished to the author by the extreme kindness of the Venerable Archdeacon Davies. The Hutchins School was opened August 3rd, 1846. Visitor— the Lord Bishop of Tasmania. Head Master—The Reverend John R. Buckland, B.A., late Student of Christ Church, Oxford. Second and Mathe-matical Master—Matthew Kennett, St. John's Col-lege, Cambridge. Third Master—The Reverend H. Abdy Middleton, B.A., Brasenose College, Ox-ford. Fourth Master — Mr. L. Trollope. The Terms are, from the 1st January, 1854 — Day scholars, under twelve years of age, £12 per annum; day scholars, above twelve years of age, £16 per annum; boarders, under twelve years of age, £60 per annum; boarders, above twelve years of age, £70 per annum; day boarders, dining in the house, £32 per annum; drawing (an extra at the option of parents), £4 4s. per annum. Each boarder is expected to bring two pairs of sheets, six towels, a knife, fork, and spoon. A quarter's notice is required before the removal of any pupil. All accounts are sent in quarterly; and any pupil whose account remains unpaid for more than a quarter will be removed. There are at present 120 scholars.

At a meeting of the Trustees of the Hutchins School, held at Hobarton, on Thursday, the 22nd day of December, 1853, the Hon. the Speaker of the Legislative Council in the Chair, it was proposed by the Hon. the Attorney-General, and seconded by the Venerable Archdeacon Davies,

"That for every sum of two hundred pounds paid to the Trustees of the Hutchins School, from the 'Newcastle Scholarship Fund,' a scholarship of the value of twelve pounds, tenable for two years, shall be founded. That in order to keep up a spirit of emulation among the students, these scholarships shall be thrown open to competition, with this sole limitation,—that one scholarship in each year shall be open to boys under twelve years of age, the other to boys above that age; the details of the examination to be left to the authorities of the School for the time being. That if the amount paid to the Trustees shall exceed the sum of eight hundred pounds, it shall form a fund to found a second prize of books, to be called 'The Newcastle Prize,' for the boy who shall stand next to the successful candidate for each scholarship."

(Signed)   R. R. DAVIES,
V. FLEMING,
R. DRY.

We are indebted to a publication called "The Churchman's Almanac," for an account of the following Societies under the immediate direction of the Bishop of Tasmania.

Hobarton Branch Society for Promoting Christian Knowledge, and for the Propagation of the Gospel. — Patron — His Excellency Sir William Thomas Denison, Knight. President—The Lord Bishop of Tasmania. Vice-President—The Archdeacon of Hobarton. Treasurer — M. Evans, Esq. Secretary—Rev. D. Galer. The affairs of this Society are managed by a committee, consisting of the President, the Vice - President, the Secretary, the Treasurer, all clergymen ministering within the Archdeaconry with the sanction of the Bishop, the lay representatives of district or parochial associations, and twelve laymen elected annually by the members from the general body. The committee meet on the first Tuesday in each month, in the Harrington-street school-room : five forming a quorum. The principal objects of the society are : 1, the building, furnishing, and repair or enlargement of churches and chapels ; 2, the support of additional clergymen in populous or remote places ; 3, the establishment and maintenance of church schools and their teachers ; 4, the supply and distribution of the books of the incorporated Society for Promoting Christian Knowledge.

A depôt for the sale of books exclusively from the catalogue of the venerable English Society for Promoting Christian Knowledge is kept at Mr. W. Fletcher's Stationery and Berlin Depôt, 28, Elizabeth-street. Subscribers of £1 and upwards have

the privilege of purchasing the books at the Parent
Society's reduced prices to members, with a penny
in the shilling added towards defraying the expenses. To all others threepence in the shilling
is charged. But to promote the circulation of the
Holy Scriptures, nothing extra is charged upon
Bibles and New Testaments. Almost every church
and school in this division of the diocese has received assistance from this useful society, which
deserves to be better supported by the members
of the Church of England.

The following statistics of the two venerable
societies, of which this is a branch, are particularly interesting, and call for gratitude to
Almighty God for His continued blessing upon
these two handmaids of the Church of England.
Issue of books, etc., by the Christian Knowledge Society from April, 1851, to April, 1852 :
Bibles, 143,482 ; New Testaments, 73,982 ; Common Prayer Books, 329,444 ; other bound books,
1,095,925 ; Tracts, 2,450,381 ; total, 4,093,214.
Since the year 1733, when the society began to
report its annual circulation of Bibles, Prayer Books,
and Tracts, it has issued one hundred and six
millions of publications. From 1840 to 1854 the
society voted £28,000 in aid of the endowment
of Bishoprics in the Colonies. Within the same
period £31,000 were voted towards the establishment of Colleges and Collegiate Institutions

in the Colonies. A further sum of £12,000 has recently been devoted by the society towards the erection of Cathedrals in the Colonies. Progressive extension of the two Parent Societies:—Society for Promoting Christian Knowledge, established 1699: receipts from subscriptions and benefactions alone: —1749, first jubilee, £1,200 9s. 6d.; 1799, second jubilee, £2,136 5s. 6d.; 1849, third jubilee, £22,723 12s. 10d. Society for the Propagation of the Gospel in Foreign Parts, established 1701:— 1701, first year, £1,537; 1751, first jubilee, £3,719; 1801, second jubilee, £6,457; 1851, third jubilee, £147,476.

Launceston Branch Society for Promoting Christian Knowledge, and for the Propagation of the Gospel.—President—The Right Reverend the Lord Bishop of Tasmania. Vice-Presidents—Rev. A. C. Thomson, W. Archer, Esq., T. A. Eddie, Esq. Treasurer—W. Henty, Esq. Clerical Secretary— Rev. G. B. Smith. Lay Secretary—W. Barrett, Esq. The affairs of the society are managed by a committee of clergymen and laymen, meeting quarterly. The objects of the society are similar to those of the Hobarton branch.

The Ripon Missionary Fund.—Trustees—The Lord Bishop of Tasmania, and the Archdeacons of Hobarton and Launceston. This fund, which is purely local, had its origin in a donation of £5,000 sent to this colony by the Bishop of Ripon, for the purpose of supplying "religious instruction to settlers in the bush." The only condition imposed was, that an account be rendered annually to the Society for the Propagation of the Gospel in Foreign Parts. This sum has been nearly doubled from other sources, and the interest alone is expended in carrying out the wishes of the original donor. The greater portion of the principal is lent on mortgage, and about £1,000 has been expended in the purchase of landed endowments. In consequence of the present high prices of the necessaries of life, the income thus accruing is found inadequate to meet the increased demand on the fund; the continuance, therefore, of the additional allowance to clergymen and catechists paid from this source must depend upon the contributions of the members of the Church of England in this diocese. Let those who profit by the present state of things not fail to. remember how hard the times press upon those who have to proclaim to their fellow-men the unsearchable riches of Christ.

Tasmanian Missionary Society.—The Tasmanian Missionary Society was established on the 27th of January, 1852, His - Excellency the Lieutenant-Governor being patron; the Right Reverend the Bishop of the diocese, president; and the Venerable the Archdeacons, vice-presidents; with a committee of management, consisting of the president

8

and vice-presidents, all licensed clergymen within
the diocese, and a number of elected laymen: the
said committee having power to add to their number, and to appoint their own secretary, treasurer,
and auditors. The objects of the Tasmanian Missionary Society are twofold: firstly, to co-operate,
as far as possible, with the Provincial Board of
Missions at Sydney in promoting "the conversion
and civilization of the Australian aborigines, and
the conversion and civilization of the heathen races
in the islands of the Western Pacific;" secondly,
to receive and forward any subscriptions given
to particular missionary societies or special missionary objects, approved by the committee. The
committee meet on the last Monday in January,
April, July, and October; five forming a quorum.

JOHN DUNN, ESQ., TREASURER.
REV. F. H. COX, SECRETARY.

Appendix [B] contains a list of all the schools
in connection with the Church of England which
come under Government aid and control. We
must also refer the reader to Appendix [C] for
a statistical account of the diocese of Tasmania,
wherein every matter is particularised.

Since writing the foregoing, the independence
of the Tasmanian Government being declared in
the British Parliament, it was resolved to with-
draw a considerable portion of the sum allowed
from home for the support of the Established

Church. The Legislative Assembly not feeling inclined to make good such a grant from colonial funds, it was resolved to make up the deficiency by a sustentation. Several meetings of both clergy and laity have been held, but as yet nothing has been determined upon; although the prevailing opinion seems to be that lay delegates should be chosen to direct the financial affairs of the Church, so far as the contributed funds extend; that congregations subscribing to the maintenance of a pastor, can choose their own, subject to the Bishop's sanction; and that every subscriber can give a vote, as well as name how his subscription is to be disposed of, either for the general fund or a particular parish. A very good feeling seems to prevail, and former disputes are likely to be forgotten, never to be renewed.

The author has also been favoured with a short account of the *Roman Catholic Church* in Van Diemen's Land, by the courtesy of the Vicar-General:—In May, 1844, there were but three churches—Hobarton, Launceston, and Richmond. In May, 1854, there were seven—Hobarton, Launceston, Richmond, New Norfolk, Oatlands, Westbury, Emu Bay; and several others were about to be erected. Divine service is also performed at stated times in Hamilton, Bothwell, Jerusalem, Brighton, Green Ponds, Ross, Campbell Town, Evandale, Longford, Deloraine, Sorell; and occasionally at

Circular Head, George Town, Perth, Avoca, Macquarie River, Great Swan Port, Spring Bay, Port Cygnet, and Franklin Settlement. In May, 1844, there were only three Catholic clergyman to attend to the colonial and convict duties. In 1854, there were one bishop and three clergymen paid by Government, and two paid by the people for the colonial duty—ten attached to the convict department in Van Diemen's Land and Norfolk Island.

In 1844, the Catholic children were very much scattered about, and many received no education : in 1854 there were two large school-rooms in Hobarton, one in Launceston, one in Richmond, and one in Westbury. These buildings were erected at the sole expense of the Catholic community. A large number of children also attend the other Government schools, but without any interference with their religious principles or practice. In 1848, a boarding-school for young ladies was established in Hobarton, in which there are at present thirty-two boarders and twelve day-boarders. In 1854 a seminary for young gentlemen was established, in which there are sixty boarders and twenty-three day scholars. There is a small community of Sisters of Charity, established in 1847, who devote their time to educating the poor children of Hobarton, and visiting the sick in the hospitals and private houses, and the imprisoned in the gaol and houses of correction.

Dr. Lillie has placed at our disposal the following remarks upon the state of the *Scotch Church* in Tasmania :—The Presbytery includes ten ministers, whose churches are distributed over the following localities : two in Hobarton, one in Launceston, one at Evandale, one at Bothwell, one at Sorell, one at O'Brien's Bridge, one at Great Swan Port, and one at West Tamar. Besides these churches, there are chapels and stations in other parts of the country, at which Divine Service is performed by the neighbouring ministers or the missionaries employed by the Presbytery. The ordinary meetings of Presbytery take place once a year, on the first Wednesday of November, at Hobarton and Launceston alternately. The ministers of the Presbytery receive exactly the same emoluments from the Government as ministers of the Church of England. Their Moderator is empowered by law to issue marriage licenses, and to give authority to the other members of Presbytery to do the same in their respective districts.

The Rev. Mr. Manton has obliged us with a statistical statement of the *Wesleyan Church* in Tasmania, by which we find it consists of twenty-three chapels, with six ordained ministers and twenty-two lay preachers. The members, or regular communicants, amount to about seven hundred. The several congregations average four thousand. There are Sunday-schools established in various

places throughout the island, at which there are
in constant attendance upwards of one thousand
children, and about one hundred teachers. For
some time there has been a very good day-school
attached to the principal chapel in Hobarton, with
an average attendance of one hundred scholars,
and one of a similar description in Launceston
with two hundred.

We have also been kindly furnished with
memoranda relative to Judaism in the island, by
Mr. J. Moss, the secretary for that community.
From them we find that in the year 1828, Sir
George Arthur, Bart., then Lieutenant-Governor,
granted two acres of land to the Jews for a cemetery. On the 9th August, 1843, the foundation
of a Synagogue, built and endowed by voluntary
subscriptions, was laid in Argyle-street, on a site
presented to them by a member of their persuasion. Another Synagogue was afterwards built in
Launceston, and endowed in a similar manner. In
regard to their religious affairs, the Synagogue of
Hobarton takes precedence of all the others in
Australia; and recently, the Rev. Herman Hoelzel
has been appointed Presiding Rabbi over all the
congregations in the south. Since his arrival a
school for teaching Hebrew has been founded, and
placed under his care. There are from forty to
fifty families of Jews resident in Hobarton and its
vicinity, who, by their own contributions, support

entirely the Synagogue and school. A charitable institution was founded in 1847, by Mr. Louis Nathan, now residing in London, for the relief of the poor; but it is gratifying to state that at present, there is not one person seeking pecuniary aid from it.

CHAPTER XII.

Knowledge of all avails the human kind,
For all beyond the grave are joys of mind.
　　　　　　　　　　　　　　　　HOGG.

The allotted hour of daily sport is o'er,
And Learning beckons from her temple's door.
. . . .
There Science from her favour'd seat surveys
The vale where rural nature claims her praise.
. . . .
When learning nurtures the superior mind,
What may we hope from genius thus refined.
　　　　　　　　　　　　　　　　BYRON.

IN our remarks upon the progress making in the
Arts and Sciences in Tasmania and its capital, the
Royal Society claims our particular notice, tending,
as it does, not only to encourage science and research of every description, but also to disseminate
a knowledge of the resources and produce of the
island in other countries.

A detailed account of the latter, as sent to the
Great Exhibition of 1851, has been kindly placed
at our disposal by Dr. Milligan, the talented Secretary of the Society, with a mention of the prizes

awarded, which cannot fail to interest the reader. See Appendix [D]. We also present extracts from the catalogue of the articles sent to the Paris Exhibition, 1855, it being too voluminous to publish entire. See Appendix [D 2].

The Royal Society was founded at a meeting held at Government House, on the 14th of October, 1843, His Excellency the Governor, Sir J. E. Eardley-Wilmot, presiding. This meeting consisted of the members of the Tasmanian and Horticultural Societies, and of many gentlemen interested in the advance of science in the colony. A portion of the Government Garden in the Domain was assigned to the Society for the formation of a Botanical Garden (already described), and an allowance of £400 a year was granted from the public treasury. In September, 1844, His Excellency announced that Her Majesty had signified her consent to become Patron of the Society, ratifying and approving all the steps taken in its formation.

The leading objects of the Society are to develope the physical characteristics of the island, and to illustrate its natural history and productions. The Society consists of a president, which post is invariably to be filled by the Governor for the time being; a council of twelve, a treasurer, secretary, and an indefinite number of Fellows. From the council, four are named by the Governor to act as vice-presidents. The president and council have the management of all the affairs of the Society. Elections are by ballot, according to liberal rules established, and special general meetings of the whole Society are held whenever any matter of moment is to be discussed, all members voting alike. The number at present is upwards of three hundred, besides honorary and corresponding members. The Royal Society seems to have a firmer footing and a wider basis than any similar institution established in the colony.

During the period of Sir John Franklin's administration, a society having the same object in view was established; Sir John being permanent president. This society comprised a few of the Government officers and a number of residents and non-residents eminent for scientific attainments and for their contributions to the natural history of the colony; it was temporarily endowed by Lady Franklin with a grant of four hundred acres of land, to aid and carry out its operations generally, but more especially to initiate a Museum. This her Ladyship built on a classic model, in a secluded but picturesque valley at the foot of Mount Wellington, three miles from the city and a mile from New Town; the reversion of the property being understood to be vested in any College or University which might be established by charter, in connection with the Church of England. We are uncertain

whether the College at Bishopsbourne fulfils all
the conditions; but there is reason to believe that
the Museum and the lands, etc., forming its endowments, have been handed over to the trustees
for that college. The funds upon which the Tasmanian Society depended for its support, in a great
measure, being thus withdrawn, and the Royal
Society having been formed about the same time
with similar objects, most of the members of the
former joined the latter, under the impression that
one strong society would more effectually accomplish its end than two, having only the same
amount of means at command, and incurring a
double amount of expenditure.

The present building in Harrington-street, occupied by the Society for its meetings and the formation of a Museum, is much too small for its
increasing collections in natural history and the
liberal donations of curiosities which it is constantly receiving. It is daily open to the public,
gratis, for inspection, and is well worthy of a
visit from the stranger.

We are glad to learn that the Government
have acceded to the wish of the inhabitants of
Fitzroy Crescent to appropriate the open space of
ground there to the purpose of building a suitable structure and forming Zoological Gardens.
The ground (comprising several acres) is peculiarly
adapted to this purpose, having a rivulet of the

purest water constantly flowing through the lower
portion; and the whole being capable—by the
exercise of a little taste, and some expenditure,
which it is to be hoped the Society will gladly
incur—of being rendered one of the prettiest and
most attractive promenades about Hobarton.

We must now take a cursory view of the
different public offices, from the papers before us.

The *Land Department*. The following is a
summary of the regulations under which Crown
land may be occupied:—Applications to be made
to the Surveyor-General, on printed forms obtainable at the police offices, describing the exact
situation of the land applied for. No lot to contain less than 500 or more than 5,000 acres.
License fee, £1 per 100 acres. On receipt of
notice from Survey Department, applicant must
deposit in the Treasury the amount of the first
year's license fee. Licenses may be renewed from
year to year, for five years, on payment of the
license fee two months before the expiry of the
current license. Survey Department to give three
months' notice of intended resumption of land,
and occupant to have the value of his improvements, by arbitration, when necessary. The Government reserves the power of granting licenses
to cut timber on occupied lands. The frontage
of a lot will be in general in proportion to the
depth of one to four. No license to be transferred

unless with the consent of the Surveyor-General. Persons occupying, or using Crown land without a license to be treated as trespassers.

The *Survey Department* is under the control of the Governor, and consists of a surveyor-general, deputy, six clerks, six permanent field surveyors, and seven draughtsmen, with salaries from £800 to £110 per annum.

The *Law Department* consists of the Chief Justice, with a salary of £1,500 a year, Puisné Judge, with £1,200, and a master, with £600; then come the reporters, clerks, Commissioners of the courts, Vice-Admiralty courts, and law officers of the Crown, Attorney-General, Solicitor-General, and Crown Solicitor. There are seventy barristers, attorneys, and solicitors who practice in common; though a few of the most eminent act only as pleaders: it is the intention, we believe, to divide the profession, as in England and Ireland.

There are upwards of 300 Justices of the Peace in the colony; but Sir H. Young, the present Governor, having issued a new Commission of the Peace, and decided that in future none shall hold the title without acting, also that no clergyman can be sworn in, the present list will be considerably reduced. There is one high sheriff for the colony, with a salary of £800 a year; an under sheriff, with £300, clerks, etc.; one commissioner of Insolvent Court, two chairmen of Quarter Sessions, and two deputy-chairmen, with their clerks, etc.; Crown prosecutors, commissioners of Court of Requests, deputy commissioners, registrars, etc. There are twelve notaries public.

The colony is divided into eight districts, and twelve sub-districts, over each of which preside police magistrates, receiving salaries from £80 to £300 a year; with district constables and police to correspond.

Next comes the *Marine Department*, with the post-offices at Hobarton and Launceston; both retain naval officers, with large salaries, under whom are the deputy harbour-masters, pilots, and lighthouse-keepers. The following are the lighthouses:—Iron Pot, entrance of Storm Bay, South Bruni, Swan Island; Goose Island; Kent Group, and Low Head. The dues collected annually for these exceed the expenses by about £1,000. There are two signal stations, with their dependencies; one for Hobarton *via* Mount Nelson to the entrance of Storm Bay, and one for Launceston from the Tamar Head to George Town.

The *Custom House Department* is under the charge of a collector at Hobarton, with a salary of £800 a year, a surveyor, with six landing waiters, six clerks, etc. An establishment somewhat smaller in number is kept up at Launceston, with clearing officers at the ports on the Huon, and the Mersey, Circular Head, and Swan Port.

At Hobarton there is also a *Caveat Board* for investigating claims and settling all disputes about land.

The *Board of Education* consists of the members of the Executive and Legislative Council, with an inspector, and a deputy inspector, clerks,` etc. There are fifty-four schools under the board, including nine at Hobarton and four at Launceston. These schools are conducted under the following (amongst other) regulations:—No particular form of religious training is allowed, but ample opportunity is afforded to parents to have their children instructed in their own religious tenets.

The Board will provide for the maintenance of two classes of schools. Those of the first class to be established in Hobarton and Launceston, and in other localities where an attendance of eighty children may be calculated upon. Of the second class, schools may be established wherever it appears likely that there will be an attendance of not less than twenty children. When the number of scholars likely to attend does not amount to twenty, the Board will consider the propriety of granting assistance (so far as the state of their funds will admit) on the principle of proportioning their grants to the sums locally subscribed.

As a general rule, at least one-third of the expense, either of building or of renting a schoolhouse and master's residence, must be defrayed from local sources. Applications for the establishment of schools must be made according to a printed form, copies of which may be obtained through the secretary. The hours of attendance shall be from nine to twelve in the forenoon, and from two to four in the afternoon. Saturday shall be a half-holiday. The ordinary course of instruction in every public school shall be considered to comprise reading, spelling, writing, arithmetic, English grammar, geography, history, and singing. Teachers entitled to charge school-fees.

There is one regiment of the line stationed in Tasmania. Head quarters at Hobarton, a company at Launceston, strong detachments at Port Arthur and Eagle Hawk Neck, under officers, and a smaller one at Oatlands under a non-commissioned officer.

The *Ordnance Department* consists of a storekeeper, deputy-storekeeper, and four clerks, one of whom is the barrack-master.

The *Engineer Department*—the office of which forms one of the neatest buildings in Hobarton, situated at the lower entrance to the Domain—is now reduced to one officer, and some clerks. Previously there were four officers and twelve sappers and miners; but two officers went home, and the remainder were removed to Sydney, the Tasmanian Government not requiring their services.

The *Commissariat Department*, lately much reduced, now consists of a deputy commissary-general,

OLD WHARF, HOBARTON.

T. Prout del.

Smith, Elder & Co. London.

three assistants, and two deputy-assistant commissary-generals.

The *Post-Office Department* is under the control of the Postmaster-General at Hobarton, with seven clerks, the Postmaster at Launceston, with three clerks, and sixty established Post-Offices throughout the country.

There are ten coaches to the interior from Hobarton, eight daily and two twice a week; and there are six from Launceston.

Of steamers, one leaves Hobarton daily for New Norfolk, one twice a week to the Huon. There are two steam-packet companies, with three vessels for the Eastern Coast every week: the Tasmanian Company have two very fine vessels, one which makes a trip every ten days to and from Melbourne, and the other the same to Sydney. From Launceston there are four steamers weekly to Melbourne and Sydney; one leaves every week for the North-Western Coast, Port Sorell, the Mersey, Emu Bay, and Circular Head; there are, besides, two small boats on the Tamar used as tug and passenger-boats.

We next pass on to the Public Hospitals and the Medical Schools for the study of surgery and medicine; upon which matters we place before our readers a memorandum kindly furnished by Dr. Hall, the resident professional and authorized Lecturer, etc., of Her Majesty's

General Hospital:—This important establishment is situated on a very advantageous plot of ground, with a handsome frontage to Liverpool-street, the rear being bounded by the cliff of sandstone overhanging the Town Creek. It is divided into three distinct buildings:—1st. The Male Hospital—a handsome, cut-stone building, two stories high, presenting one of the finest architectural ornaments of the town, in the centre of an ornamental shrubbery. It has eight large well-ventilated wards, holding twenty beds each, with a good operating room and some smaller wards; and at the rear are two covered balconies running the whole length of the building, and commanding a beautiful view of the town, harbour, and adjacent country. Here, on wet days, the convalescent patients have ample room for exercise: on fine days they can extend their rambles amongst the flower-beds and shrubs. It has only been built a few years. 2nd. The Female Hospital; the original building, two stories high, and capable of accommodating about eighty patients. 3rd. The Infirmary; a commodious one-story building, where invalid females are treated: it has at present sixty inmates, but can accommodate considerably more. Many of the patients are upwards of seventy years of age, and one recently died aged 105. The outbuildings comprise the resident medical officer's, the matron's, and the superintendent's quarters, with ordnance and `drug stores, offices, dispensary, dead-house, kitchens, laundry, etc. Patients of all classes are received; free people paying fees to the Government of five shillings a day, assigned servants one shilling a day, and the same for paupers paid for by the Colony. The medical staff consists of two military and two civil practitioners, one of the latter being the resident medical officer.

By the statistical return [Appendix E] of the establishment for 1853, the nature of the diseases most prevalent in this healthy climate will be easily seen, with the relative amount of mortality. But it must be borne in mind, that this being the principal hospital in the island, numbers of hope-less cases are sent here. The whole number of patients that can be accommodated is about three hundred, and the arrangements are scarcely sur-passed by any hospital with similar accommodations in Great Britain. As a field for acquiring medical knowledge, it possesses eminent advantages : the opportunities for studying morbid anatomy cannot be equalled by any other hospital in the Southern Hemisphere. The resident medical officer takes pupils on the same plan as the large Dublin hospitals. The establishment, on the whole, is a credit to the comparatively infant colony. Some of the most able and successful practitioners of Tasmania and Victoria were *élèves* of this institu-tion. Possessing as it does such ample means for

expanding, it will doubtless become ultimately the
medical college of the southern colonies.

There are also in Hobarton the public hospital of
St. Mary's, and a *Lying-in Hospital*, under the supervision and attendance of medical gentlemen of much
skill and practice. There are sixty-five practising
medical men in Tasmania, and twelve chemists in
Hobarton and Launceston.

Nor are the inhabitants of the good city without
professors and masters in the elegant accomplishment
of music; for there are several of no mean repute,
and whose talents, judging from the multiplicity
of their engagements, their frequent concerts and
musical *soirées*, are not unappreciated by the Tasmanians. A glee club has been organized under
the direction of Mr. Tapfield, organist of Trinity
Church, which has met with considerable success,
and is patronised by some of the principal families:
the meetings of the club, each alternate week,
when members can introduce two or three friends,
are of a very *recherché* and pleasing character.
M. Del Sarte has also contributed much to the
improvement of musical taste, and his concerts
are always crowded. The Mechanics' Institute,
under the tuition of Messrs. Salier and Russell,
have formed a class for music at a very reduced
rate for its members, and moderate fees for all
who wish to become pupils. Besides these gentlemen, there are others of no less taste and talents;

and in the person of Mr. Packer, a fine vocalist and skilful pianist, the city possesses an unrivalled artist.

There are two theatres in Hobarton; and the principal one, the Victoria, is constantly visited by "stars," who seldom fail to draw crowded houses.

Periodical horticultural exhibitions are held in the New Market, and prizes awarded of considerable value, which tend to create a very laudable emulation amongst the votaries of Flora and Ceres, and to improve the horticulture of the colony.

The Antipodes can also boast of many good draughtsmen and masters of painting, but none of more exquisite taste and elegance of style than the talented Bishop of Tasmania, the friend and patron of everything tending to improve the colony. Yet it is to be regretted that greater inducements are not held out to the artists who not unfrequently visit the island; and we do hope that, ere long, a Public Gallery may grace the city, and a School for Painting and Sculpture, which will give a stimulus to public taste, and promote the study of arts that can hand down to posterity representations of scenes and persons to be looked on with pride and regarded with exultation.

The moral and intellectual growth of the colony is also greatly assisted by the "Fourth Estate." Indeed, the Press of Tasmania (with some slight exceptions), both by its moderation of tone and the intellectual ability displayed in its original matter, affords a strong contrast to the general character of the colonial press, and bears a favourable comparison with its more immediate continental neighbours. This may be ascribed to the early infusion of a correct and sound literary taste, by the influx of educated and scientific gentlemen connected with the Government; whose efforts for the moral and physical advancement of the colony, even from its very commencement, were greatly assisted by a succession of Governors of singular ability. As a proof of this, we may refer to the Royal Society, whose papers and proceedings bear ample evidence that the germ of a vigorous and healthy intellectual community has been planted in this remote colony; which may in time mature into a "Modern Athens" in the Southern Hemisphere, and be the means of rousing the whole Australasian group from that intellectual torpor, which, during the present devotion to Mammon, seems to pervade it.

It may well be asked, what will be the consequences, if the counteracting influences necessary for the development of the better part of man be not sufficiently numerous and powerful to overcome evil tendencies? Or where should we be more likely to find those influences exerted with greater effect than in a community like Tasmania, where such a high tone has been preserved during a long period of depressing circumstances? It is to be hoped that the conductors of the Press may maintain and increase their reputation for moderation and ability, and be careful not to compromise their position and usefulness by descending to personalities and party warfare, destructive alike to private happiness and public prosperity.

The wants of every section of the community —religious, political, and social—are supplied by the newspapers of Hobarton and Launceston; for, besides the sheets devoted to the general topics of the day, there are some which discuss controversial topics, and others which advocate temperance as the panacea for every social evil.

In Hobarton, there are no less than seven newspapers, as well as publications of humbler pretensions; two being published daily, and the remainder at more or less frequent intervals during the week; and in Launceston, besides two bi-weekly papers, ably conducted, there are several minor productions which need not here be particularised.

CHAPTER XIII.

Oh ! bright occasion of dispensing good,
How seldom used, how little understood !
To nurse with care the thriving Arts;
Watch ev'ry beam Philosophy imparts.
. . . .
Freedom has a thousand charms to show,
That slaves, howe'er contented, never know.
The mind attains beneath her happy reign,
The growth that Nature meant she should attain.
The varied fields of science, ever new,
Opening and wider opening on her view,
She ventures onward with a prosp'rous force,
While no base fear impedes her in her course.

COWPER.

OUR limits will not permit us to give an enlarged
statement of the different institutions and societies
of the colony ; and yet there are many that would
demand some notice from us, denoting, as they
do, the rise and progress of the Arts and Sciences
in Tasmania. Dr. Lillie has furnished us with the
following statement of the *Mechanics' Institute,*
which we gladly insert as it was received from him.

This Institute is one of the oldest in the colony ;
and, by its steady progress and its present high

state of prosperity, has given the best proof of its adaptation to the wants and circumstances of the community. Its officers consist of Patron, Vice-patron, President, and Committee of Management. It now numbers upwards of four hundred members. Its funds are principally derived from the subscriptions of its members and an annual grant of £150 from the Government, on the condition that at least an equal sum shall have been obtained from its own resources.

The Institute contains a lecture-hall, library, reading-room, laboratory, committee-room, etc. A course of lectures, delivered weekly, is given during the winter season every year, to the extent of about twenty lectures. Occasionally, paid lecturers have been engaged, but in general the lectures are gratuitous. The subjects of the lectures are for the most part scientific and literary, but chiefly the former; embracing different branches of Mechanics and Natural Philosophy, Chemistry, Natural History, Physiology, etc. The lectures are well attended. The library contains about 2,200 volumes. During the year 1852, the number of volumes lent from the library was 5,925. In 1854 this number was increased to 8,952: an important fact, as showing a growing taste on the part of the public for reading. The reading-room contains, besides newspapers, all the leading English literary and scientific journals, and a great variety of dictionaries and books of reference. According to last year's report, "the attendance in the reading-room has increased to so great an extent, that it has been with some difficulty all the visitors have been accommodated."

The Institution possesses a valuable collection of Philosophical Apparatus for illustrating the various departments of Mechanics, Chemistry, etc., including a complete oxyhydrogen microscope. Besides the lectures, there are also weekly classes for Music and Drawing.

The following extract from the Report of the Committee will show the flourishing condition of the Institution. "The Committee are highly gratified by finding that the financial condition of the Institution is not only better than at the close of last year, but will bear to be compared with former years. Twelve years ago, the Mechanics' Institute was encumbered by a debt of £70. There was then no paid librarian or curator, and the number of books in the library did not much exceed five hundred. Since that period, above £200 have been expended in apparatus and chemicals; £600 have been laid out in building and alterations; the number of books in the library has been nearly quadrupled; and for several years, there has been an annual outlay for the salary of the librarian and curator. And now, after many struggles in past years, the Institution is entirely free from debt. The debt reported at the last anniversary has been paid, and there now remains a surplus in hand of £15 0s. 1d." The report for the year ending January, 1855, is equally gratifying. The annual income of the Institution, from all sources, amounted at that date to £753 9s. 5d.: its expenditure to £599 2s. 4d.; leaving a balance in favour of the Institute of £154 7s. 1d.

The *High School* of Hobarton is situated, as remarked in a former chapter, in the Domain, and is justly considered one of the prettiest buildings in or about the capital. It was originated by a Company, and established with a capital of £5,000 in £25 shares. This institution has for its immediate object the instruction of youth in the various branches of learning, as taught in the superior mathematical and classical schools in England; its ultimate object being the extension of its organization concurrently with the growing wants of the community. It aims more particularly to obtain for itself the privileges of a chartered corporation, so as to confer on the Tasmanian youth all the advantages derived at any of the European universities.

It has been long felt by the friends of education in Tasmania that an establishment conducted on liberal principles, and free from all sectarian influences, was much required to meet the demand of the rising population, not only of this, but of the neighbouring colonies,—a College which would eventually rank with the universities of the Mother Country, — where youths of every denomination might obtain degrees fitting them for every profession. It was also considered that the beautiful climate of the colony would be a further inducement for the parents to send their children here, when the College obtains such repute as it is confidently expected the High School will deserve; it having all the advantages attainable in Europe, whither many children are annually sent from India and Australia. Altogether in Tasmania there are, in addition to the public ones enumerated, one hundred private schools, at which are being educated upwards of 3,000 children.

The next Society that comes under our notice is the *Midland Agricultural Association*, established in the year 1838, for the improvement of stock, agriculture, and rural economy in general. There are three fixed meetings in the year : one at Campbell Town in January, for electing a committee of management; another at Ross in July, to appoint judges for the show meeting, which takes place at Campbell Town in October. Subscription to this Society, £2 per annum.

Among other Societies which have been formed from time to time for similar objects, this alone has maintained its ground. It procured last year a professor of agriculture from England, and the establishment of a model farm and cottage, for teaching the youth of the colony the theory and practice of farming; and as soon as the plan is matured, the Professor will no doubt make of it a very valuable and useful institution.

We have already, in a previous chapter, in speaking of the Royal Society of Van Diemen's Land, alluded to its embracing horticulture as one of its leading objects. In addition to this, we cannot pass without a review of the *Launceston Horticultural Society* for the introduction and acclimatizing of plants for England and other countries, for experimental research; also as a recreation to the colonist, and to encourage a taste and love of gardening; and lastly, a station, where the most valuable and ornamental plants might be collected and distributed throughout the country. Subscription, half-a-guinea per annum; Government grant £100 per annum.

In Launceston there is a club, styled the United Service Club, composed of Her Majesty's Officers of the Army and Navy resident on the northern side of the island; but all officers are eligible who hold or have held commissions in either of the services. There are many honorary members. The mode of election is by ballot, and the club is supported by an annual subscription.

We can only briefly enumerate the different societies, space not permitting us to give a more particular account of them. In Hobarton we find a Gardeners' and Horticultural Society; the same also in Launceston. For the colony generally, an Ornithological Society. In Launceston a Cricket Club. In Hobarton a Chess Club; also an Immigration Society. In Launceston, St. Andrew's ditto. At Ross, a Wesleyan College. In Hobarton, a Ragged School, also a Maternal and Dorcas Society; at the formation of the latter Society its object was to assist poor married women during confinement, but the funds being increased, relief is now extended to all cases of distress. There is also a Strangers' Friend Society at Hobarton, for relieving the sick and indigent; and a Lunatic Asylum supported by Government at New Norfolk. In Launceston, a Building Investment Society was established last year; and a Philharmonic Society was established about the same time.

In the year 1839 was formed the Licensed Victuallers' Society, the objects of which are to protect and aid its members, and promote the general interests of the trade.

At Hobarton, a Mercantile Assistants' Association was originated in the year 1847, for the mutual instruction of the members in the various branches of literature, science, and general useful knowledge. Subscription, 10s. per annum.

St. Patrick's Benefit Society was instituted at Launceston in 1848, for the purpose of raising a fund to secure for its members, in case of sick-nesss, pecuniary weekly allowance and medical aid; and in case of death, a certain sum to the family, to defray general expenses.

A Launceston Printers' Benefit Society was also instituted for a similar purpose in 1849. There are other societies established among us—such as Masonic, Odd Fellows, Rechabite, and Total Absti-nence Societies, etc.

There are sixteen offices of Insurance Com-panies ; eight in Hobarton, and eight in Laun-ceston. Seven of these are colonial, the remainder being branches and agencies of English associations. There are established in Tasmania, three Banks, belonging exclusively to the colony, the Com-mercial, Van Diemen's Land, and Tasmania; two Branch Banks also, one of Australasia, the other of the Union Bank of Australia : each of the above has separate establishments in Hobarton and Laun-ceston. There is, besides, a Savings' Bank in each city.

Hobarton and Launceston are municipal cities; each council consisting of a mayor, with £600 a year salary, and six aldermen, whose term of ser-vice expires every three years; also a town clerk, town surveyor, and city inspector and collector. Latterly their powers have been much increased, and additional grants given to them.

In October, 1855, the new Constitution was

proclaimed in Tasmania; and, but for certain political disputes—principally referring to the powers
of the Legislative Assembly in demanding a particular inquiry into certain alleged abuses in the
convict department, which has ever been under
the entire control and pay of the Home Government—it would have been now in force; but the
Governor, Sir H. Young, was compelled, after
repeated unavailing remonstrances, to prorogue the
House and refer the matter to royal decision.   It
is not our province to enter into a detail of the
merits of the case; but we are aware that much
valuable time has been frittered away by these
political squabbles, delaying for a time, we fear,
the advancement of the colony.

The new Constitution is to consist of two
Chambers, the Upper and the Lower House. In the
Upper there will be fifteen members, including a
President, elected by the country generally, divided
into districts: voters for the Upper House being
£50 freeholders.   The Lower House is to consist of
thirty members, in proportion to the population of
the districts, and voted for by the £50 freeholders,
and £10 freeholders.   The officers of the Crown,
viz., Colonial Secretary, Attorney-General, Solicitor-
General, and Colonial Treasurer, must be members
of the Lower House.

The present Governor, Sir Henry E. F. Young,
arrived in Tasmania on the 10th of January, 1855.

His staff consists of an aide-de-camp, private secretary, and clerks, etc., six mounted police as a body guard, and four soldiers as servants and orderlies. Under the immediate control of the Government are the following departments, with their various offices and clerks :—Colonial Secretary's, Colonial Treasurer's, Auditor-General's, Public Works, Government Printers, and Immigration.

From the statistics of the colony, we find that the number of immigrants during the year 1855 was—

Great Britain	3,900
Victoria and Foreign States . .	5,625
Total . .	9,525

The value of imports in 1855 was upwards of £3,000,000, and of exports £2,000,000. The number of vessels entered inwards 1,220, with 298,612 tons; the number cleared outwards 1,200, with 296,612 tons. The return of ships engaged in the fisheries is 10 vessels, 3,700 tons; the number built and registered, 10 of 400 tons and upwards, and 90 with a total of 11,340 tons; the number of steamers 14, with a total of 1,760 horse power.

The revenue of the colony amounted to £298,784, the expenditure £276,650; the return of land revenue £113,335, expenditure £86,620. Return of land sold and rented during the year 1855:

2,804,183 acres sold, and 2,284,214 rented; remaining still unsold in the colony 12,482,214 acres.

In 1855 there were in crop upwards of 50,000 acres of wheat, 10,000 of barley, 40,000 of oats, and 12,000 of potatoes; producing, wheat 990,500 bushels, barley 225,000 ditto, oats 610,240 ditto, potatoes 43,000 tons, hay 23,860 tons. The live stock in the colony was—horses 17,450, horned cattle 105,420, sheep 1,941,308, pigs 24,598.

A return of public schools shows 54 male teachers and 10 female. Children on the books 2,300 males and 2,126 females, for which was voted by the council £10,000.

There are several public libraries, reading-rooms, and circulating libraries. There is also the Australian Smelting Company, the Launceston Ship-building and Shipping Company, Douglas River Coal Company, the Mersey Coal Company, the Tasmanian Building Association, the Tasmanian Navigation Company, and lastly, yet in their infancy, the Hobarton and Sydney Navigation Company and the Launceston and Circular Head Steam Navigation Company.

By an Act of Parliament in the year 1825, incorporated by Royal Charter, was established the Van Diemen's Land Agricultural Company, with a capital of £100,000 in 10,000 shares. To this Company was granted 400,000 acres of land under certain stipulations; which, we regret to say, have not been fully carried out. The territories of the Company are situated in the following places in the north-west quarter of the island, comprising 150,000 acres at Woolnorth, 20,000 acres at Circular Head and the coast adjoining, 60,000 acres at Emu Bay and Hampshire Hills, 10,000 acres at Middlesex Plains, 150,000 acres at the Surrey Hills, and 10,000 acres estimated quantity of good land in Trefoil, Walker's, and Robin's Island. In our descriptive tour to Circular Head we will treat more at large of the stations of the Company.

CHAPTER XIV.

Where shall that land, that spot be found?
Art thou a man? a patriot?   Look around!
Oh, thou shalt find, howe'er thy footsteps roam,
That land *thy* country, and that spot *thy* home.
Man, through all ages of revolving time,
Unchanging man, in every varying clime,
Deems his own land of every land the pride,
Beloved by Heaven o'er all the world beside;
His home the spot of earth supremely blest,
A dearer, sweeter spot than all the rest.

MONTGOMERY.

THERE is, perhaps, no greater difficulty for an author to overcome, than that of avoiding offence when constrained to make remarks on a community. And yet, ungracious as the task is, it must be performed.   In Hobarton, as in most other places in the world, having a considerable population, society is composed of several sets, and these sets here, as elsewhere, run into, as it were, distinct circles; all, however, contributing to form one harmonious social system.   There is no absolute line of demarcation except between the extremes—

HOBARTON, FROM THE WEST.

the highest and the lowest, the educated and the ignorant. There is no aristocracy of birth, and but little affectation of exclusiveness; nor an aristocracy of talent. Neither can there be an aristocracy of wealth, where the working man, favoured by a lucky turn of the wheel of fortune, may vindicate his claim to the first position: and the small tendency that does exist towards exclusiveness affects but few except the individuals who cultivate and encourage it.

Society, then, in Hobarton, is in a state of transition; yet the principal part of the community are those whose aim is peace and good-will; who, indifferent to the patronage of the exclusive few, and despising the tale-bearer, live contented and happy in their families, and endeavour to make all around participate in their happiness: using the world but not abusing it, and mixing in the society of their compatriots with kind and friendly feelings. Viewing all things on the brighter side, they strive to make their city a pleasant resting-place for the visitor, a happy home for the stranger.

Words fail to extol as they deserve, these the bright gems of Tasmanian society; but we cannot censure too severely those who allow petty jealousies and differences of rank and station—of politics, and, alas! also, of religion—to interfere with their better feelings. Yet as the great majority are of a nobler spirit, these differences and

disputes, and the disunion they engender, will
soon vanish. It is most pleasing, in making
these observations, to see a more amicable feeling
gaining ground; and, in glancing over the annals
of the past years, to perceive how society has
advanced, and how little is seen or known of
that which many a writer prognosticated — that
its tone would be deteriorated by the numbers
of freed convicts. It is gratifying to state that
the case is far otherwise, and that no such evil
has arisen; for, in whatever point of view we
regard the community at large, we cannot fail to
perceive a high tone of morality and virtue prevailing. Indeed, it seems to have been overlooked
by those who indulged in these evil prognostics,
that the first act of every freed convict would be
to hasten from the colony, where the associations
are almost exclusively of his evil deeds and punishment; and from the returns we find that as those
depart the free immigrants arrive.

Colonial society in general differs in its characteristics from the society met with in old countries:
and very naturally. New communities, composed
of the most ardent and adventurous spirits of the
land from whence they emigrate, shoot a-head of
the mere conventionalities of life, and engage, ener-
getically, from morning till night, and day after
day, in the actual concerns of worldly existence.
They are ever active and bustling in matters of

business; and in social intercourse they have a certain freedom and heartiness of manner, which are more pleasing than the straight-laced ideas and formal restraints which trammel the Old Country.

Society in Hobarton and Tasmania generally has, from the very commencement of the colony, possessed, with some drawbacks, many great advantages. Originally a penal settlement, the principal inhabitants long continued to be exclusively officers of government; and when free immigration was allowed, the majority of those who availed themselves of the privilege were retired officers from the army and navy, with a few capitalists, and a sprinkling of the mercantile classes from Leeds, Liverpool, and London; who thereby secured to themselves broad acres in freehold of the richest land in the finest climate of the world. It thus happened that the colonists, being men who had held authority in their former positions in life, and filled high places in society, they felt it a duty incumbent on them to exert a control over their own actions and conduct, and maintain an elevated tone of manner, so as to avoid even the appearance of an evil considered —as Lord Stanley avowed in the House—likely to accrue from the cause above alluded to. The presence also of a highly educated class, from the earliest period of the colony, contributed to this beneficial influence; and there can be no

question, that, in addition to her beautiful climate
and picturesque scenery, Tasmania can boast of
as agreeable and cultivated society as can be
found in the southern hemisphere.

We cannot conclude our remarks without a
testimony of veneration and esteem for one class
amongst us, whose goodness of heart and virtu-
ous deeds are unknown to most, though of abundant usefulness—whose sole aim in life seems to
be philanthropy, and who, with but little at their
disposal, freely give—who labour constantly and
untiringly in the field of humanity, comforting
the distressed, healing the broken-hearted with
visitations of kindness and love—who teach youth
and direct their young minds in the way of duty.
These, though they labour on in that unostenta-
tious charity that alloweth not the right hand to
know what the left hand doeth, still have their
reward: the blessings of the fatherless and the
widow, of the once destitute and needy, now
happy under their care—repay them more than
all the world could give.

Viewing, therefore, the society of Hobarton in
all its lights and shades, whilst we see somewhat
to condemn, we find much to admire. The Anglo-
Saxon race is everywhere energetic, enterprising,
and improving. We have amongst us the germs
of virtue and true nobleness. A spirit of emulation is rife amongst us. Our merchants assume a

place in Europe, not dreamt of before; goodly ships
daily visit our ports; our land fast increases in
value; the industrious and sober earn much more
than a competence; and, within the last year, a fresh
impetus has been given to trade of every kind.
Still it is the imperative duty of every member
of our society to labour in the great work for its
advancement; and, proud as they well may be
of their adopted country, to assist each other in
the endeavour to make all contented and happy:
being assured, that to accomplish this end, we have
only our own hearts to rule—the principle being
the all-enduring, never failing one of charity and
peace.

March, 1856.—We have left Tasmania for a
time only, for we earnestly hope to return to its
fertile shore and fine climate. Our sojourn there
has been such as soldiers say, "most agreeable,"
and we left our kind and hospitable friends with
sincere regret. The society of the city is still progressing, even as we foresaw some two years ago.
Many who left about that time, with the intention
of remaining in England, have returned to spend
their fortunes there. Some few, we grieve to say,
who had amassed wealth, have lately left, with
the feeling of all Britons—a longing desire to
return to the land of their nativity. A few have
gone on account of political feelings, involving
dissatisfaction at the conduct of our rulers; who

are not free from blame. We earnestly hope such disputes will never recur, and that the pledges of one Governor and Government given in Council, will ever be held sacred by their successors. Since the opening of steam communication to Sydney, and the more constant and regular trips to Victoria, Hobarton has had an influx of visitors; principally during the summer months, when the Tasmanian climate offers a most grateful change from those cities.

The new Constitution and the independence of the State, promise well for the future greatness, and speedy advancement of Tasmania. A more liberal line of policy respecting the waste lands will be adopted, and greater inducements held out to *bonâ fide* settlers; so that we can well close this chapter with the motto of the colony, "Advance, Tasmania."

CHAPTER XV.

Though sluggards deem it but a foolish chase,
And marvel men should quit their easy chair,
The toilsome way and long, long league to trace,
Oh, there is sweetness in the mountain air,
And life that bloated Ease can never share!
More bleak to view the hills at length recede,
And, less luxuriant, smoother vales extend;
Immense horizon-bounded plains succeed,
Far as the eye discerns, withouten end.

BYRON.

IN order to change our subject, and not to trespass too much on the patience of our readers, we returned from our tour to Marlborough to say somewhat of the capital. We must now conduct him back to that district; and, again indebted to a friend who formed one of an expedition to discover the river Gordon and its rise, we copy from his notes, and in his own words give an account of the trip; feeling assured that the truthfulness and simplicity of the style, incapable of any improvement from us, will please the most captious reader.

Having obtained the necessary supplies of bacon and biscuit, tea and sugar, tomahawks, and other indispensables for a bush expedition, I left town on the 16th of November, with my man Bullock, a pensioner from the 96th (who accompanied me at his own particular request, thinking I was not able to take care of myself) and proceeded as far as Hamilton, where I was joined by Mr. C. Forster on the 18th. On the following day we went on to the house of Mr. Gellibrand (son of a former attorney-general who was lost in the bush at Port Philip), on the Dee. Here we were most hospitably entertained; and early next morning we bade adieu to our kind friends, put our packs on Forster's old Arab " Mameluke," and walked by his side as far as a place called China. There a girl of fifteen ferried us across the Derwent, (the men being engaged in shearing, and the colonial fair ones being accustomed to such manly exercises), and showed us the way to her father's hut, where we made an excellent leg of mutton look particularly foolish, and prepared the packs for carrying on our own backs instead of that of the old horse, whose services were dispensed with as it was impossible to take him further. A little girl about seven years old guided us as far as the Broad River, where she left us. We crossed the river near where it enters the Derwent, and after enjoying a delicious bath in its cool water, found our way to the Repulse, a smaller stream, which also runs into the Derwent; and on which a log hut had been erected as a depôt of stores for the service of a party of surveyors.

The only stores we could discover proved to be a quantity of yellow soap. The storekeeper, a stout, healthy-looking bushman, insisted on our taking up our quarters at his hut for the night, offering his services to set us on the marked-tree track the next morning; and then, without further delay, put a "damper" to bake for our future provision on the road.

We were nothing loth to rid ourselves of our packs, to which we were not yet accustomed; they were soon thrown off. I adjourned to the stream with a fishing-line, and in about an hour captured enough of the finny tribe to make an excellent supper. We tried to shoot an opossum; but the night was too dark, and we were unsuccessful. It being very warm, we preferred the bush air to the smoke and shelter of the hut, and, laying our rugs on the ground, slept soundly until daybreak the following morning.

21st November.—Our host's "damper" and our bacon afforded an excellent breakfast; and before sunrise, our packs were on our backs and we were off. I must now describe the contents of our packs. Each man had his rug, generally of opossum skins, which are preferable from their warmth; though

Forster's—which was of wallaby—proved far more
effectual in keeping out the rain. In my own
rug was rolled twenty pounds of smoked beef, ten
pounds of bacon, some few articles of clothing, and
other necessaries. Forster carried a damper weighing ten pounds, and more bacon, etc.; Bullock,
twenty pounds of biscuit, tea, sugar, and a fryingpan. We had a half-gallon tin pot for boiling
tea; and each man had his pannikin. These, with
my little gun, a supply of powder and shot, and
two tomahawks, completed our outfit. Our dress
consisted of a blue serge shirt buckled round the
waist, long gaiters, and the thickest boots that
could be made.

My servant Bullock, having carried a knapsack
for some five-and-twenty years, was, of course, expected to be most lively under his burden; but, as
was remarked to me afterwards by a shepherd who
had been an old sailor, he had always been accustomed to "plane sailing," and had never learnt
"traverse sailing," as he called forcing one's way
through the scrub. I remarked that Mr. Bullock
lagged behind very much: sometimes he was quite
out of sight, and we had to wait for him. It struck
me that if he went on to the really difficult parts
and was knocked up, we should be obliged to
stop too; and probably find great difficulty in
getting him safe home. After volunteering, as he
did, to accompany us, he was, of course, un-

willing to go back so soon; but, after another trial, we found that he was not equal to the work, and we persuaded him to take off his pack and return with our guide to the Repulse.

Forster and I now made a new arrangement of our knapsacks, taking biscuit from Bullock's, and relieving our own of a large proportion of bacon and other commissariat stores. We then wished "good bye" to our guide and our deserter, and proceeded alone on our journey. I forgot to say that we had an old dog with us, which had been lent me at Hamilton, to supply us with kangaroos; but which we afterwards regretted having brought, for he ate our beef and bacon, and killed nothing.

The day was very hot, and for some time we suffered greatly from thirst. On coming to a water hole, I was imprudent enough to drink a large quantity of water, and then tea, which made me so ill that we could not continue our walk for about two hours. In the evening, we encamped on a little green spot by the side of a stream, where there was a little bark hut; made, I suppose, by the party who marked the trees some weeks ago. The chief difficulty in our walk consisted in getting over fallen trees, whose diameter was sometimes greater than my own height; or, worse still, having to crawl under them, which, with our packs on our backs, was no easy matter. This sort of walking continued througout the marked-tree track; and I think I may say without exaggeration, that in some parts, for miles together, there was an obstacle of this sort every ten yards.

We spread our rugs on the grass by the side of the stream, and were just going to sleep, when it began to rain; this induced us to shift our positions to the shelter of the little hut, which happened to be at hand. The architecture of our abode, however picturesque, was not of a style which afforded any great degree of comfort; but it certainly kept some of the rain from us, and we passed the night tolerably well.

Friday, 22nd November.—It rained all day, and we had a most disagreeable march. At one place we stopped to make a fire and a pot of tea; but after using a whole box of matches, we were obliged to give it up. In the middle of the day, we were more successful; and during a short interval of fine weather, managed to dry some of our things. We encamped this evening on the banks of the Florentine, a deep sluggish stream, about sixty feet wide. I was so fatigued by the day's walk that I could not eat, but slept the greater part of the night; although it rained hard, and I was wet through. Poor Forster, who was not so fatigued, could not sleep at all. We had very great difficulty in lighting our fire: we collected dry twigs, and bark, from under fallen or

out of hollow trees, cut chips with our tomahawks
from the hearts of dead saplings, and even then
were sometimes an hour before we could get a
blaze to warm us. We were very much annoyed
by leeches; in a day we might have collected
enough to stock an apothecary's shop: they at-
tacked the dog as well as ourselves.

Saturday, 23rd.—Still raining, and we had to
pack our wet things in our wet rugs, and proceed
on our journey, with ardour as much damped as
everything else. The rain soaked into the skins
and fur of the rugs, and increased their weight
very much. We had expected to reach the Gordon
to-day, but Forster felt the want of his night's
rest so much that we were obliged to stop earlier
than usual, at a place where there were marks
of a former encampment; and from which we expected to have a gentle stroll the next morning
to the river, and then spend the rest of our Sunday
quietly on its banks.

Sunday, 24th.—After another cold wet night,
in which my rug proved its utter incapacity to
keep out the rain, we packed up and started. To-
day's walk turned out, after all, to be by far the
most fatiguing we had had,—over logs and under
logs, and falling every now and then from the
slippery bridges that they form in wet weather.

We passed through a forest of fern trees, varying in height from ten to thirty feet; then up a hill

11

so steep, that the trees which grew on it seemed
to be climbing up themselves, and holding on for
support by their upper branches instead of their
roots. The foliage of some of these trees—the
sassafras, the myrtle, and the native laurel—is
very beautiful. The waratah grows here, too, in
great perfection: it has a flower not unlike the
honeysuckle in shape, but in thicker clusters and
of a deep red colour, and with a leaf like that of
the rhododendron. After descending the hill on
the other side, we at last emerged into the long-
looked-for open country; but saw no river Gordon
winding at our feet, as we had expected. A large
extent of marsh, covered with long, coarse, tufted
grass lay before us, occasionally diversified by
patches of yellow scrub. Here, there being no
trees to mark (the marked-tree track being at end),
we had to make our way as best we could to
the Gordon.

At first we went wrong; and after forcing
our way through a mass of detestable yellow
scrub, growing higher than our heads, which
we fancied led us in the direction that had been
described to us, we held a council of war, and
determined to retrace our steps. The next time
we made a better hit, and, after remounting a
scrubby hill, discovered a belt of small gum
trees winding through the valley. This, we had
no doubt, marked the course of the river. To

reach it we had to walk over some miles of heavy marsh, but at last accomplished our task. We found that we were right in our anticipations of finding the river among the gum trees, and encamped a little before sunset on the banks of the Gordon, here about 150 feet broad, apparently deep; and very rapid.

Monday, 25th.—A fine hot day.   We swam the river; and I ascended a bleak, rugged mountain, whose blocks of granite, glancing in the evening sun, had given us the idea, as we approached it the preceding evening, that it was a mountain covered with snow. From this, however, I found that it was entirely free; and it was only towards evening, when the sun's rays struck obliquely on the sparkling rock, that it presented this singular effect. The sides of the mountain between the rocks were covered with epacris and small flowering shrubs.

On Tuesday, Forster ascended the same mountain, and collected specimens of the rocks and of the flowers.   Some of them we attempted to preserve; but in the discomfort which we suffered afterwards, most of them were forgotten or thrown aside.   From the summit of this mountain we had a most extensive view of the surrounding country. We discovered a curious natural arch, formed by an immense block of granite.   The hills to the westward were covered with huge boulders of rock, grouped in all sorts of fantastic shapes; one group bore a striking resemblance to the keep of Dover Castle, and some of them were apparently balanced on a point. Forster employed himself on Monday in setting fire to the scrub and long grass of the marshes, which a few hours' sun seemed to have thoroughly dried, and in the evening the whole country was in a blaze for miles round. We protected our own camp from surprise by burning a space all round it. Here we saw four very fine kangaroos, but could not get near enough to them to have a chance with either dog or gun.

Wednesday, 27th.—Last night it rained again, and we passed a wretched night. It was still raining in the morning; but we crossed the river by a ford that Forster had discovered, and proceeded some ten miles up the right or west bank of the river. The grass and scrub having been burnt on this side, the walking was much better. We had some difficulty in crossing streams, tributaries of the Gordon, which were all much swollen from the rains. Another cold wet night. We had greater difficulty than ever in making a fire; but Forster's perseverance at last succeeded.

Thursday, 28th.—A fine morning, but rain came on in the afternoon. We walked nearly as far as what is marked in Frankland's chart the head of the Gordon; but instead of running north and south, as in the chart, it comes up from the south-west, rising, I should think, near the Frenchman's Cap. Our plan being to make our way to Marlborough by Lake St. Clair, we wished to keep a due northerly course; but the river was so much swollen that we saw no way of crossing it, and continued to follow it upwards in order to go round its source. In the evening it rained in torrents; but after repeated attempts and discomfitures, we contrived to light a fire in a hollow tree, and thence to convey it to a convenient encampment. I forgot to remark, that during our walk through the marked-tree track, we observed a quantity of fallen timber in different stages of petrifaction: in fact, wherever a tree had fallen in a damp situation, it showed some signs of it; sometimes presenting, when broken, a milky-white glutinous appearance, which in others had become hardened to a sort of flint. I regret that we did not bring specimens; but, in the wet, disagreeable weather that we had, our love of science was swallowed up in love of self, and we grudged every additional ounce that was added to our wet heavy packs.

This reminds me of an anecdote I heard of a man, who attended Dr. Milligan, the secretary to the Royal Tasmanian Society, in one of his expeditions, and whose duty it was to carry the Doctor's knapsack. Packs in general decrease in weight according to the consumption of beef and

bacon; but this man found to his surprise that,
whenever the doctor returned his pack, after having
made up its contents, it was heavier than before.
One day, having ascended a steep mountain, Dr.
Milligan requested the man to collect specimens
of the rock "basalt" on its summit. This he positively refused to do, declaring that he could get
plenty of "bay salt" down on the sea coast, without going up steep mountains for it.

During the first part of our walk, I remarked
small boulders of what I considered to be iron-stone,
in the neighbourhood of the Florentine. These were
succeeded by fragments of white stone with blue
veins, resembling marble; and about the Gordon I
found pieces of granite, some a coarse conglomerate,
and others fine, and of a pink colour. The rock on
the mountain that we ascended on the other side of
the Gordon was composed entirely of slabs of granite,
lying nearly parallel to the face of the hill, which
was very steep. The base of this mountain, as well
as the sides of the hills rising from either side of
the Gordon, were quite honeycombed with round
cells, which appeared to be the abode of fresh-
water lobsters. We caught and boiled one about
the size of a prawn, and liked it so well that at
one time we formed a project of an extensive
attack on their habitations.

Friday, 29*th*.—A fine morning; but the river so
much swollen, that we saw no prospect of being

able to cross it : we walked some miles further
up, trying everywhere for fords, but found none
practicable. At last, having held a consultation
and examined the state of our commissariat, we
determined to cross it in the following manner. I
was to swim across with a line, formed of all our
straps and handkerchiefs tied together, and fastened
at the other end to our packs joined together with
cord, and carrying my gun on the top. Forster
was to remain behind, and steer them across. The
packs had already proved their floating capabilities ;
for yesterday, in crossing a stream by a fallen tree,
mine, which I had taken off and was pushing
before me, fell into the water, but swam like a
duck, and was caught lower down. We effected
our project, and found ourselves on the other side
with our rugs and what little remained of our
provisions.

In the passage, however, we lost two valuable
articles,—our powder, and one of Forster's gaiters ; both of which, with some heavier articles,
he had thrown across to lighten the raft. They
cleared the river, but fell into a water-hole on the
other side ; the powder was lost at once, but the
gaiter floated until we tried to regain it with a
long stick : it sunk directly it was touched. I
also lost about a pound of bacon—all that remained—from not strapping my pack properly.
The powder was an irreparable loss, because, al-

though we did not expect to see game, we might
have shot parrots and cockatoos; for our provisions
were getting very short.

The success of our plan of crossing the river
cheered our spirits, and we walked briskly up
a bare hill, expecting to see from its summit a
clear way before us to the northward. We were,
however, disappointed: nothing was to be seen
but hill after hill, covered with the dense scrub,
which we knew it was almost impossible to penetrate. We descended again to the valley—went
up another hill lower down the river—saw the
same prospect before us—again descended, and
encamped by the side of the river, thoroughly
disheartened, and wishing we had never heard of
the "new country."

To return by the same way we had come
appeared now to be our only course: but here
again we were in a dilemma; for the left bank,
on which we now were, was almost impracticable, owing to the thickness of the scrub; and
if we crossed the river here, and walked down
the same way that we had come up, we should
not be able to re-cross it lower down, opposite
our former encampment, unless the water should
subside very considerably in the meantime. We
now examined our stock of provisions. There
were seven biscuits left, and about four pounds of
salt beef. We took each a little morsel of beef,

without biscuit, for supper, and managed to make a fire; but sleep was out of the question, for it rained in torrents. We sat or stood by the fire all night, with the rain running out of the sleeves of our coats.

Saturday, 30*th*.—The river rose so much during the night, that our encampment, which had been so high above it on the previous evening that it was with difficulty we could reach from the banks to get water, was now gradually becoming an island. All thought of crossing the river was now at an end, and we had to think of some other way of getting back. At sunrise the weather became clear, and we went up another hill to take fresh observations. From this point we were gratified by seeing a line of marshes stretching northward, with comparatively short intervals of scrub; and in this line we determined to make an attempt to extricate ourselves from our cage.

We returned to our insulated camp and partook of a particularly light breakfast; each took possession of one biscuit, which was to last the whole day, and we, having given the dog a bit of beef, shouldered our packs, and trudged off. After walking a few miles nearly due north, we came to a surveyor's encampment, which appeared to have been occupied not more than ten days ago. We kept the same direction about two miles farther, and then inclined to the eastward, hoping to avoid a thickly wooded hill

which stood before us; but we only became en-
tangled in another far worse bit of scrub, in which
we had great difficulty in getting along: narrowly
escaping breaking our bones every five minutes, but
never stopping to inquire whether either of us
was hurt. It was too serious a business to allow
time for speaking, and we thought of nothing but
how to get on. The compass was of great use to
us here; and, with its aid, we at last, after about
five miles of this scrambling, managed to extricate
ourselves: at the top of a steep hill that we had
ascended, we were greeted with the cheering sight
of an immense extent of marsh stretching out before
us as far as the eye could reach. While getting
through the scrub, Forster nearly trod on a large
black snake; but we were not able to kill the
villain.

We continued our walk northward along these
marshes until the sun got low, and then encamped
among a grove of high gum-trees, which we
hoped would afford some shelter from the cold
wind and rain, and sometimes hail, which came
down in torrents. We had more than our usual
difficulty in lighting a fire to-night, but Forster's
perseverance gained the day. We made our camp
inside a hollow tree, with the fire outside. Forster
made a sort of bed for himself, like a coffin, with
sheets of bark, and managed to sleep pretty well;
but, for my own part, I preferred standing outside

by the fire, although I had had no sleep the night
before.

  Sunday, 1st December. — Daybreak was wel-
comed by me most heartily. I made some tea,
pulled Forster out of his coffin, and soon after
sunrise we had packed up and were off. The
weather cleared up, and we managed to dry most
of our things before starting. About two miles
further on we crossed a stream, which we flattered
ourselves was the Guelph, but which we were
afterwards told could only be another branch of the
Gordon. About eight miles further we crossed the
real Guelph, and found ourselves on a sheep-run.

  We now began to look about for shepherds' huts;
and a few miles beyond we discovered one, but it
was deserted; the shepherd having gone down to
Hamilton with his sheep for shearing. The wool
has to be taken down on the sheeps' backs, because,
as yet, there are no roads to those distant sheep-
runs. Sometimes many hundreds are lost on the
way. In this hut we found a bag marked " T. F."
containing flour; but Forster was so confident of
finding another hut, better supplied, if not inhabited,
before night, that we did not take any. " A bird
in the hand is worth two in the bush," thought
I, and left it most unwillingly. We could now
clearly distinguish all the mountains about Lake
St. Clair, and shortly afterwards obtained a view
of the lake itself, with the river flowing out of

it. We knew that a bridge had been lately thrown across for the passage of sheep, and our only anxiety now was to reach the river near that point.

We walked the whole of this day, from shortly after sunrise till sunset, without stopping for more than five minutes at a time; and at last we encamped near the banks of the Derwent, thoroughly knocked up, and not a little disappointed, at having found neither the bridge nor a hut to sleep in. Forster had hurt his knee, and I my ankle, in yesterday's scramble; and to-day's walk had made them worse, although we did not feel it much until we stopped. We had now left the country of our enemies, the leeches: one night, on the banks of the Gordon, I pulled one out of my ear.

Monday, 2nd.—The night was fine, and we enjoyed a good rest. I awoke, however, before daybreak, very cold, and found my boots and the ground covered with a white frost. I soon made a good fire, and drove the frost from our camp; and then, having boiled water and made tea, I contrived with some difficulty to arouse Forster, who slept soundly. The sun rose brightly, and everything looked so cheerful that our spirits rose too; and, although suffering from our wounds, and as stiff as hard-worked coach-horses, we managed to bend our legs by degrees, and, after finishing our last biscuit, made up our packs, and soon found our way to the river's bank. We walked about two miles down the stream, following sheep and cart tracks, which we imagined must lead to the bridge; but seeing no signs of it in that direction, we retraced our steps, and after walking some miles up the stream, at length discovered the object of our search.

We knew that we were now only twenty miles from Marlborough, and with a track all the way: but we were both very lame, and got on but slowly. About three miles beyond the bridge we lost the track, but at last succeeded in finding it again. The day was very hot; and Forster's knee and my ankle were both so bad, that we began to doubt whether we should get to Marlborough that night. We had no biscuit; the sugar had been out some days; and the tea had been so soaked by rain that there was very little strength in it. Still, we had enough salt beef left to last us another day; and, if the worst came to the worst, we had the dog (poor fellow! he had not much flesh upon him), and an untanned opossum rug—an article of food very frequently made use of by thorough bushmen.

But we were soon relieved from all such culinary cares; for, while sitting down on a fallen log, what should we see coming across the marsh but a man—yes, a living man, with a pack on his back;—the first human being we had seen since we took leave of Bullock and the storekeeper at the Repulse. We immediately set out a loud " cooee," and gave chase. The man proved to be a shepherd, on his way to some distant sheep-runs. His pack was soon undone; and the nicest piece of white bread and a pat of fresh butter, rolled in a snow-white cloth, were produced. What became of the bread and butter, I need not say. When it was finished, our kind friend, who said he was as glad " as fifty pound " that he had met us, took us to a neighbouring hut; and there we stayed all day, feasting on the fat of the land. There, too, we slept that night; for, after once stopping, we were too stiff to move.

Tuesday, 3rd. — Forster's knee was so much better that he was able to walk to Marlborough. My ankle was worse instead of better, and so much swollen that I found walking quite out of the question. Our host, the hutkeeper, served as a guide to Forster, and brought me back a horse, the property of the police magistrate, or rather constable (for he is nothing more), the sole inhabitant of the township of Marlborough. I was at a loss how to show some substantial token of gratitude to our host; for my rug, the fryingpan, and the greater part of our kit, had been given to Ben, the man who found us and brought us to the hut. At last, I thought of a small compass, which seemed to please him; but it had got so rusty from the damp, that, in spite of my endeavours to polish it, I fear it will be more likely to mislead than to be of use to him.

I was not long in reaching Marlborough; for, although the country is very rough and covered with sharp rocks, the horses bred in this part are so active and so well accustomed to it that you may ride at full gallop, with very little more danger of a summersault than with an English horse over an English park. At any rate, my guide was in a hurry, and I was obliged to follow at his pace. We were nearly bogged crossing some streams, but managed to extricate ourselves by desperate exertions on the part of the horses. My new host, Mr. Lascelles, the constable, was away driving a team of bullocks with provisions for a surveying party in the neighbourhood. Forster went off early the next morning, and I was left to take care of myself, without a soul to speak to. Mr. Lascelles' library was not very extensive; the only books I could find being "Handy Andy" and Sir John Franklin's "Expeditions in North America." Not being able to move from the sofa, (there *was* a sofa, though I cannot think how it ever got there,) I amused myself by reading the latter, thinking the subject rather appropriate; but found it rather dry amusement after all, for it was a bare journal, written in a most uninteresting style.

Thursday, 5th.—Mr. Lascelles came in about

noon, and released me from my solitary confinement. He is a son of a late colonial secretary, and of good family. Although a functionary of the common law, he exercises a sort of martial law of his own; which, if not strictly regular, has the effect of keeping this district in good order : indeed his services are so much esteemed by those who have been in the neighbourhood, that they have subscribed a considerable sum annually to keep him from accepting any more lucrative appointment elsewhere. One virtue, that of hospitality, he possesses to an unlimited extent. In the evening Forster returned from his run, (about eight miles off,) on horseback, leading a most miserable Rosinante for me, the property of his shepherd.

Friday, *6th*.—This morning, Lascelles, who is an universal genius, or, at any rate, a jack-of-all-trades, shod our horses. We wished good-bye to him and Marlborough, and started for Mr. Gellibrand's, about forty miles distant ; whence we had set out on our expedition. After riding twenty miles at a snail's pace—for neither of our nags were very spirited, and mine required constant beating and spurring to keep it going at all—we reached Victoria Valley, where there are some huts, and a most comfortable little inn, kept by a tidy little woman, Mrs. Stock. Here we had an excellent dinner on mutton chops and tea, and I borrowed a fresh horse. We got over the remaining twenty miles, and rode up to Mr. Gellibrand's house just as it was getting dark on the evening of the seventeenth day since we left it. We were kindly and cordially received—told how parties were on the point of setting out in search of us—pitied for the hardships we had suffered, and rewarded for our trouble by finding ready listeners to the recital of our adventures.

Saturday, 7th.—I bade adieu to my kind friends over-night, and at daylight proceeded alone on my homeward journey, leaving Forster to be taken care of by the fair Miss Gellibrands. The man who made the saddle on which I had been perched all yesterday, and which was to convey me some thirty-seven miles farther (to New Norfolk) to-day, deserves to be hanged, drawn, and quartered. I put a sheepskin over it, and tried to put a cheerful countenance on my own visage. At Hamilton I stopped to give my horse and myself a feed; the former at the inn stable—the latter at the table of Mr. Fenwick, the police magistrate; who, in addition to a good breakfast, offered to replace my tattered garments with a suit of his own clothes. I got to New Norfolk just in time for the coach to Hobarton, where I arrived about 7 p.m., and for a whole week afterwards never wished to set out on another such expedition.

CHAPTER XVI.

The scene is steep'd in beauty: and my soul,
No longer lingering in the gloom of care,
Doth greet Creation's smile. The grey clouds roll
Even from the mountain peaks, and melt in air;
The landscape looks an Eden! Who could wear
The frown of sorrow now? This glorious hour
Reveals the ruling god! The heavens are bare!
Each sunny stream and blossom-mantled bower
Breathes of pervading love, and shows the power
That spoke him into life hath blessed Man's earthly dower.

RICHARDSON.

ERE we turn our steps towards the city of the North, we must conduct our readers a little eastward to visit Swan Port and the Douglas River: and as this seems to us like travelling on a beaten track, our notice of it will be very limited, choosing rather to refer our readers to the work of the talented Mrs. Charles Meredith—"My Home in Tasmania,"—whose elegant and graphic descriptions of her wanderings and bush life, which we have no pretensions to equal, cannot fail to be highly interesting to every reader.

The tourist would do well to pause and admire the lovely scene stretched out before his view, as, leaving New Town (before described), and turning to the right towards Risdon Ferry, he passes the pretty gothic residence of Colonel Hamilton, R.E., with its beautiful gardens, opposite the gardens and house of Mr. Roope, already spoken of. To the left along this road are three or four handsome villas, with ornamental gardens; and a little retiring from it to the left is the residence of the chief police magistrate: also the rich homestead and grounds of Mr. Read. Before you reach the ferry, for some two miles, you pass, hanging over the river, the pretty house and romantic gardens of Mr. Jones, from which place you have a panoramic view of the Derwent. The fine bay of New Town here opens to the view, skirting which you turn towards a narrow part of the river, where a ferry-boat conveys you across. On the opposite side is Grass-tree Hill, which commands Hobarton and its harbour. This is the property of Mr. Gregson, before spoken of; near to which is Richmond Park, the estate of Mrs. Lord, one of the most valuable in the colony.

Richmond, a small village nine miles further on, is situated in a flat valley; and, though very unlike its prototype, it has the appearance of a neat village of the old country, with a good hotel and a square-towered church, also a pretty chapel.

Near Richmond is Campagnia, the very fine place of Mr. Villeneuve Smith, brother of the attorney-general. Both these gentlemen are large landholders in the district, and, being men of capital and enterprise, do much to improve the locality.

The coal river runs through the valley, along which is the large property of Mr. Butcher, called Lowlands; also Glenare, the extensive domain and run of Mr. Dixon; besides several places of wealthy settlers, along the vale, with rich farms and comfortable homesteads. It was through this valley that the late Governor, Sir W. Denison, was anxious to run a new line of road to Launceston, by which the range of hills would be avoided and the way lessened by twelve or fourteen miles. A short time since a bill was passed in the Legislative Assembly, directing a line of road to be surveyed for the purpose of connecting Launceston and Hobarton by railway; this survey is now going on, and it is along the line, as designed by Sir William, that the engineers have decided to proceed.

Hence to the next village, of most euphonious title, yclept Jerusalem, the road—if such it may be called, being little more than a track through an uncultivated, and for the most part uninhabited, district—would weary the patience of any of the pilgrims bound to the capital of Palestine.

SHOUTEN   ISLAND.

We next pass on to the Eastern Marshes, a wild and desolate-looking country for many miles in extent, till we reach the Sugar Loaf, where a road winds along the ridge of the mountain-top. A wide extent of hills and dales is spread out to view, with the sombre forest in the foreground. The Schouten Islands appear stretching along the coast; and a view of much beauty and extent, embracing hill and dale and the outspread sea, repays the wanderer for the toils and difficulties of the way. There is a good working coal-mine here, of the same description as that at the Douglas River.

Three steamers call weekly at Swan Port, near these islands, on the main land; a rapidly rising township. Many settlers have been induced to purchase land there, and it has now become a favourite locality. Miles of the large tracts of land in the neighbourhood have been cut up in small lots, and sold with great advantage by the original possessor, and considerable benefit to the community generally. A good road is also in formation to connect this district with Richmond; thereby throwing open large tracts of country of which at present little is known.

Little Swan Port is the first resting-place on the sea-shore, formed on an inlet of Oyster Bay. From thence the road runs along the sea-coast, beautifully described by the authoress before mentioned. Passing over the rocky hills, we arrive

at Swanseaa nd Waterloo Point; and thence over
a good road, which extends for nine miles along
the extremity of the bay, we pass the head of
Swan Port, a broad and rather open arm of the
sea; behind which there is a considerable lagoon,
named Moulting Bay, from being the resort of
numerous flocks of black swans and other wild
fowl.

There are several excursions from this point,
which our space will not admit of detailing: we
therefore turn our steps to Douglas River, the road
to which passes first through the highly cultivated
tracts of country belonging to the Meredith family,
to Amos, and others; and which, from its minute
subdivisions, separated by beautiful quickset hedges,
reminds one more forcibly of an English country
landscape than any other part of the island.

Further on the tourist espies the Swan River,
and then the range of hills dividing this tract
from the vale of Apsley, where there are extensive sheep-runs and valuable agricultural land,
chiefly in the hands of the Lynes, etc. Near the
head of the Apsley River is the rich vale of St.
Alban's, subdivided into various agricultural farms;
and a few miles further is the new and rising
township of Bicheno.

Distant from this about four or five miles are
the coal mines of the Douglas River Company.
Several seams of coal have been found here, and

the company are now working two, of four and
five feet, at points about two miles apart; the
persistence of the seams throughout the interval
having been ascertained by borings. The quality
of the coal is bituminous. Some of it cakes well;
and by recent experiments in Hobarton, it has
been found to yield an average amount of gas,
not inferior to the gas coals of England: it
will no doubt, ere long, prove extremely valuable
to the colony. There is a tram-road, nearly completed, from the coal shafts to the shipping place,—
decidedly one of the most important works in the
island. The terminus is at Waubb's Harbour,
where there is shelter under a small island for
vessels of 200 tons; and the Company are now
building a jetty, and are about to lay down moorings to give additional security and every facility
to vessels coming here to load.

Returning to New Town, the road to Launceston leads over a gentle declivity, passing on
the left a handsome block of buildings, which
comprise the pretty parish church in the centre,
flanked by the Queen's Orphan School, with the
vicarage and its gardens in the rear, overshadowed
by the lofty peak of Mount Wellington. On the
right is seen New Town Park, the residence of
Mr. Carter. The house is a neatly built mansion
in the comfortable English style; the grounds are
tastefully laid out, and kept in beautiful order,

speaking highly for the good taste of its hospitable, and worthy proprietor. The New Town Race-course, with its commodious stand-house, half-a-mile further on, affords the lovers of the turf a fair field and a frequent opportunity of testing the mettle of their steeds—and of their pockets. Opposite the race-course, are two very pretty places nestling under the hill side amid luxurious gardens; those of Mr. Henry Best, the Editor of the " Courier," and of Mr. Hopkins, a retired merchant of Hobarton, of considerable property: his mansion in the city is the finest within its limits. On the right, after you pass these, is the residence of, probably, the largest landed proprietor in the world, Mr. W. J. T. Clarke.

This gentleman some years ago, having amassed considerable wealth in cattle dealing and sheep runs, finding an old Government Proclamation to the effect that any one paying down £20,000 should be entitled to a special survey of 20,000 acres of any part of Australia he chose to fix upon, went to the Victoria Government, referred to the authority, which there was no gainsaying, and paid down his £20,000. Immediately the survey was ordered; which he took care should comprise the richest tracts of the colony, and as near as he could obtain it between the city of Melbourne and Geelong. Besides this extensive property he is the owner of several sheep runs

and estates here; and some of the most productive
land in Tasmania also belongs to him. Yet,
strange to say, the house at which he principally
resides is not to be compared to the cottage of
the farmer renting his 100 acres; nor is his household or establishment in better style — accumu-
lation being his only idea: this is fully borne
out by his general character and appearance. Such
men are the ruin of an infant colony, and the
sooner they leave, and their rich lands become
divided amongst more useful men, the better.

His character forcibly reminds us of Dr. Watts'
lines :—

"Proudly poising what he weighs,
   He swells amidst his wealthy store,
In his own scale he fondly lays
   Huge heaps of shining ore."
. . . .
"Let a broad stream, with golden sands,
   Through all his meadows roll;
He's but a wretch with all his lands
   Who wears a narrow soul."

The road leads through the pretty village of
O'Brien's Bridge, already described; and passing
on through the richly cultivated slope from the
mountain ridge, which extends from Mount Wellington to New Norfolk, you cross the Derwent
at Bridgewater by a very fine viaduct, constructed
by Government at an immense outlay.

On the other side, from the village of Bridgewater—boasting of a large hotel—a magnificent
view is obtained of the winding Derwent, with the

long range of mountain scenery in the distance.
Six miles further on, cantering over Brighton
Plains, the valley of the Jordan opens to the view.
The high-sounding names of this poor little village
of Brighton and the miserable little stream lead
the visitor to expect something more worthy of
their cognomens. However, great as the disappointment may be, on proceeding to the brow of
the hill above the hamlet, a splendid prospect
charms the beholder. On one side, the little
stream, like a silver thread, winds through a
luxuriant and verdant valley, above which the
rich cultivated lands of the colonial military settlers appear; on the other side, you pass a quaint
little church of nondescript architecture, remarkable
for its curiously devised portico. Opposite is the
pretty residence of Mr. Forster, who dispenses law
and justice to the extensive district of Bagdad.

This plain, which is of considerable beauty,
extends for some miles between two ridges of
thickly covered mountains. On the right is the
extensive property of the Butlers. A fine building
of stables and offices in the foreground partly
eclipses their cottage residence; which, though
small, is nevertheless remarkable for the great hospitality ever to be found within its walls. On the
left of this estate is that of Mr. Lord; passing
which, one cannot fail to admire the neatly farmed
lands of Mr. Hayes.

Cornucopia, the residence of Dr. Lempriere, adjoins; and, though it boasts no architectural beauty, being a plainly built modern mansion, yet few houses in the colony can vie with it in the profuse hospitality and kindly welcome ever extended to the stranger by its worthy host and his most amiable lady.

Leaving with regret this friendly roof, we proceed through a mountain gorge and the hamlet of Bagdad to the very prettily situated village of Green Ponds—celebrated in Tasmanian lore as the honeymoon retreat: it derives its name from a large marsh and low swampy soil of rich alluvial land in the valley.

Three miles from Green Ponds is Mount Vernon, the property of A. F. Kemp, Esq., an old officer well known in the colony, enjoying the soubriquet of "the Father of the Settlers." His estate comprises about four thousand acres, principally of luxuriant pasture land, running along the valley watered by the Jordan; which, like the Nile, constantly overflowing its banks, increases much the value of the land by its never-failing irrigation. Mount Vernon is justly celebrated as a dairy farm, the butter from which is in considerable repute in the Hobarton market.

The road leads by a winding ascent for some miles to Spring Hill, where a landscape of wide extent spreads itself before the view, Mount Wel-

lington towering in the background and bounding
the horizon. Beyond this, at the foot of the hill, is
the very charming residence of Mr. E. Bisdee, well
named "Lovely Banks." To the left, through a
pretty valley, is the road to Hutton Park, the
property of Mr. J. Bisdee.

The next village *en route* is Jericho; and if it
derives its name from any similarity to the city
overthrown by Joshua, it must surely be from the
aspect of that place after its fall. It is of little
note, though watered by the Jordan. To account
for the Eastern nomenclature in this locality, which
seems so irrelevant, it is on record that the first
settlers were some soldiers lately arrived from
Syria, where their regiment had been stationed
during the Egyptian campaign.

Before you come to Jericho the road to Bothwell branches off; it is a rising country village,
and several comfortable homesteads surround it.

Running diagonally through the island, from the
south to the north-west, is an elevated mountainous
district, which has Mount Wellington for its southern extremity, and Cradle Mountain, or Valentine's
Peak, for its culminating point to the north. About
the centre of the island it widens to such an extent
as to form an elevated plateau, some three or four
thousand feet above the level of the sea, having
Table Mountain and Miller's Bluff for its eastern
turrets, and extending westward from forty to

seventy miles, to where King William's Mountain and Barm Bluff form its western towers. There is great variety of climate and soil in different parts of this plateau; but all of it being more or less elevated, has a much colder climate than the centre and east parts of the island: besides which, having no shelter from the south-west, whence comes our cold and wet weather, there is more rain and snow than to leeward of this great natural barrier.

Many residents in Tasmania have little idea of the quantity of snow that is to be seen in the more mountainous parts. There are snow-drifts which do not entirely melt all the summer, out of which little rivulets run, as from miniature glaciers. Such I have seen on the shady side of King William's Mountain, Mount Field, etc. Snow covers the Great Lake Plains, St. Patrick's Plains, and King William's Plains, for days, and sometimes for weeks, together.

Considering the number of Scotch settlers that we have, I am surprised that this district is not called the Highlands; instead of that, however, it is called the Lakes, from its numerous and extensive sheets of water: they differ, however, from their English protonymes in being all at the top of mountains instead of at the bottom.

Nearly the whole of this tract is occupied by flocks of sheep in summer; and some of the stronger flocks remain all the winter in the best parts of it. Comparatively but little of the land is private property, the high upset price preventing its purchase; but it is leased by the crown in large lots of from 500 to 5,000 acres. There is also another difficulty to deter buyers, as may be supposed: an ascent of two or three thousand feet is no easy matter; though numerous bullock carts go up and down every season along the three roads or tracts by which it is approached. The Hobarton resident would no doubt choose the Bothwell road, which is by far the most easy of ascent; but it has no particular features of interest. The track has the river Clyde winding in deep ravines on the left, and Table Mountain on the right; but it is seldom that a distant view can be obtained through the extensive forests of gum trees that line the road.

So gradual is our entrance upon the table land that it is difficult to fix the precise spot; but soon after crossing the Clyde by a small wooden bridge, Lake Crescent comes into view. The Crescent is best seen from the tip of its north-western horn, when Table Mountain forms a noble feature on its southern side. A narrow piece of land separates Lake Crescent from Lake Sorell, a beautiful sheet of water some fifteen miles by ten, and connected with Lake Crescent by a narrow, deep channel; over this channel private enterprise has placed a

substantial bridge, but private interest keeps the
gate locked, unless armed with the talismanic sig-
nature of G. C. Clarke.

Crossing the bridge and skirting the lake,
through fine park-like scenery, we arrive at a
pretty cottage erected by that romantic gentleman, Mr. O'Meagher, one of the Irish rebels,
who resided here on parole during a considerable
part of his captivity in Tasmania, dividing his
time between his yacht and his library.

The lake abounds with ducks and teal, also
black swans; now and then a pelican is to be
seen : these last sometimes alight when driven
inland by storms, but do not stay long. Lake
Sorell is cut deep, and considerable portions are
frozen over in winter, but not sufficiently to
bear.

Leaving Lake Sorell and travelling to the westward, through fine, open, well-grassed forest, we
reach Interlacken, the out station of Mr. G. C.
Clarke, who owns and rents a very large quantity
of land in this neighbourhood. Nothing strikes
the traveller in summer so much as the green
fresh looking grass at the lakes, when compared
with the scorched and withered appearance of the
lower country. Near Interlacken, clover and rye
grass, green and luxuriant, proclaim the abundant
moisture ; wheat has been tried, but seldom ripens ;
of oats and barley I have seen excellent crops,

and such turnips and cabbages as would do credit to Covent Garden Market.

Ten miles from Interlacken we reach St. Patrick's Plains, through which runs the Shannon river; in summer only ankle deep, but in winter a roaring cataract. Here commence the dead forests; the spectre-like trees bleaching in the wind and rain, and strewing the ground with their bark and branches, have a ghastly and dismal look: when camped near them on a windy night, the noise of their constantly falling limbs is like the firing of guns at a distance. I shall not forget the look of my man's face one windy night, when I was comforting him with the improbability of their falling on us, as he said, "but what brings all these down?" pointing to the ground already thickly strewed with dead timber. It was very remarkable that, on passing this place some time afterwards with a friend, and relating the man's expression, we turned off the track to see the place, and found that the tree to whose roots my tent had been attached, was torn up, and several limbs recently strewed about: this would at least have frightened us, had we been there at the time.

This reminds me of an escape that I had from a falling tree in another part of this colony, which I will stop to relate.

I had been in the bush several days with W. O. C. looking for wild cattle, when, after a

very wet day's walk, we camped on the banks
of a small rivulet. W. secured our only toma-
hawk, and supplied himself with a few strips of
bark to keep the wet from him, both above and
below. By the time I had got a fire and made
tea it was dark, so I wrapped myself up in my
rug and went to sleep. About midnight I found
that my body was acting as a dam against the
side of the bank, down which the rain was pour-
ing; indeed, it was about three inches deep in
water all along my upper side. This was not to
be borne, and as the fire had gone out I was
at infinite trouble in rekindling it. I at length
succeeded in making a fire in a hollow tree, and
for some time I sat inside in my shirt; but as
the fire grew I was obliged to turn out, and
when daylight appeared, the tree was in a roaring flame. It burnt very much up the trunk,
and as it was not a convenient fire to boil our
tea, or make a cake, I made another fire lower
down; and, the rain having ceased, I laid down
before it on my rug, with a dog on either side
of me. I must have been half asleep when I heard
a sound of creak, creak! A momentary glance
at the tree showed me it had split up fifty feet
or so, and was balancing round on the top of the
splinter ready to fall where I lay! I had only time
to shout to my companion and spring towards the
creek, when thundering down came the burning

mass, scattering the fire in all directions. One limb, a foot thick, had pinned my rug to the ground, and killed one of my dogs that was lying by my side; the other dog was so frightened he ran away, but found his way home some days afterwards. This escape taught me never to trust to a tree on fire, as you never know the time or direction of its fall.

But to return to the Great Lake. Five or six miles of rough walking in a northerly direction up a wide, wet, wintry-looking marsh, the gum-trees getting more and more stunted, the grass coarser, the soil thinner and more strong, and we are on the very edge of the western mountain. Three thousand feet below, like a mass at our feet, lie Deloraine and Westbury, with many a small farm and clearing. There is one bridle path down this part of the range, but dangerous and difficult. On a sandstone ledge some distance down, is the skull of a horse, set up in memory of a narrow escape of one of Mr. Field's stock-keepers, whose horse slipped off the ledge and was killed; the rider, by agility little short of the miraculous, clinging to the rock and saving his life.

There is a saddle, or hollow, in the mountain range on the eastern side of the Great Lake, over which the traveller may reach Arthur's Lakes, about eight miles distant: rocks and trees make the journey anything but agreeable, whilst large beds of moss, some crusted over so as to bear a man's weight, others soft and wet like sponge, are dangerous obstacles to the unaccustomed horse; or, should it be winter time, the snow will make the passage impracticable for days together. About this part of the district the cider tree is very common: it is a species of eucalyptus, the sap of which is collected by the shepherds and hunters from notches cut in the trunk; when drank fresh it tastes like honey and water, but soon ferments and turns sour.

Arthur's Lakes are, perhaps, the least attractive, though likely to be the most useful of all the lakes. They are bounded by gently undulating hills, covered with the brown-green foliage of the eucalypti, and without sign of life or animation: as far as I could learn they are without fish, and not a sail or a boat relieved their wide expanse. This affected me with unmitigated melancholy, and I could not help thinking of the lovely lakes of Westmoreland and Cumberland, as contrasted with the great round dull ponds before me. Out of these lakes (there are four which claim the name, two large and two small) the Lake River derives its supply; forming but a shallow stream in summer, but a fearful torrent in winter.

A small dam at the mouth of the lake, with a regulating sluice, would, at a trifling expense, equalise the summer and winter flow, and enable

the extensive agricultural expanse of Norfolk
Plains (2,000 feet lower down) to be laid under
irrigation; but whether labour and capital will
ever be cheap enough in Tasmania 'to cope with
·this grand project, before it is complicated by
innumerable disagreeable obstructions under the
name of vested interests, is a problem difficult of
solution. Several other rivers in the colony have
similar advantages, equally apparent and alike
neglected; as they must be whilst land is cheap
and labour dear.

From Arthur's Lakes, four miles of a bridle
track 1,000 feet lower down, take us into Job's
Den, a curious basin of 2,000 or 3,000 acres in
extent, into and out of which the Lake River
appears to have cut itself a channel.

There are two more hills to descend alongside
the Lake River before it emerges into the open
valley (where stands the pretty residence of Mr.
Parker) and the rich plains of Longford, filling
with riches and abundance that thriving township.

There is no place worthy of remark till the
large and flourishing town of Oatlands is reached;
and which is said to be built on the most elevated
table-land in the island, excepting Bothwell and
Marlborough, and about midway between Hobarton
and Launceston. To the right of the township
there is a large lake, along the shores of which,
by the forest-clad hills, are several pretty places.

Oatlands is an inland town' of some importance, returning a member to the Legislative Assembly. Three miles from the town is the residence of the present member, Mr. Anstey, of Anstey Barton, situated in a beautiful valley; an amphitheatre, encircled by a romantic chain of hills surrounds it. From the high situation of the town the winter is very severe. The houses are built of fine stone, abundant in the neighbourhood. There is a good hotel at Oatlands, and annual races are held there.

CHAPTER XVII.

The morn is up again, the dewy morn,
With breath all incense and with cheek all bloom,
Laughing the clouds away with playful scorn,
And living as if earth contained no tomb—
And glowing into day. We may resume
The march of our existence; and thus I,
Still on thy shores, fair Leman! may find room
And food for meditation; nor pass by
Much that may give us pause if pondered fittingly.
CHILDE HAROLD.

As the tourist or the traveller stops awhile at Oatlands, the half-way resting-place to the goodly town of Launceston, so has our pen paused: now we resume our description.

Four miles from Oatlands is situated the pretty place of Mr. O'Connor, St. Peter's Pass, with good house and fine gardens; beyond which is a fine valley of well cultivated land, and the comfortable residence of Mr. Harrison and his son, remarkable for its very beautiful and blooming gardens. The little village of Tunbridge is scarcely worthy of note, save in the contrast it affords to its English namesake. The extensive Salt Pan Plains are traversed wearily, and without interest,

till we come to the *cottage ornée* and grounds of
Captain Horton. This gentleman is possessed of
considerable property, and his philanthropic anxiety
to benefit the colony has induced him to build, at
a large outlay, a very fine College, endowed by
him in conjunction with the Government, for the
purpose of educating youth, and conferring degrees
in every profession. This imposing structure is now
nearly completed, and, being situated near the public road, is an object of much interest to the tourist.

In this neighbourhood, also, is the residence
of Philip Smith, Esq., another large landed proprietor. We need not enter upon a detailed
account of Mona Vale, the magnificent property
of Mr. Kermode, it having been so ably described
in Colonel Mundy's work, " Our Antipodes."

The village of Ross, celebrated for its unrivalled

freestone, next greets us, with the meandering Macquarie encircling it: a neat bridge over which leads
to the town.   Unfortunately, owing to the pecu-
liarity of Tasmanian rivers, the Macquarie constantly overflows its banks, carrying away in its
impetuous course bridges, houses, etc.: hence the
skill of the engineer is constantly in requisition
for new inventions to meet the difficulties and
interruptions of transit caused by these frequent
inundations.

After leaving Ross we pass the charming seat
of Mr. Horne, in the *cottage ornée* style.   From
thence a straight and level road, without a turn
or hill for seven miles, leads to Campbell Town,
where, to use the words of the poet Crabbe,

> "They are of those whose skill assigns the prize,
> For creatures fed in pens, and stalls, and styes;
> And who, in places where improvers meet
> To fill the land with fatness, have a seat"—

for it is here the annual cattle shows are held.
The neighbouring gentry, men of considerable
property and substance, are far in advance, and
take the lead in all the agricultural projects of
the colony.   We must make Campbell Town
another halting place in order to conduct the
reader on some excursions of interest in the neighbourhood: and certainly the principal feature of
the town being its four fine and comfortable hotels,
is enough to induce a short sojourn here.   Sometimes, also, the lovers of Terpsichore are accus-

tomed to while away the hours in the festive dance within the fine Assembly Rooms.

Our first excursion is to Falmouth; and though the way can scarcely be called a road, as it leads through the bush, and has never been under the superintendence of M'Adam, it cannot fail to please and interest. Selma, the very pretty place of Mr. M'Kinnon, is passed on the left hand; and proceeding along the banks of the South Esk, a winding stream through hill and dale, you come to Avoca, "where the sweet waters meet,"—the St. Paul's and the South Esk,—a most picturesque and charming spot, and worthy of the name it bears. The hospitable mansion of Mr. S. Lord, with grounds of considerable beauty and extent, commands a splendid view of the vale, with a high range of hills in the background.

This part of the country is so beautifully and graphically described by the authoress already spoken of in a former chapter that we must entreat forgiveness for here inserting an extract from her work.

"The first part of our next day's journey was through a beautiful valley between fine ranges of wooded hills, one of which, from its high round form, is named St. Paul's Dome. Our road lay along the opposite declivity, overlooking the vale and its snug farms and cottages, green lawn-like fields, and the bright winding river of St. Paul's, outspread in fair array before us, as we drove pleasantly along St. Paul's Plains, fully appreciating the comfort of hard firm ground, albeit sometimes rough with rocks.   My attention had for some time been engrossed by the outline of the distant hills on our left, and watching the changes of effect caused by the passage of clouds across the sunlight, when, on looking again to the right, I involuntarily uttered a cry of astonishment and delight.   Beyond a sort of promontory, in which one hilly range abruptly ended, had arisen, as if by enchantment, a living picture of the sunny Alps,—a distant lofty expanse of crag and battlement and peak, all white and dazzling in the silvery snow, amidst which the steep sides of some mighty buttress-like rocks showed black as jet; and the deep blue unclouded sky crowned the glorious scene, which, I suppose, was yet the more charming to me as being wholly unexpected.   My new friend was the Tasmanian Ben Lomond, the lordly chief of a great mountain group in the north-east of our beautiful island."

We are again indebted to Mr. Gell, before alluded to, for the following description of wild cattle hunting, which we copy in the words of his letter to us:—

"I will now give you an account of a chase of a very exciting character: indeed I can only compare it to fox hunting, though it is more dangerous, and requires greater personal vigour and presence

J. P. Gell, delt.

Smith, Elder & Co. London.

BEN LOMOND.

of mind. You will hardly believe me when I tell you that wild cattle are the objects of our pursuit; but, indeed, very few are aware of the difference that exists between the sluggish animals in our farm-yards and their wild brethren in the bush, or would believe that there is as much difference between tame and wild cattle as between a sweep's donkey and a zebra. The ancestors of the cattle of Van Diemen's Land were imported from England, Sydney, and the Cape. Some of the wildest I have seen resemble the Cape buffaloes, in their dun colour, high shoulders (sometimes adorned with a sort of mane), narrow arched backs, and drooped rumps; as Loudon says, 'More in the coach-horse line than fitted for the shambles.'

"These again have been crossed with the Devon and Hereford cattle, and the produce seem to gain in speed and ferocity. But it is not the breed but the training that makes these cattle what they are; for they are in perfect training, and always on the look out: if a stick does but break, they are off in a trot, and the sight of a dog or a man, sends them away at a gallop. When they are much disturbed they only come out to feed at night, remaining concealed during the day in thick scrub, or along the banks of rivers in the long grass and ferns. From time to time the cattle born wild are joined by some unruly bullock escaped from his master's tame herd, and so

long as he remains in wild company he shows as
much determination, and more cunning to avoid
capture than his wild companions; but when once
overtaken he does not resist with the same ob-
stinacy of spirit as a wild beast, which will often
die rather than submit.

"Most of the wild cattle owe their origin to
stragglers from the herds of Messrs. W. Field,
E. Lord, and Stains and Fry; but they have not
failed to lead away numbers from adjoining herds:
and be it remembered that the produce of a wild
bull is with difficulty tamed, though brought up
in the milking yard. It will thus be seen that
they are not acceptable neighbours; as, besides
deteriorating the tame breed, they have been
known to visit grain fields, eating and destroying
all night, and getting away before dawn: they are
continually breaking down the fences and causing
flocks of sheep to intermix. It is, therefore, an
object to get rid of them, and were it not for the
almost inaccessible places in which they herd, it
would, perhaps, be easiest to shoot them; but
this would involve the total loss of flesh and hide:
besides, it is not so easy to shoot so wary an
animal, who will carry away as much lead as you
may be able to give him, if not placed in the
head or heart—and the forehead of a bull will
turn a ball. Most I have seen killed were shot
behind the shoulder.

"The young Tasmanians, who are excellent horsemen, prefer hunting these cattle with horses and dogs; and on a fine morning in June (our winter) I started off with C. on a cattle hunting expedition. But I have not told you what C. is like; he is tall, and stout for his age (and the natives come early to maturity), six feet one inch high and about eleven stone weight, with fair hair and blue eyes, like the rest of his family. In his straw hat and leathern leggins he is not unlike the young farmer of England, except that his easy seat and thorough identification with his horse proclaim him to be perfectly at home in his saddle. He carries a whip with a handle about twelve inches and a lash of about nine feet long (from the thickness of the forests in Tasmania the whips with lashes of twenty-four feet, common in New South Wales, would be useless); the end of the lash is pointed with a silken cracker, formed of about a skein of silk twisted together. The force of a blow from one of these weapons may be estimated from the fact that an apparently slight touch from the cracker will break to shivers a common wine-bottle, or draw blood through the thickest bull's hide.

"We will next take a look at his horse; and at first view we are not much enchanted. The grey appears to have a rough coat, his legs look terribly scarred, the marks of stubbs are seen

in his hoofs, and a thong of bullock hides round
his neck does not improve his appearance; but
on further observation, I see he picks his way
with great quickness and activity, over logs,
brushwood, stump holes, and other obstructions,
that would puzzle your English hunter: with
short joints, firm sinews, attentive eye and ear,
he carries his master easily and safely.

"I was mounted on a somewhat similar animal,
but stouter and slower. At our heels paced two
dogs, one in colour and appearance a Scotch colly,
or sheep dog, but much larger than the generality;
the other a surly-looking mastiff, tall, bony, and
short-tailed, of a grizzly grey colour. For a long
time we rode on in Indian file without speaking
a word; at last my friend looked earnestly on
the ground, and coming to a soft spot, I saw the
marks of the cloven foot. C. said in a whisper
that they had not been long gone. When I looked
round, I did not at all fancy the place for a gallop.
On our right rose the western mountains; we were
on a spur of them, but almost cut off by a gully
of unknown depth, that I could trace round the
hill to where I supposed the river to be. I could
see nothing but tops of trees, except a small clearing about six miles off; rocks sticking up amongst
the rich red soil, and wattle trees with their low
branches seeming to shut the road on every side.

"'Look out!' cries C. The dogs are on the

scent, and in a moment I see nothing but the
grey's silvery tail whisking through the trees along
the top of the hill, like a shooting star. My horse
gets his head down and away we go. The first
bough sweeps off my hat and scratches my face,
and I learn to keep my head to my horse's neck.
My horse never leaves the track of the grey, and
in a moment we come to the brow of the hill.
Surely, I think, the horses cannot go this pace
down that hill, over stones, holes, logs, and trees—
a cat could not keep its balance! But, positively,
C. sits back and spurs; he gains on me: perhaps
I held the reins a *leetle* too tight. Safe over the
creek at the bottom, I soon overtake him, and
we both pass the dogs in the ferns across a flat.
Rising the hill opposite, for the first time I see
the white tuft of a beast; I next distinguish two
or three sidling along the hill a little higher up·
I gain confidence up the rise, and begin to use
my spurs, though the pace is tremendous; all at
once a burnt out stump hole takes the grey up
to.the shoulders; one plunge, and horse and rider
are sprawling beneath me: an inch more and I
should have ridden over them. ' Go on !' shouted
C., who was not hurt; so taking a pull at my
horse, to avoid a tree, I find that he has a
mouth, which I doubted before. I now see, fifty
yards a-head of me, a black animal steaming along,
with his head low and tail straight out. What

my horse is about I don't know; I only see the
animal and wish my spurs were sharper.

"We come to a thick clump of saplings; I can't
thread them, and I can't knock them down. I
get my horse's head on the wrong side of me,
and as I broach-to, with a lurch that requires
all my sticking powers, my friend shouts, 'Take
a rein in each hand,' as he glides past, steering
the grey as easily as a dowager would her bath
chair. I next see and hear his whip, bang, bang,
quick and heavy on the rump of the bull. Strange
to say, so far from the brute going faster, he
shortens his stride at every stroke, and my friend
is able to get near enough to him to take him
by the tail; when, with a sudden jerk and a dex-
terous movement of the horse, over goes the bull
on his side. This takes the running out of him,
and I now find that he is more disposed to run
at us than away *from* us: that seems dangerous,
so I keep my distance. But young Tasmania,
backing his horse towards the savage and now
desperate brute, provokes him to follow in the
direction of home; the grey all the while keeping
his eye on the enemy. At last the bull stands
at bay under a tree, tearing up the ground, bel-
lowing, and smashing the saplings all round. What
fury in his blood-shot eye! what rage in his roar!
He trembles with fear and ferocity, and waits
for breath to make a more deadly plunge; but

before he can regain his power, up comes the mastiff and, with one snap, seizes him by the ear. In vain he tosses and roars; the dog brings him on his knees: in a' moment the rope is transferred from the neck of the grey to that of the bull, and made fast to a tree. There he was left, until two strong quiet bullocks were brought up and the bull yoked to them; then in process of time, though never thoroughly tamed, he would become a serviceable working bullock."

This short account may give you some idea of wild cattle hunting in Van Diemen's Land; but each day has its own adventures and escapes. Every year the wild herds are decreasing; the leasing of the crown lands, and their being stocked with sheep, starves out the wild cattle and makes them more easily caught.

An undulating tract of country extends to the township of Fingal. On the road to it you pass Tullochgorum, the residence of Mr. Grant, a gentleman of considerable property. In this locality gold is found, and with untiring perseverance it is still sought for, though the specimens are—

"Like angels' visits, few and far between."

Fingal is one of the prettiest villages in the colony, situated on a hill-side, with the South Esk flowing in the valley; and pre-eminent in the village is seen the very neat cottage of Mr. Aitkin, the Police Magistrate. One and a half miles from

14

the hamlet is Malahide, the whilome residence
of a scion of the noble house of Talbot. Five
miles further is the large and fine mansion of
Killymoon, the seat of Mr. Von Steiglitz, in the
German style of architecture, where hospitality
in true old country abundance is ever to be found.
There is a coal-seam in this part of the country;
but there being no road yet made, the mine is
not worked. There are also some large dairy
farms and fine pasture land around.

Cullenswood is a very nice village on the road
to Falmouth, about twelve miles from Fingal. The
house and gardens of the clergyman, Mr. Parsons,
with a neat church on the summit of the hill,
have a very pleasing effect. Mr. Legge, also one
of the largest landed proprietors in the district, has
here a fine house, which is seen from the road.

The tourist cannot but hasten to the most romantic view in the island, now appearing before
him, in St. Mary's Pass. Winding along the side
of a densely wooded hill is cut a road, overshadowed by lofty trees. Beneath, the beautiful
sassafras trees fill the valley, intermingled down
the vale with the no less beautiful and romantic
looking fern trees, dipping into the rushing torrent
which flows through the glen. On the opposite
side rises perpendicularly a similar hill, thickly
studded with lordly forest trees up to the summit,
reminding one forcibly of the Glen of the Downs

in the Emerald Isle. Rounding the hill side, the mighty ocean appears, thus adding another lovely feature to this charming. spot; yet, as you proceed, descending amidst the forest, it is lost to sight until you come upon the town of Falmouth. This town is becoming esteemed of some importance, and has opened a good produce trade with Hobarton, from the very fine dairy farms in the neighbourhood.

Some distance from Falmouth, on the coast, is the embouchure of the Scamander. The scenery on both sides of this fine river is very wild and beautiful; but there are very few settlers here, and the region has been but little explored.

We must now return to Campbell Town, and commence another chapter.

CHAPTER XVIII.

The vapours round the mountains curled
Melt into morn, and light awakes the world.
Man has another day to swell the past,
And lead him near so little, ere he last.
But mighty Nature bounds us from her birth:
The sun is in the heavens, and life on earth;
Flowers in the valley, and splendour in the beam;
Health on the gale, and freshness in the stream.
Immortal man! behold her glories shine,
And cry exultingly, for they are thine.

LONGFELLOW

FEW countries in the world have more diversified
and picturesque scenery so closely adjoining as the
fair isle of Tasmania; for though many parts are
tame and uninteresting, their extent is not great,
and the eye is soon relieved by a beautiful back-
ground of mountain range, or some winding stream
or verdant valley. Such is the lovely vale of the
Macquarie, where nature's beauties are richly spread
before the view, and the river flows gently on
through a most picturesque valley extending to the
western tier and lake.

A road leading from Campbell Town to the Plains, passes the charming residence of Mr. Harrison, Merton Vale, and also the chaste Italian villa, Rosedale, belonging to Mr. Leake, M.L.C., the gardens and grounds of which are laid out in beautiful order. What is most remarkable about the latter edifice is the change effected by Mr. Blackburn (an architect of this colony) who, from a plain cottage has converted it into a beautiful villa in the Italian style, without detracting from its convenience.

Mr. Leake, with a young family, emigrated, in 1823, from Hamburg, where he had been a British resident for seven years, being originally from Hull, and a merchant by profession. As a colonist of Tasmania he belongs to the successful class; for many years he has been a magistrate of the county, and a member of the Legislative Council. He was among the first who imported the fine-woolled Saxon sheep from Germany; and some of his family have extensive property in South Australia.

In the midst of the plain is a pretty Scotch Kirk and manse, surrounded by the park-like scenery of the district. Seen in the distance is the fine seat of Mr. Allison, Streamshall, situated on the banks of the Macquarie River, in a splendid alluvial valley, which, for fertility and beauty of scenery, can hardly be supassed. The owner was, in early life, a sailor; he commanded a ship at

Copenhagen under Nelson, and also on the American coast, where the information he was enabled to furnish led to the action between the "Shannon" and "Chesapeake." After the war, he commanded a ship of his own in the merchant service, and finally settled with his family in Van Diemen's Land, in the year 1822; where he has been successful: his family are principally married, living in peace and harmony with all around, and looking up to him as their head. Two of his sons are Justices of the Peace, and one is a Member of Council. This family forms a good example of what can be done, in a young colony by union and industry—occupying at present among them some eighty thousand acres of land, and grazing upwards of thirty thousand sheep—all created from limited means at the commencement; fully proving the axiom that "union is strength," and that "industry seldom fails to meet its just reward."

In the early days of the colony Mr. Allison, sen., resisted an attack made upon him by three armed bushrangers. The struggle was a desperate one; but the bushrangers were finally victorious, leaving Mr. Allison for dead in front of his own door: they inflicted many injuries upon him, especially with the butts of their guns upon his head; from which, we regret to say, he still suffers, though thirty years have passed. Had he permitted the bushrangers to rob him quietly, they, no doubt, would not have injured him; but he had too much spirit to submit to this: there was in him too much of the true-hearted sailor of the old war to brook this indignity.

These circumstances prove that, although we find the generality of the old settlers very comfortably placed, they have had to struggle hard, and to bear much from murderous attacks of the natives and bushrangers, and from other sources of annoyance and danger in the colony. To illustrate this position further we will mention an occurrence which happened to two of this gentleman's sons, the eldest and youngest, at one of their remote sheep stations. We give the sad history in the words of W. Race Allison, M.L.C., who, at our request, has kindly furnished them :—

"The time for shearing our flocks at Cape Portland, which is one hundred and fifty miles from home, had arrived. The run is upon the coast of the sea. I generally go myself to superintend the shearing at this station. There had been a great many deaths among young persons from scarlet fever. My youngest brother was not strong; I feared he might take the fever. I mostly go by myself, because I do not like to subject my brothers to the risks from fording the large rivers we have to cross at their bar mouths, at low tide, - just where they join the sea, and from other causes. Still I thought that this time I would take

my youngest brother, about seventeen years of age,
with me, thinking the trip might do him good,
and keep him out of the way of the fever.   We
shall see how man proposes and God disposes.

"We started from home on horseback, in high
spirits, February, 1853.   We crossed all the seven
rivers safely, and got to the Station Hut well on
the fourth day.   The shearing passed over well and
pleasantly: the sea air gave the boy increased
strength.   There were a lot of horses running wild
in the neighbourhood, and among them was one
that a poor man, who had a large family and lived
in that quarter, had given £70 for, and he could
not catch him or get him in.   Feeling for the man,
we got up a party of all the horsemen we could
muster among our own people and others, and
started, eight in number, to try and catch this
horse.   My brother went with us on horseback,
for he could ride as well as I could.   We fell in
with the wild horses.   The moment they saw us
away they went, as hard as they could split, and
we after them.   We kept sight of and followed
them about ten miles—crossing a very rough scrubby
country, full of blind creeks, right into the heart
of the forest.   Several of the wild horses, the
worst, knocked up and fell back.   But the horse
we wanted, a very fine one, still kept the lead.

"We now came out upon an open country—the
wild horses in full view; our overseer was in front

of me. I heard my brother's voice cheering, and giving the 'view halloo.' I had not seen him for eight miles before ; he was now a few hundred yards behind me. I felt proud to see him enjoying himself, and riding so well up. We kept galloping as hard as we could. I looked round quickly again at him to see if he was gaining upon me. Just as my eyes fell upon him, he rode against a tree, and, shocking sight ! seemed to me to be smashed to pieces, and to fall headlong dead. The thought at once struck me—what could I do with him in that forest, alone? I spurred my horse to endeavour to overtake the overseer, and called to him, for God's sake, to stop, as my brother was killed. But I could not gain upon him, or make him hear me. The thought now occurred to me, that if I go any further I shall never find the place where his body has fallen. I pulled up my horse and galloped back. A fearful sight it was. There lay my poor brother, to all appearance dead. The right cheek, which had struck the tree, and the neck were skinned and completely raw ; the left jaw was broken in two, the blood running out of his mouth. The right knee had also struck the tree, which had broken the thigh just above the knee, and the upper thigh bone was protruding through the flesh about five inches. I let go of my horse, and took my brother in my arms. There was no appearance of pulse or respiration : he seemed dead.

"I wiped the dirt off the protruding bone, and, with a strong effort, pulled the leg straight, and returned the bone into its place. I don't know exactly what feeling actuated me; I believe I thought I was laying him decent in death. I sat upon the ground, and took his shoulders upon my knees, resting his head upon my breast, in such a way that the blood should not run down his throat. I pulled his shoulders back, to give the lungs the best chance to play again if any life remained, and chafed his temples and hands.

"For ten minutes he lay as dead; he then gave a deep sob. Whether his last breath had then fled, or whether this was a sign of returning life, I could not tell. For five minutes he did not breathe again. I thought all was passed, and I felt mad with anguish. In that wilderness alone, what was I to do? I felt I had not strength to remove his shattered body; I thought I would stay and die beside him. A merciful God directed it otherwise. His respiration feebly but gradually returned. He opened his eyes and looked at me. The relief I felt no tongue can tell. Hope returned again, and I fervently thanked God.

"My brother's horse, without any rider, galloped on, and came up with the overseer (a prisoner lad, who had served his time with us) about two miles on: when he saw the horse without a rider, he at once guessed something was wrong,

and, with the tact of a good bushman, dismounted,
took up the tracks of the horse's feet, and traced
them back, step by step, to where my brother
and I were. The poor fellow put his arms round
my brother's neck (who was a great favourite
with all the servants), fell upon his body, kissed
him, and wept like a child. After a few moments
thus spent I told him to get on his horse, gallop
round in all directions, and try to muster some
of the other men, that we might carry my brother.
to the nearest shepherd's hut, distant about seven
miles. He found some of them, and we made
a handbarrow or bier out of saplings, with our
girths, whips, and stirrup-leathers. We made him
a soft bed of heath, and laid him upon it. I bound
the leg steady with two pieces of bark and our
handkerchiefs, and, after many hours carrying, we
got him safely to the hut; sometimes he screamed
with pain, and at others he slept for a few minutes
as peacefully as a child. I started the overseer to
Launceston, distant one hundred and twenty miles,
for a doctor, directing amputating instruments to
be brought, as I felt sure the leg must come off.

"I knew four days must elapse before I could
get medical assistance, and that every hour was of
the deepest moment: I knew if I left my brother's
leg unset as it was, it would be in a fearful state
before that time; indeed I felt there was no alter-
native—that I must set the leg, or he must die.

I asked the shepherd's wife to get a bed for him, which she did, giving up her own for that purpose; meanwhile I got a saw and tools, and made splints out of a twelve-feet deal picked up on the beach. I set the leg: his screams and appeals to me not to hurt him so much, were fearful; none of the men could bear it, or stay in the hut: several of them fainted. The poor woman, however, kept her firmness, and held him tight at the head of the bed, while I stood at the foot, pulled the leg out, worked the ends of the bone into their places, and set the leg. I never felt so determined, though it went to my heart, for I knew that his life, under Providence, depended upon my firmness and success. Under other circumstances I could not have witnessed such an operation upon a stranger, far less have performed it myself upon my own brother. This over, he became comparatively easy. I gave him a dose of castor oil, which happened by good chance to be in the hut. I tore a blanket into long strips, and, dipping them in cold water, applied them continually along the whole course of the leg, to keep back the inflammation all I could, until the doctor should come. I bound up the broken jaw the best way I knew how, and, when he was laid comfortable, I went out, felt very sick, sat down under a fence out of sight and fainted.

"The doctor came with one of my brothers

on the fourth day. The leg was white, cool, and but little swelled; the continual cold application kept back inflammation, and rendered amputation unnecessary. The doctor said I had done all that could be done under such painful circumstances. Thank goodness, my brother recovered; though he is still lame. But that is not of much consequence; those of us who are not lame must work for those who are: his life was spared, that was everything. For nine weeks I fed him with a teaspoon. He could not move the jaw, or open his mouth. I did not leave him one hundred yards; my bed was dried grass on the floor of the hut—my bed-clothes my opossum-skin rug.

"In fifteen weeks I took him home in a covered-in cart, which I drove most of the road myself, for fear of further accident; his leg being still very bad, discharging immensely where the bones came through: I had to dress it six times a day to keep it clean. Some of the matter got into a small scratch on my thumb, caused the arm to swell, brought on fever, and made me suffer very much for a month or more. Nothing could exceed the patience with which my brother bore his sufferings, or the attention and kindness of the poor shepherds and people around; many of whom had been prisoners, but whose conduct proved their hearts were kind and good. One poor fellow brought me, from a distance of thirty miles, a bottle of brandy to put in water to bathe the leg.

"Though eighteen months have passed, I still fancy I see the horrible sight of my brother striking against the tree. For weeks I could not get the vision away from my eyes: sleeping or waking it haunted me. The agony of suspense I endured for three weeks, until I knew he was out of danger, cannot be conceived; for, besides my own natural affection for my brother, I had this feeling—that I had taken their youngest child away from my aged parents, and that I could never return him to them alive; therefore I could not bear to see them again. Providence mercifully ordered it otherwise.

"I would not have given any description of the matter, which is most· painful to me to recal, only I wish to show that we never should cease to exert ourselves, or give up to despair, even when all looks hopeless around us.

"The gentleman who was then our Governor, Sir William Denison, with that sincere kindness and true Christian feeling which eminently characterise him, did not forget us, remote as we were; he felt for the situation in which we were placed, and wrote me the kindest letters of consolation and advice, sending them weekly ninety miles by special messenger, and receiving my replies, until I wrote him that my brother was out of danger : acts of genuine kindness which will never be forgotten while our memories last ; and for which may God bless him.

" It is the greatest mercy that I happened at the moment to see my brother fall; had the accident happened either sooner, or later, in all probability his body would never have been discovered in that wilderness—that would have been dreadful indeed : in fact, from the way in which I found him lying, a few moments more must have destroyed his small remains of life; for, without assistance, he must have died. The whole circumstances, though most painful, were mercifully directed by our Great Master."

Returning to the town, one cannot fail to admire the elegant cottage of Dr. Valentine, built in the Elizabethan style.. His upright character and steady perseverance in disinterested exertions for the welfare of his adopted country have gained for the worthy Doctor a name far better than riches.

One mile from Campbell Town in the midst of a large plain, is Ricarton, a fine modern house, the seat of Mr. Davidson, a gentleman of very large property, ever kind and attentive to the stranger. Near Ricarton is Quorn Hall, a fine large mansion, with extensive park and beautiful grounds, the residence of Mr. James Lord,—who is rightly named, he being a very extensive *lord* of the soil. This district abounds in good agricultural farms and some capital sheep-runs.

The next township on our road is Cleveland, a very unpretending hamlet.

Leaving the main road for a while, we must turn a few miles to the left, till we enter the lovely valley of the Esk, leading from Avoca, before spoken of. The plain extends far away to the base of the lofty Ben Lomond, which rises majestically in the distance. Clynevale, the residence of Mr. Crear, is very beautifully situated on the river, with splendid gardens and shrubberies, and having a charming view of the finest scenery of the Esk.

There are some fine pasture lands in this district; and capital sheep runs, spreading away to Ben Lomond and back again to the Macquarie Plains. As the wool of these flocks is considered among the best, and constitutes the chief article of export, I here insert an account of the Sheep-shearing, furnished to us by the kindness of a gentleman in that neighbourhood: I give it in his own words.

"The season for shearing is from the middle of October to the end of March; the time occupied on different farms of course depending on the number of sheep, the number of shearers employed, and the convenience of the place. A shearer, working twelve hours a day, will shear from fifty to one hundred sheep, and as the price has ranged for the last three or four years from fifteen shillings to one pound per hundred, the wages for shearing are higher in proportion than for any other farming work. Still there are some drawbacks, as the shearer often loses much time in going from place to place, and at the end of the summer has to engage for low wages during the winter season. There is always a stand made at the beginning of the shearing season for the price, and the unlucky sheepholder who begins first has sometimes the mortification of seeing all his shearers troop off just as he has got his sheep washed and perhaps ready to shear.

"The usual trial of skill between master and man goes forward somewhat in the following way:—Suppose the sheep in the pens, shearers scattered over the floor, wool winders and wool pressers in their places. The master comes in, and, with as careless an air as he can assume, says, 'Now, my lads, hit in.'—'What's the price?' asks the Spokesman, a bush lawyer.

"Master: 'Oh, thirteen shillings is what I hear.'

"All: 'Thirteen shillings!'

"Spokesman: 'Why, Jack says they're a giving thirty shillings over the water; it war a pound last year, and now all the shearers is gone to New Zealand, it's a going to be twenty-five shillings this year.'

15

"Master: 'Pooh! nonsense! Who can afford to give such a price as that? I hear fifteen shillings is the price at Port Philip, and we can't afford to give so high a price as they do.'

"Spokesman: 'Why, look at the price of wool; it's higher now than when you give a pound last year.'

"Master: ''Tis not as if it did you any good: you'll spend all the money in drink.'

"Wag: 'We lays it out in houses (*sotto voce*) public houses.'

"Master: 'And as to shearers, there's lots of them knocking about that would be glad to take a flock like mine, so many ewes and lambs and hardly any rough sheep.'

"Spokesman: 'Ah, they says they are shearers! but when they gives in their tally, it'll be five-and-twenty, or thirty: as to me and my mates, we've been a shearing these ten years; but it's time we give up when masters talks of thirteen shillings.' (putting up shears and commencing to put on coats).

"Master: 'Well, I'll go as high as fifteen shillings and two lots of cider, and no thanks to you: you are a greedy set.'

"Spokesman: 'There now, just as if we cared! only how can one go for to show oneself on a township, and have it cast up as we lowered the price? we darna go for to do it.'

"Master: 'You may depend upon it nobody about here will give more; but if anybody round about gives a pound I will: but mind, now, the price is fifteen shillings.' (Exit master.)

"Spokesman (to the rest): 'Well, how's it to be?'

"Man, who has not got a shilling, and has borrowed money to buy his shears: 'The cove says he'll give a pound if anybody else does.'

"Man, who left a good place, and has got five pounds in his pockets: 'A pound is the price we agreed to have.'

"Thirsty man: 'But cove says we're to have two lots of cider.'

"At this juncture an old ewe, with very little wool on it, comes round to the front of the yard.

"'Good morning, marm,' cries the wag; 'you're the shearer's friend, I should say: you and me's partners.'

"'Come, Jack,' says his mate, 'don't you be a eagle, hawking 'em at this rate: no picking, say I.'

"This induces a rush for the sheep, and before the Spokesman can get out, 'That's not a fair start,' there are several sheep on the shearing floor, and busy shears at work: the most stubborn grumble, and at last get a sheep, saying, 'Well, I think the cove would ha' given the pound if we had a stuck out.'

"In a few minutes in walks the aforesaid 'cove,' pleased to see a commencement made, knowing that the men are now in his power. 'Clip close, my lads; all the wool but no skin. No racing; let's have a steady stroke:' whilst the men, with backs bent and shears bright and sharp, click, click away, plunging the shears up to the hilt in the wool, with a rapidity and precision only attained by long practice. Talking is not allowed in most shearing sheds, when there are many shearers employed; but it is hardly possible to put a stop to it altogether.

"Many are the rows before the business is over; the most prolific source of disturbance being the quantity and quality of the food. English farmers would hardly credit the quantity eaten and wasted by a party of shearers; two pounds of meat per day, unlimited bread and vegetables, still they find something to complain of: a cook that pleases them must be a clever artist indeed.

"Constant attention is necessary on the part of the master, to see that the sheep are well shorn. Each man keeps his own tally, and the master counts all the sheep shorn each day, and compares them with the tallies. The fleeces are rolled up separately, and sometimes classed: about one hundred are put into a bale, (generally by means of an iron screw,) branded, and shipped to the London market.

"Tasmania wool ranks high in the English market, principally in consequence of frequent and judicious importations of European sheep; coupled with the facilities for getting up the wool in a clean state, which this well-watered island affords."

Returning to Cleveland you traverse over a good, though long and dreary, road, through a stunted forest, for several miles, till the Esk once again breaks on your view; and the bridge of Perth is before you, forming a pretty foreground to the fine village on the hill above. Here, again, the skill of the engineer has been put to a severe test, for the inundations of the Esk are sometimes fearful. The bridge is now in a very sad state, though it is being repáired; the foundations of the piers are shaken, and it has been deemed necessary to send to England for an iron one: which it is to be hoped will have better luck than its predecessor. Perth is a neat country village.

Here three roads meet, so we must again turn off a little to visit Longford and its fertile neighbourhood. This town is three miles from Perth, beautifully situated at the junction of the South Esk and Lake Rivers, over which a curious looking bridge of piles has lately been erected. Longford is the most thriving settlement of the colony, and has an appearance of comfort and well-being seldom so visible in an infant state. In the town are three steam mills, large stores for grain, and several good hotels. There is also a very fine church, which cost, even in its present unfinished state, ten thousand pounds. In its oriel window is some stained glass by the famous Weims, of Newcastle.

This district is called Norfolk Plains, from its first settlers being from Norfolk Island, and obtaining in lieu of their holdings in that settlement small grants of the fine land along the Esk. There are, however, but few of the original possessors now to be found here: for the most part their tenements were purchased by more enterprising men, who built comfortable homesteads on the smaller allotments, and obtained Government grants of land in the vicinity.` Norfolk Plains is with justice named the "garden of Tasmania," and nothing reminds the stranger more forcibly of his own dear native land than the beautiful hedgerows of the blooming thorn; particularly on the farms of Messrs. Archer and Willmore.

To the south of the town is the Cressy estate, belonging to a company in England, and consisting of twenty thousand acres, mostly splendid parklike land: it is to be regretted that so magnificent a block of land is not subdivided and more cultivated, with a greater number of resident proprietors. This estate however, has been sold within the last year, subdivided into farms from one hundred to five hundred acres in extent. It may give some idea of the value of the land when we state that the average price throughout was £9; although the greater portion of it was unreclaimed forest land.

Eight miles over the Plains brings you to the village of Bishopsbourne, near the College already described. From thence the distant view of the western range is very grand and imposing, being five thousand feet above the level of the sea. Amidst the table land on the range are several lakes,—one called the Great Lake, seven miles broad and ninety miles in circumference; from which lake the river Shannon takes its rise. Along the base of the tiers are several pretty places, which our space will not admit of particularising. Amongst the proprietors are found the names of Archer, Walker, O'Connor, Parker, Fletcher, and Gatenby.

Three miles from Longford is Woolmers, the residence of the late Mr. T. Archer, and well worthy of a visit from the tourist, on account of its beautiful and valuable collection of paintings, and the very fine and extensive gardens. Near to this mansion is Rhodes, the complete farming establishment of Mr. Walker; and further on, situated charmingly on the river, with its tastefully laid out grounds, gardens, and conservatories, is Woodhall, the seat of Mr. J. Bonney, which is always in magnificent order, no expense being spared to keep it so. The last place we note in this locality

is the very handsome place of Mr. J. Archer,
Panshanger, on the Lake River: it rivals in beauty
many a noble domain in England.

Returning to Perth, and taking the road to
the right, you come to Evandale, four miles distant,—a very improving township of rich agricultural land. Five miles from the village is the
large and handsome domain of Mr. James Cox,
of Clarendon, who has been at considerable expense
in importing fallow deer to the colony, of which
he has now above a hundred in his park; he has
also domesticated the large forest kangaroo, great
numbers of which are to be seen throughout his
extensive property. The residence is a spacious
modern building; and justly is the truly noble
owner famed for his courtesy and hospitality.

About two miles from George Town (of which
we will speak hereafter) is the summer residence of
Mr. Cox, Marianville, a very pretty place at the
entrance of the Tamar, and seldom without an
influx of visitors, when occupied by the family.

About five miles from this place is the village
of Lymington, on the Nile, where a neat church
and school-house have been built by Mr. Cox, and
endowed by him with two hundred acres of very
valuable land.

Proceeding up the Nile towards Ben Lomond,
we come to another settlement, where a church
has been erected. Close by is the Camperdown

estate, adjoining which is Patterdale, formerly the
residence of Glover, the artist, now in the hands
of Mr. James Crear. The scenery all along this
river is exceedingly beautiful. Again we turn
our steps to Perth, and, gaining the main road,
wend our way to the city of the North. Ascending a hill above the town, a magnificent panorama
is spread out to view.

In the valley beneath is Launceston, very remarkable for the order and regularity of its streets.
Beyond is the extensive vale of the Tamar, through
whilch the meandering river is seen winding its
way until, lost in the woody hills in the distance,
it hurries on to the sea. Launceston is an exceedingly pretty place, situated at the confluence of the
North and South Esk, which here form the Tamar.
On one side a bold craggy hill hangs over the
city, down which, through a deep gorge, rushes the
impetuous South Esk.

From this height is a very splendid view of the
whole city and neighbourhood, which well repays
the toil of the ascent. Descending the other side,
the busy haunts of man are hidden, and the eye is
charmed by the very beautiful miniature lake before
you—the wild crag and forest around, and the dashing torrent beneath, forming a very pretty cascade:
it is one of the most enchanting scenes possible.
From the summit, on the one side, is seen a large
and busy town: hundreds of vessels crowding the

wharves; steamers and ships hastening to and
hurrying from the port: all is life and bustle, the
crowded streets exhibiting all the turmoil of daily
toil and traffic. A few steps, and the scene is
changed: you are in a wild desert, surrounded
with the primeval rock and native forest, with
naught save the sound of the cataract rushing over
to disturb you. Man is here alone with nature and
nature's God, and, with sublime thoughts of His
power and goodness, forgets the busy scene in the
divine beauty of the one before him. From another
hill on the opposite side, called Signal Point, a
very fine view is also had of the city, and an extensive landscape, shewing the windings of the North
Esk, so often to be met with all through the
surrounding country.

Launceston contains about eight thousand inhabitants. The streets are well laid out and
regularly built. There are churches of every
denomination, law courts, public buildings, banks,
etc.; some fine shops, well supplied; large and
handsome stores, with wharves and quays, but
subject to inconvenience from the rise and fall
of the tides. The town is situated forty miles from
the sea, and the navigation is extremely difficult;
though vessels of seven or eight hundred tons
often come to the port. There are two good hotels,
and some sixty altogether. A very prettily laid
out botanical garden, before spoken of, quite close

to the town, affords a *recherché* promenade. Several very beautiful suburban villas, and a great many fine gardens, are also to be met with.

Launceston is fast rising in wealth and importance, sending three steamers every week to Victoria and one to Sydney. There are also small steamers daily running to George Town, the seaport town outlet, which, though now but an inconsiderable village, will soon rise to greatness.

The society of Launceston is said to be less formal, and more free from the trammels of etiquette, than its southern rival; and though, from the long, low, flat, and marshy land of the vale, fogs are prevalent, yet it is considered a more healthy place than Hobarton. This marsh, however, has been lately drained, chiefly by Government, under the talented administration of Sir William Denison; and has been cut up into allotments, which realized large sums. It is contemplated to build a wharf right round this vale, facing the town, converting the interior (previously covered with water during half the year) into streets, warehouses, and valuable gardens; thereby adding much to the health, beauty, and wealth of the city.

There are some very beautiful walks and drives all round Launceston, and some very fine places in the neighbourhood: none more deserving of notice than Newenham, formerly the residence of W. A.

Gardner, Esq., whose extreme hospitality and kindness was proverbial in Tasmania. This gentleman
possessed extensive property, which his truly
philanthropic spirit devoted to the best purposes;
he was the promoter of everything tending to improve his country, and the liberal patron of every
matter, grave or gay. But, alas! he is now no
more. In June, 1855, he was suddenly seized
with inflammation of the chest, supposed to be
the effects of a neglected cold, and though every
attention was paid, medical skill proved unavailing.
His loss is severely felt by all, more particularly
as he had been but lately returned as Member
for Cornwall; and from his extensive property
and munificence, his talents and energetic habits,
together with the love he at all times evinced
for his adopted country, it was but reasonably
inferred he would have become a leader in the
House, and a warm advocate for every measure
tending to advance the colony. Having personally
known him, and experienced his kindness, we de-
plore his loss as that of a friend. Newenham has
now changed hands, owing to the amiable family
of Mr. Gardner leaving Tasmania: Mr. De Little, a
merchant of Launceston, has become the purchaser.

One of the most charming trips in Tasmania
is down the Tamar to George Town. Along the
river side all the way are handsome places, or
fine romantic hills, which, as the course of the river

leads from one defile to another, opens some pretty spot to view. Here a neat village is seen slumbering in a tranquil valley; there, some handsome mansion appears; anon, you are lost in the woody highlands overtopping the narrowing stream; again, an estuary opens to view, and wild scenery enchants the eye, till at length the open sea spreads itself before you, and George Town is gained.

The entrance to the river is dangerous, on account of several rocks and shoal water; but buoys are carefully laid down, light-houses have been erected, and skilful pilots are ever ready to conduct the stranger ship to anchor and safe moorings. The distance to Victoria and the entrance to the heads from George Town is one hundred and eighty miles; and the trip has been made from Launceston to Hobson's Bay—some two hundred odd miles—in sixteen hours; which, considering the difficulty of navigation in the forty miles of dangerous river cruising, speaks well for the state of transit to the sister colony.

Several projects are now in embryo for clearing the river, and building quays and wharves; and a very few years will no doubt improve this city wonderfully. There are many large landed proprietors living in the neighbourhood, and many merchants of wealth within it. The great desire to advance that is now abroad will very soon tell in such a place as this, where there is so wide a field for improvement and speculation; and as Hobarton is daily increasing in importance amongst the cities of the Southern Hemisphere, so will Launceston also take up its position. Nor will its honest and industrious citizens hold back with niggard hand the wealth that is now in their keeping. The day for hoarding is gone by; and as the go-ahead principle prevails, we prognosticate great things for the fair city of the north.

CHAPTER XIX.

Heavens! what a goodly prospect spreads around
Of hills, and dales, and woods, and lawns, and spires,
And glittering towns, and gilded streams, till all
The stretching landscape into smoke decays!
. . . .
Rich is thy soil and merciful thy clime,
Thy streams unfailing in the summer's drought;
Unmatch'd thy guardian oaks; thy valleys float
With golden waves; and on thy mountains flocks
Bleat numberless.

THOMSON.

GLADLY would we linger on the enchanting scene spread in panoramic view before us as we leave the fair city of Launceston; but having already exceeded our limits, we hasten on to the unexplored regions of the north-west coast, which abound in riches still unknown, with goodly ports as yet seen but by a few, with lordly rivers hitherto untraversed, and with mineral wealth still hidden and unsought for.

Ere we enter upon the Forest Country and the wilds of Devon, we pass through a rich and well-cultivated district. The road from Launceston to

Deloraine, on the confines of the woods whither we turn our steps, leads over a long acclivity of gradual ascent, from the top of which we gain a very charming view of the city and the surrounding country. Five miles brings us to the neat and snug village of Hadspen, where we again see the South Esk. Over it is thrown a curiously-built bridge of piles; and though it is raised some twenty to thirty feet above the level of ordinary high water, yet sometimes the stream rises above and carries all before it. This is a smiling and fertile valley, and many comfortable farm houses appear along the river side.

After you pass Hadspen, the pretty grounds and mansion of Entallez rises before you; it is the property of the Rev. Mr. Raibey, a very enterprising gentleman of large property in the colony, and one who tends much, both by precept and example, to keep a good feeling alive in his neighbourhood. On the opposite bank of the river is the extensive property of the Landon family, known as Meander Rise, and containing upwards of eight thousand acres.

From hence the road leads through a wood for three or four miles, till the Vale of Carrick appears, in which is a very fine race-course. Carrick is a village of some note, the land in the neighbourhood being very rich and highly cultivated; it boasts, however, of but little beauty save the view from the other side of the hill, which, with a pretty mill, and the little gurgling stream stealing away into the forest, makes a sweet scene for the landscape painter. Over this hill the road leads again through the thick forests till you reach the cleared land to the right of the Quamby estate. This, the most extensive and valuable property in the colony, belongs to Mr. Dry, the Speaker of the House of Assembly.

The house of Quamby is some distance from the road, but seen on the rising ground has a fine aspect. Since the foregoing was written, Mr. Dry has retired from political life on account of ill health: a matter of deep regret to all. On his resigning the Speakership, the House unanimously voted to him an address for his ability and courtesy; and to prove their veneration for him, requested he would permit them to possess his likeness: he acceded to their request, and his portrait was painted by an eminent artist, Mr. Conway Hart. The picture now graces the lower House of Parliament. Mr. Dry, ever foremost to advance the best interests of his country, previous to his departure for England, allowed his country house at Quamby to be used as a church until one is built; Archdeacon Davies being about to form a parish in that locality. Mr. Dry has further given over to trustees a portion of land for a church and glebe, etc.; also the annual sum of £400 as an endow-

ment. The neighbouring gentlemen having added
their contributions, this will be the best supported
parish in Tasmania.

On the other side of the road is the large and
fine mansion, beautiful park, and well-farmed lands
of Hagley, the residence of Dr. Richardson, whose
kindness and hospitality to the stranger are no less
pleasing than the well-informed mind and courteous
manners of the bestower. The house is very prettily
situated in the midst of a large park, well laid
out with handsome trees; and the interior corres-
ponds with the ideas one forms on the first view
of the place, which certainly cannot fail to be aught
but favourable. The Quamby estate extends still on
the right for a considerable way towards Westbury.

The town of Westbury is surrounded with some
fine land and several pretty places; one in particular, a handsome cottage, with neat gardens
and grounds, the residence of a retired officer of
the army. A very fine valley extends from the
village to the domain of Mr. Field, who possesses,
with his brothers, some very considerable extent of
property: they are besides the largest stock holders
in the colony.

The road from Deloraine to Westbury leads
partly through the forest, where are some clearings
of the grants lately made to pensioners. Some
good farms are also passed before you come to the
property of Mr. T. Archer, whose house, is in the

cottage style, with deep verandahs. Its situation
is pre-eminently beautiful, on a rising ground, most
tastefully laid out with elegant gardens, of which
the worthy proprietor is justly proud. A rich vale
spreads away, bounded by the wild forest, which
has a most pleasing effect. The fine cultivated
lands in this sweet oasis are remarkable for their
richness and beauty : justly is it named the Retreat ; and if profuse hospitality, kindness, and
urbanity can make a perfect retreat, it is there
to be found. On the opposite side of the road is
the domain and very pretty place of Mr. Rooke, an
extensive landed proprietor, who has a fine brewery
adjoining his premises, and who rivals his kind
neighbour and brother-in-law in hospitality to the
stranger.

Two miles further on you come to the very
neat and rising village of Deloraine, the last town
ere we enter the wilds of the north-west. Its
houses are very well built of brick, and it boasts
of two or three good inns ; the largest one very
prettily situated on the other side of the river,
on a rising ground, commanding a fine view of a
large low plain, through which flows a rapid
stream. The bridge over the river Meander
through the town is of piles, of very novel construction. Beyond the valley are two or three
handsome places; one in particular, Mr. McArthur's,
of Calstock.

Leaving the village you strike into the Black Forest, and wander through the wild for several miles until you reach the Whiteford Hills, and the clearing and extensive farm of Mr. Charles Field.

A considerable change has taken place in this part of the country within the last year: a good open road has replaced the old bridle tract, which was often difficult to find; good bridges have been erected over the rivers, and planked causeways over the dangerous swamps; a township, called Elizabeth Town, has also been laid out, surveyed, and sold, close to the farm of Mr. Charles Field, above alluded to. Some houses are already finished, and more are in progress; and as Mr. Field is a gentleman of large property, and anxious to improve it, we have no doubt the place will continue to advance. The road is about to be continued to Tarleton, twenty-five miles further on, by this route.

Leaving Mr. Field's to the right and skirting his farm lands, you enter on a road, once begun, but never completed, by the Government; it extends some four or five miles till you reach the Derwent. This river is here fordable in summer time; but should a luckless traveller take this way after a heavy fall of rain, he will have to retrace his steps some three miles, and, taking a circuit over the stony hills, at length come on the native plains. After fording the river you find a level road along the vale for some miles; then passing a fine rich farm, you again ford the river, here more than two hundred yards across, and at lowest four feet deep, with a rapid current. After the second ford, you enter upon the Native Plain, a beautiful spot, here and there richly planted and gently undulating, full of flocks and herds. It is rented from Government by Mr. Field. After a charming canter across it for six miles, you again enter the forest, and proceed by a bridle road over hill and dale, till the Derwent once more greets your longing eye. Opposite the river is the comfortable hotel of Mr. Parsons, who is also the district road-surveyor; he is a most respectable and well-informed man, and at his house the stranger will find good cheer and moderate charges, rendered more agreeable by the courtesy and attention of his amiable helpmate.

One mile further on is the fast rising township of Tarleton, situated partly on the low ground, on an island formed by the Derwent, called Ballyhoo, and on the bank opposite. Near to it are the now lucrative and well-worked coal mines of Messrs. Nicholas and Williams. The indefatigable energy and indomitable skill of the latter, ably assisted by the enterprise and capital of the former, has at length been attended with success; and in the face of geologists' partial opinions, and repeated failures, the Welsh miner has conquered.

The mines are in full work, and the coal is justly esteemed as the most valuable in the colony : being especially adapted for steam or smelting purposes. Tarleton is seven miles from Torquay, at the mouth of the Mersey, and is navigable up to the island.

We must now conduct our reader back to Elizabeth Town, and resume the track towards Port Sorell. Crossing a small rivulet you pass over a low plain of two or three miles in length, and entering the forest, again follow on the track; which is here with difficulty regained : over hill and dale you wander, still surrounded with the seemingly interminable forest, and nought but a blazed track to direct you. Here and there a gurgling stream comes dashing down some hill, and a plank or two afford you the means of crossing. For nearly thirty miles the way is thus pursued, and still no resting-place appears. Suddenly the scene changes, and as the hopes of the weary stranger are sinking with the setting sun, the loud barking of a house-dog proclaims that a home is at hand, and the hospitable residence of Mr. Douglas receives you with warm welcome and friendly cheer.

Leaving with grateful remembrance this friendly family, you reach Port Sorell, four miles distant, a place (for a town it cannot be called) on the mouth of a river of that name.

But here we must pause awhile to particularise

the rivers of this part of the coast; a description
of which, together with much valuable information,
has been kindly placed at our disposal by Mr.
Sprent, the talented and energetic conductor of
the Trigonometrical Survey of the island.

"There are no less than eleven rivers between
the Tamar and Circular Head. Of these, the largest
is the Mersey, which discharges more water into the
sea than the North and South Esk at Launceston.
Vessels of 300 tons can easily enter the Mersey,
which is navigable for a considerable way; but its
capabilities are not yet fully known. The Forth is
but little inferior to the Mersey. The Leven will
admit vessels of from one to two hundred tons.
The Cam and Inglis have good entrances twelve
to fourteen feet over the bar. All these rivers
have sand bars; but as the tide in the Straits
rises about ten feet, they have considerable depth
of water when at the full. The bars, however,
are subject to frequent changes: they have the
shallowest water upon them in summer, when the
inner force of the river is the weakest; and the
deepest in winter, when the "freshes" are sufficiently powerful to force a passage. The prevailing
wind being from the north-west to south-west,
there is not much difficulty in getting in and
out; and there is very good anchorage within all
these rivers, and but very few rocks or shoals to
impede navigation. In another point of view

these rivers possess great advantages as water powers. The Mersey is a large and powerful stream of near sixty miles in length: it has a great fall, particularly some distance from the sea, having fine sites for mills, and giving power to any extent. The Mersey and the Forth have a fall of several thousand feet. The Leven has a fall of fifteen hundred feet in a distance of twenty miles. The Blyth, Emu, and Cam have a considerable fall, but have not been much explored. The Inglis and Black River are also fine rivers, and have considerable advantages. Altogether in this part of the coast there is sufficient water power for the machinery of a large manufacturing country.

"With regard to the land through which these rivers run, it is of a very varied character. At Port Sorell and Badger Head the rocks are of dirty quartz, and the land is very poor and barren. Continuing southerly over the Asbestos Hills, this range culminates at about ten miles southward of Badger Hill, where, from the heavy timber, the land assumes an appearance of superior quality. The soil of some parts near the Mersey is of a rich alluvial character. Coal is also to be found there, and a seam of dysodile, or combustible schist; which, by late experiments, has been proved to be more valuable than coal in making gas. Emery has also been discovered in this locality. Several saw and other mills are being erected on the banks of the Mersey, and hundreds of settlers are daily flocking to this part of the coast."

Near the Forth and Leven the land is heavily timbered, but, for the most part, is of very superior quality. The expense of clearing it, however, is enormous; being computed by some to cost nearly fifty pounds the acre. The want of labour is a great drawback to the coast being more settled, as also are the many impediments and delays attending the surveying of the allotments : before the survey it is impossible to find out even the *locale* of your property. It is to be hoped, however, now that new life and vigour are being given to the commerce of the coast and the value of the land is rapidly increasing, that Government will be induced to offer more remunerative contracts to surveyors; and by building one or more bridges over each of the rivers, with a road along the coast or the interior, confer a real benefit on the district, and one which is certain to repay the outlay in the end.

From the Leven to the Blyth the land is rich, but very heavily timbered, and most difficult of clearing. The headlands, of which there are a great many jutting into the sea, are bold, rocky, and precipitous. Between them are deep sandy bays, some of very considerable extent : the one between Port Sorell and the Mersey is five miles in one continuous break, with a mag-

nificent sandy beach the whole way. These headlands, however, very much impede the traveller,
who, when passing over a winding bay on the
trackless sand, with difficulty finds the blazed track;
which he must recover, in order to pass inland,
and avoid the rocky point, otherwise impassable.
About six miles from the coast runs a range of
rocky hills, known as the Dim Range, which rises
to a considerable elevation in some parts. The
lands are scrubby, with heath and barren soil.

Port Sorell, as before-mentioned, boasts of but
few houses; but there are several inlets and townships along the shore of the river, which is very
broad and fine at its entrance.

The road from the port, leading still through
the forest, is over a light sandy soil : occasionally
a glimpse of the sea is caught when you ascend
some hill. About three miles from Sorell you open
upon the cleared land and very fine property of Mr.
Thomas and his sons. Here, on the upper grounds,
which gradually rise from the sea in undulating
beauty, is one of the prettiest cottages in the
colony, belonging to Mr. S. Thomas. Lower down,
and partly hidden amidst a thick shrubbery with
very handsome gardens, is the very comfortable
home of the elder Mr. Thomas, North Downs.

A fine valley, of good pasture land, stretches
away beneath, till you reach the beach already
spoken of. Crossing this, you come to the banks

of the Mersey, where is a good and comfortable
inn. The want of a bridge is here much felt, the
traveller having to swim his horse after a boat;
which is not always a safe proceeding.

Torquay, on the mouth of the Mersey, is fast
rising into importance, and the township assuming
the appearance of a town; two or three streets
have been commenced, besides several detached
cottages, a court-house, police-barrack, etc. One
very good wharf has been built by Mr. Stephens.
A considerable number of good clearings are
amongst the suburban lots; for though the soil of
the town lots immediately adjoining is sandy
and bad, the suburban lots are of fine valuable
land, and the produce from their cultivation is
repaying a hundred fold. Along the river side,
extending to Tarleton, before spoken off, are several
good clearings, saw-mills, and some substantial
houses. On the opposite bank, facing Torquay,
another township is laid out, Fromby; most of
which has been sold. Near it is the valuable
property of Mr. B. Thomas and his brother, who
are both actively engaged in clearing and building
on their several estates.

Some three miles further bring you to the
River Don, a small winding stream, which is fordable near the comfortable farm-house and mills of
Mr. Drew. This property is now of considerable
extent in cleared land; which, being of the richest

quality, well cleared, and farmed with great care, fully repays the original outlay. The Don can be entered by small craft of from fifty to one hundred tons, at high water. There are two or three clearings above Mr. Drew's, on the river, and a road leads between it and the Mersey to Tarleton, by which you pass the coal mines of Mr. Dean, now in full operation. Mr. Dean having accepted a contract to furnish the Adelaide Smelting Company with 20,000 tons of coal annually, he has constructed a tramway two miles to the Mersey, about three miles above Torquay.

About two miles on this side of Tarleton are the extensive works and buildings of the Mersey Coal Company; but they have not proved so successful as those of Mr. Williams, or Mr. Dean. Private enterprise seems to succeed better in Tasmania than companies; an example of this is but too evident in the operations of the Mersey Coal Company's mines; where, although considerable sums have been expended, there has been little or no return—owing, we suppose, to the conflicting opinions of too many directors. It is now generally acknowledged that coal abounds along this tract for many miles. Every month this coast is receiving fresh hands; the dense forests are being felled, and farms rich and fertile are yearly appearing, making this district the Devonshire of Tasmania.

Five miles through the forest, with an occasional canter on the sands, bring you to the Forth, which is fordable at low water over the bar; too often, however, this is a ticklish matter, as particular care must be taken to hit the time exactly: an hour before or after the turn of the tide, the attempt is impracticable, and a difficult and dangerous swim rewards the hardy adventurer. Such was once my misfortune; but in giving the following account of this adventure from my notebook, I must premise that such accidents need not again occur, there being now so many settlers along the coast, and hospitable houses ready to receive a belated traveller.

"I left Torquay at 1 p.m. (March, 1854) alone, having failed to procure a guide. I had an order to the police of the district to furnish me with one; but neither order nor promise of gold could induce any one to accompany me. Having ridden three miles through the forest and scrub by a bridle track, I reached the Don, which I easily forded, and was then kindly entertained by Mr. Drew. After a ride of six miles, alternately through forest and along the beach, as evening was approaching I reached the Forth; on the other side of which I was informed there was an inn where I could put up at for the night.

"I had come since morning from Port Sorell, a distance of some five-and-twenty miles; a mere

nothing on a good road, but very fatiguing
when riding through a dense forest, and often
with difficulty regaining the track. I was also
told I could cross the Forth at low water,
which would be about sundown; and as I
neared the river, the weariness of my steed
increased my anxiety to reach the halting-place,
more particularly as the shades of evening were
fast closing upon me. At length I made the
river; but it seemed some five hundred yards
across, and as a heavy surge was breaking over
the bar, my courage did not feel equal to the
task. I, therefore, pursued my course along the
banks, lustily ' cooeing;' but no answer coming to
my repeated calls, I returned to the mouth of the
river, and, preferring a swim to a night in the
bush without anything for myself or horse, I at
once plunged into the boiling surf. My poor steed
got on well so long as the waves did not break
over her and the footing was safe. Spur, whip,
and voice I freely used, and I had passed about
half across, when, alas! a large and powerful wave
rolled over me with such violence as to unseat
me; and my poor mare, losing her footing at
the same time, was floundering alongside. The
tide was setting strongly outwards, swiftly im-
pelling us towards the sea. Hope nearly deserted
me. I clung in despair to the mane of my steed,
until a stroke from her fore foot drove me under

water : on rising to the surface I saw her, with her head directed to the land, freely swimming towards it. Fortunately, her long flowing tail struck me as she passed, when, with the instinct of self-preservation, I grasped it, and was thus pulled safely to the shore, feeling more dead than alive. A weary ramble to find the inn restored warmth to my benumbed limbs, and a roaring fire soon dried my drenched clothes and made me feel myself again."

A tolerable inn here awaits the weary wanderer, and means have been adopted by the Government for facilitating transit along the coast, and ensuring to the traveller safety and comfort in his toilsome way.

Five miles from the Forth is the Leven, and the very prettily situated township of Ulverstone. This river is dangerous as a ford, though it is often crossed at low water; but the traveller is chiefly indebted to the extreme kindness of one of the settlers here, Mr. Beecroft, who has a very neat house and cleared lands in the wilds above Ulverstone, and is ever ready to show hospitality, and furnish his boat and assistance, to take any one over the river.

The Leven, as before mentioned, will admit vessels of one to two hundred tons. The scenery up the river is exceedingly picturesque; its course is very tortuous, forming large bays, skirting the

base of the high blue mountain range and the
Leven forest. This contains the finest land in
the colony; most of it is allotted and sold by
the Government, and many settlers are established
in comfortable clearings; and although the expense
at first starting is very great, yet it fully repays
the venture. The timber also is very fine and
valuable, and a road has lately been surveyed
through the forest; it is also proposed that a steamer
shall call weekly at Ulverstone. Last year a
regatta club was formed; it was held on a broad
estuary above the *débouché* of the river, which is
well adapted both for sailing and rowing.

Entering the wild forest again, you have some
ten miles of a hardly discoverable tract, till you
reach the Blyth: this is a most dangerous ford, as
its bar is of shifting sand, and seldoms remains
long with the same channel near the sea; where
the fords are always most practicable.

From the Blyth to Emu Bay, near the coast,
the land is not so good; but in the interior, and
as the forest becomes of larger growth, it very
much improves, and is well watered with an infinite number of rivulets and creeks.

From the Emu to the Cam the land is more
open and settled, it being, for a considerable part,
the property of the Van Diemen's Land Company.
Like a very beautiful amphitheatre, surrounded
with high sheltering forest-clad hills, is Emu Bay.

The town of Birnie is laid out on the northern extremity, where a headland, as before described, runs out into the sea a considerable distance; it continues for more than a mile, forming a reef of rocks as the limit of the bay, and a good situation for a lighthouse. This place is described by Colonel Munday as a green-house with its windows open all the year round, so equable is its climate. 'Tis, in truth, a very pretty spot, and well calculated for a fashionable and healthy watering-place.

Within the bay to the eastward, and on the other side of the Emu, which enters the sea half-way in the bay, is the new-formed township of Wyvenhoe; which, we trust, will one day rival many a town as yet more esteemed than this very pretty, but little known, locality. It was in contemplation to form a military settlement here; the particulars of which are given in Appendix [F]; and although this project is now entirely abandoned, the author leaves the note.

At that time there were some three to four hundred soldiers of the 99th Regiment quartered in Tasmania, who were entitled to their discharge; and as war was not then in contemplation, the Home Government were disposed to grant considerable bonus to soldiers retiring and becoming settlers; but when war was proclaimed discharges were prohibited.

The author, who was the promoter of the scheme,

17

purchased the block of land from the township
of Wyvenhoe to the banks of the Blyth, containing about three thousand acres of land, with
the intention of settling there himself. The interior of the estate of Wyvenhoe, so called after
the township, has not yet been fully explored;
but judging from what has been traversed, one
half of it is considered to be of rich alluvial soil,
and having a frontage of four miles and a half
on the sea, and being bounded on the east by
the Blyth, and on the west by the Emu, with
several creeks and rivulets subdividing it, it is
but reasonable to suppose that one day it will
become most valuable. The clearing has commenced; a farm is established about a mile from
the township and seaside, several farm - houses
have been erected, and about one hundred acres
are under cultivation. At the back of the clearing
runs a deep creek, with sufficient water power
for mills. Besides the pre-eminent beauty of the
site, on a plateau three hundred feet above the
level of the sea, and protected from the east by
the higher range of Roundhill, it possesses every
requisite for a most desirable residence.

The difficulties at the onset were many, and
the cost of clearing the land, at the very lowest
calculation, was £14 per acre. Some of the township lots, which were purchased before the estate,
are cleared and prepared for building on. Most

of the remaining lots have been purchased by other parties; and as the Van Diemen's Land Company are about to extend their township of Birnie, in the bay, along the opposite bank of the Emu River facing Wyvenhoe, we feel sanguine as to its future importance. A crane, with a sliding car, extending forty feet over the sea, for the purpose of landing goods and passengers in inclement weather, has been erected on the western point of the bay; where a steamer calls twice every week to and from Launceston.

Birnie is a town belonging to the Company, who have built stores close to the sea, for the purpose of renting them to the farmers of the interior, to facilitate the transport of their produce. They had engaged to build a mole and wharf, but it is not as yet erected. There is a good hotel here, a church, etc. The inhabitants of the neighbourhood and township are estimated at three hundred. Near the township is Quashy Bungo, the cottage of Mr. Maitland Ware, in which the wandering tourist will find a home and much kindness and hospitality. Above, in a charming situation, commanding a very fine view of the bay and township, is the residence of Mr. William Gibson, the *custos rotulorum* of the district, and who rivals Mr. Ware in courtesy and urbanity.

The town allotments of Birnie, till very lately, were to be sold at reasonable prices, as well as

the suburban lots of fourteen to fifty acres; but,
from a mistaken policy, the Company will not now
dispose of their lands. A track, or as it is there
called, a road, leads from Emu Bay into the interior to the Hampshire Hills, some twenty to
thirty miles distant, a block of land of twenty
thousand acres, also belonging to the Company.

Ascending the hill alongside the Emu, you
pass through the cleared land of Mr. Gibson's
property, and, skirting the farm of Mr. Rouse,
you enter on a tract of land, now used as the
Company's grazing farm, but which was originally
cleared by settlers, since removed to Birnie.

The way from thence leads through a dense
forest; the ground gradually rising till you reach
the Hampshire Hills and St. Mary's Plains, where
there is a large extent of open country and good
pasture land. At the former place the Company
have laid out a large sum of money in farm-
houses, gardens, and other improvements.

The author is indebted to a young friend and
brother officer for the following notes upon the
trees and shrubs of Tasmania :—

"The greater part of the island is still covered
with timber; in some parts so thickly set with
scrub, as to be almost impenetrable. Various as
are the trees, they all possess one characteristic
feature, in shedding their bark and not their leaves;
thus presenting in all respects a great contrast to

those of the 'Old Country.' The indigenous trees are mostly exogenous, amongst which the *Eucalyptus* occupies the most prominent and by far the larger division. Its species are very numerous, of which I may mention *E. globulus*, or blue gum; *E. gigantea*, or stringy bark; *E. piperita*, or peppermint tree, etc. It is only the former of these, of which I shall give any detailed description, as the others resemble it in their general features, though variously prized according to the value of their timber.

"The *E. globulus*, or blue gum tree, so far as Tasmania is concerned, if not the whole world, may well be styled the Giant of the Forest, attaining as its maximum height 350 feet, maximum diameter 34 feet. Not a part of this tree is useless; its bark, which peels off in long ribands, is used for tanning, and some of it is exported; its timber, great quantities of which are exported, is valuable for ship-building; its leaves, by distillation, yield an esential oil similar to cajeput; and the tree yields a red, highly astringent gum, identical with that formerly supplied from Botany Bay as gum kino. The branches are irregular, leaves alternate, lanceolate, acute. The genus, though to be met with in all parts of the island, is principally confined to the south. It derives its name from its floral development, having a lid, which is eventually removed by the escape of numberless stamens situated around the edge of a conical indehiscent pericarp.

"Next in importance is the Huon Pine, *Dacrydium Franklinii*, which grows in great abundance at Macquarie Harbour, and more luxuriantly on the banks of streams than in dry places. Its timber is soft, and is principally used for cabinet work; also for boat-building.

"This part of the country is very thickly covered with heavy timber, densely set with scrub and brushwood; amongst which I may mention the Macquarie Harbour vine. As its name implies, this place is its principal habitat, where it is to be seen in great profusion, throwing its slender arms from tree to tree, and extending them sometimes as much as twenty-five feet in a year. Its leaves are alternate, and in their axillæ are the small, white, dichlamydeous flowers. The fruit is a pale yellow berry, pleasantly acid, called native grape.

"Along the more northerly part of the western coast is the celery-topped pine, *Phyllocladus aspleniifolia*, generally seen in groups in cool moist situations by the margin of rivers, and on the rich loamy flats so frequent on the top of the greenstone ridges to the westward. Its wood is of a white colour, of a medium density, and used for house fittings; also for masts and spars for ships, although rather heavy for the latter purpose.

Maximum height, 150 feet; maximum diameter, 2 feet.

"Along the eastern coast, occupying a belt of country a few miles in width, extending from Spring Bay northwards, nearly to Falmouth, is another of the coniferæ, used for the same purposes as the preceding, namely, the Oyster Bay Pine, *Callitris Australis*. It forms a handsome pyramidal tree, rising to one hundred and twenty feet in height when full grown, and attains a girth of four to seven feet at three feet up. The main trunk is usually short where clear of limbs, as it sends out long horizontal branches on all sides, almost from the ground, gradually shortening up to its fine-pointed top. A smaller species, *Callitris Gunnii*, which forms a particularly handsome shrub, and grows in picturesque groves along the banks of St. Paul's river, upon a portion of the South Esk, and on the Meredith River at Swanport.

"The most extensively diffused trees, next to the *Eucalypti* are the *Acaciæ*, which are met with in all parts of the island, flourishing most luxuriantly in the open pasture lands. Of these the first that will engage our attention is the *Acacia dealbata*, or Silver Wattle. This tree attains the height of sixty to one hundred and twenty feet, ramifies alternately a few feet from the ground, and measures in circumference, when full grown, from four to

nine feet, at four feet from the ground. Its leaves
are doubly pinnatified; inflorescence a spike, flowers
yellow, polygamous. Very closely resembling this
species, is the *A. mollissima*, or Black Wattle,
which, though of the same girth, does not attain
more than two-thirds its height. It flowers later
in the season; its timber is harder and darker,
as are the leaves; the legume of both species is
small, and the seeds are proportionably so.

" The handsomest of the genus is the *A. verti-
cilata*, or Prickly Mimosa, from thirty to fifty feet
in height: branches irregular, provided with spines,
much largest and longest, however, around the
axillæ; pinnæ deciduous, oblong, ovate, obtuse,
petiolated; a very small spine may be detected
at the apex. Inflorescence a raceme, bearing sometimes forty flowers, rather irregularly disposed
around the flower stalk; corolla white, calyx five-
toothed, obscurely bilabiate, the upper lip very
slightly two-toothed, covered by the reflexed vexil-
lum; the under one deeply three-toothed, colour
green, spotted with red; stamens of unequal length,
the legume containing about nine kidney-shaped
seeds, often remaining till after the reappearance
of the flowers.

" The largest of the *Acaciæ* is the *A. mela-
noxylen*, which sometimes attains a height of one
hundred and thirty feet, a diameter of four feet.
Its timber is dark brown, and used principally

for cabinet work. There are several other species
in Tasmania. The most inferior is the *A. sophora*,
or booby alla, which grows invariably straggling,
branchy, and procumbent; it flowers freely early
in the spring, and bears long pods, which used
to be eaten half roasted by the aborigines.

"We now turn our attention to some trees
of a very different nature, *Casuarina stricta* and
quadrivalvis, commonly called He and She oak, and
sometimes known by the name of beef-wood, from
the wood, which is very hard and takes a high
polish, exhibiting peculiar maculæ spots and veins
scattered throughout a finely striated tint: both
trees attain a height of thirty feet, diameter one
foot six inches. They are to be met with in all
parts of the island; and if in one locality more
than another, it is in lofty, rocky situations.

"There remains yet a great number of trees
of which we have not given any description;
many of them called by the primitive settlers by
the names of trees familiar in the ' Old Country,'
on account of some fancied resemblance they bore
to them. Such are the native cherry, or *Exocarpus*,
cuprusiformis, the fruit of which is a small drupe,
with the stone at one end; native laurel, *Anopterus
glandulosa*, a beautiful evergreen shrub, with white
campanulate flowers; the myrtle, *Fagus Cunning-
hamii;* the cedar, *Anthrotaxis selaginoides;* the
iron-wood, *Notelia lignetrina;* white-wood, *Pittos-*

porum bicolor; pink-wood, dog-wood, or *Bedfordia salicifolia,* etc. All are used more or less for cabinet work. The sassafracor, *Athnosperma moschata,* is used for flooring and house fittings; its bark is highly medicinal. This is, perhaps, in point of beauty, one of the first trees of Tasmania. It grows generally in moist shady situations, attaining sometimes one hundred and forty feet in height, and three feet in diameter. Rosewood, a species of acacia, and box-wood, *Bursaria spinosa,* are graceful flowering shrubs."

The grass-tree, and fern-tree, have been treated of elsewhere in this work.

Upon the low grounds along the coast the rocks are almost always of a primitive character, and the soil is sandy and barren. But immediately upon leaving the parts adjacent to the sea, the volcanic soil appears, the rocks being of a trap and basaltic kind. This forms into ridges, and runs down to the sea, forming headlands before mentioned. Near Emu Bay is found granite and syenite rock; also in some places, quartz and slate.

The way to Circular Head from Emu Bay leads in a devious track along the sea-coast and over precipitous densely forest-clad hills, having several dangerous fords to cross on your way.

But as Circular Head is our final resting-place, we must devote our concluding chapter to the last day's journey there — first conducting the reader to the inland mountains and country to the westward of Emu Bay, beyond the Hampshire Hills

CHAPTER XX.

There is a pleasure in the pathless woods—
　There is a rapture in the lonely shore—
There is society where none intrudes,
　By the deep sea, and music in its roar.
I love not man the less, but nature more,
　From these our interviews, in which I steal
From all I may be or have been before,
　To mingle with the universe, and feel
　What I can ne'er express, yet cannot all conceal.
. . . .
Farewell!—a word that must and hath been—
　A sound which makes us linger;—yet—farewell!
Ye who have traced the pilgrim to the scene
　Which is his last, if in your memories dwell
A thought which once was his, if on ye swell
　A single recollection; not in vain
He wore his sandal shoon, and scallop-shell.
　Farewell! with him alone may rest the pain,
If such there were—with you, the moral of his strain!

　　　　　　　　　　　　　　　BYRON.

To the admirer of nature and the lover of the
sublime and picturesque, given to wandering in
the primeval glades of the trackless forest, no
place in the island affords a finer field than
Emu Bay; and as the inhabitants of this retired
spot are ever ready to supply the stranger with

every information and cordial hospitality, one's taste in that way can be gratified to the full extent. The naturalist, geologist, and botanist could here spend many a day in researches among the vast woods and towering hills, which teem with the objects of their pursuit and study.

Ere we proceed to our destination we must conduct the reader back to the Don, in order to describe the midland road that leads from Deloraine to this point, and also to the Hampshire Hills. For the most part the former track is over fine level plains, of a light sandy soil, which, with the well-trained and all-enduring horses of the bush, you are able to canter over all day. During the summer weather this route is far preferable, and there is more than one comfortable halting-place on the way. But in winter, or after heavy rain, it is almost impracticable; and the traveller has often to wait for days ere the rivers are fordable: which, at other times, there is no difficulty in crossing. By this route you cross the Mersey twice, and at the upper ford, a track, called the Company's Road, leads in a westerly direction along the head of Emu Plains—a large wild tract of open country, of rather scanty and poor herbage —till you enter on the Middlesex Plains, of far superior quality, watered by the Forth and its tributaries. These are the property of the Van Diemen's Land Company, but now rented by the

Messrs. Field, to whom previous reference has been made.

Crossing this plain, you again enter the thick forest, and pass over several high hills. Seen in the distance, to the north, is the lofty peak of Mount Tor; also Bluff Mountain. To the left, crossing Hounslow Heath, you see a very high headland, and ford the Vale River, which runs into the Mackintosh; supposed to be a large and navigable river, running into the sea above Macquarie Harbour.

Crossing several small streams, and through some deep ravines thickly covered with scrub and the myrtle tree, you turn towards the north for some miles; then taking a westerly direction through more open country, you at last reach the Company's station on the Surrey Hills, now tenanted by the herdsmen of the Messrs. Field, who have innumerable herds of cattle and flocks of sheep grazing on the fine pasture lands they rent from the Company. Mr. Sprent, than whom none have seen more, or have a clearer knowledge of Tasmania, states, in his notes:—"From Middlesex Plains towards Cradle Mount the country rapidly rises, forming Hounslow Heath, an extensive barren plain, covered with very coarse grass, the rocks principally quartz. Beyond this, you enter Cradle Valley through a sand heath scrub, to the foot of the mountain, which may be ranked amongst the highest in the colony. The Barn Bluff, not far distant, is also of great height. There all is barrenness in every direction; but still it is a country highly interesting to the geologist, though little so to the settler.

"Returning by Hounslow Heath to Middlesex Plains, you meet land of a far different character, generally of a volcanic description. Ten thousand acres belong to the Van Diemen's Land Company; but there is also in this locality a considerable quantity of very valuable crown land. This land is very elevated, and forms part of the high table land running southerly to Cradle Mount. To the southward of the Company's boundary the country is poor and heathy, full of large and abrupt ravines. To the south-east is a very high range of hills, terminating in Black Bluff. This is the highest point towards the north, being four thousand feet above the level of the sea."

From the Black Bluff you have a most extensive view over an immense tract of country, of very different features and character. Here you see extending before you, spread out in grand panoramic display, miles upon miles of thickly forest-covered hills. The rich grass-covered plains of Middlesex lie at your feet to all appearance, though many a weary league from you. Beyond the towering range of lofty mountains on the other side, are barren heaths and desert wilds; and over

the country, far and near, you can trace the several
courses of many rivers, the deep ravines and protruding rocks, and an immense forest still bounding
your vision, rising over the Eldon group, far away
to the west.

Leaving the Black Range, and following the
Company's track, which is not always easily to
be found, you pass over the Vale of Belvoir,
a very beautiful valley, with the Lake Lea at
the upper end. A stream from this lake forms
one of the tributaries of the. Forth, whilst at the
other side another stream issues, which, taking a
south-westerly course, probably runs into the Pie-
man, or King's River.

The Surrey Hills contain one hundred and fifty
thousand acres, part of the grant to the Van Diemen's Land Company. It is a very singular tract
of country; in parts fine good land of a volcanic
character is found, with rich alluvial soil, covered
with grass, and well sheltered for grazing purposes,
intersected by numberless rivulets and deep gullies.
Amidst these hills, the Hellyer and Arthur take
their rise ; also, on the western side, the Huskisson,
running into the Mackintosh. Beyond this range
is a wild and undiscovered country of very varied
character, if one may judge from the extensive
landscape seen from the top of Mount Bishcroft,
to the west of the Surrey Hills.

Thence the track leads through the centre of

the Company's land, over the Hellyer, till you reach the Cam, here a small stream, and enter on the Hampshire Hills, before spoken of; conspicuous from which is seen the lofty height of St. Valentine's Peak, to the west.

The timber around this part of the country is chiefly myrtle, the soil is good, and the rocks are volcanic; though, in some places, they appear of the primitive character. Small gravel quartz has also been found in this locality.

We now proceed on our way to Circular Head, chiefly along the sea by Parish's Harbour, a small safe cove for boats, till you ford the Cam, at low water, four miles distant from the township of Birnie and Emu Bay. The Cam is a small river; but at high water can be entered by vessels of from forty to fifty tons, with free navigation and good anchorage for several miles. The land near the sea is very inferior, but a little inland its nature changes considerably, and the volcanic strata commences. There is some very high land along this coast, rocky and precipitous, covered with thick forest; and as you approach the Inglis, passing over the extreme end of a long chain of hills which run inland, you meet heathy land, poor and ferny. The Inglis, also fordable at low water, is not so large as the Cam. You again touch on some good land, and several clearings beyond the river.

The promontory of Table Bay runs out to sea-ward; it is high level land, with a bold bluff cliff, but affording good shelter from westerly gales. Five hundred acres of this level promontory, now densely covered with forest, is reserved for a township. Within the last year several settlers have come to this very beautiful spot, and the land proving of the best description, more will soon follow. The town-ship of Wynyard, on the Inglis, has lately been surveyed and sold, and the Messrs. Alexanders, large and enterprising landholders up the Inglis, cut up a part of their property, and sold it to great advantage.

On the side of the high promontory of Table Bluff is the clearing of the Rev. F. Hales, elevated some three hundred feet above the bay, which it overlooks; it is fine rich land, and commands a very beautiful prospect of the sea and coast for many miles. In the interior, towards the Inglis, is the clearing of Messrs. Pennefeather, five brothers of a highly respectable family in Ireland, who immi-grated here twelve months since, and have now conquered the first and most arduous difficulties of bush life with a most praiseworthy and ener-getic spirit. There are several other gentlemen of good families in this neighbourhood, well edu-cated men from the Old Country, forming an aristocratic and literary oasis in the wilds.

From the Inglis to the Sister's Creek, or rivulet,

for about six or seven miles along the coast, the land is good; but after this it becomes of a wretched sandy soil, bearing some muscular grass trees, and stunted honeysuckles of a very peculiar appearance.

From the Sisters to the Detention River the country is almost a desert; and standing on the high hill near Rocky Cape, you can see nought but barren hills running inland for many miles.

From Detention River the land is poor and unpromising; but the hills further to the westward being covered with good timber, there may be better land in the interior, though it has never been explored. These hills are of slight elevation, and not of difficult access. Between the Black River and Deep Creek, the Company have a block of land of twenty thousand acres in extent, a promontory connected to the mainland by a narrow belt—our destination, Circular Head.

But ere crossing the isthmus which conducts us there and to the town of Stanley, we must visit Woolnorth, another large tract of the Company's land, and Cape Grim, the north-west point of Tasmania. From the Deep Creek to the Duck River the land is poor and heathy, and from the high ground it appears to run inland of the same barren and useless description. The Duck River empties itself into a large bay, with a good entrance, well-sheltered and land-locked. This bar-

ren and heathy country continues to the Montague
River, which forms the boundary of the Woolnorth Station, of one hundred thousand acres in
extent. A great part of it, however, is low and
swampy. Standing upon Mount Cameron, the
highest land on the western coast of Woolnorth,
an extensive tract of heathy plains and barren
country stretches out before you, looking easterly;
but to the west and north the soil assumes a
more volcanic character. There are several thousand acres of good grass land extending to Cape
Grim, near to which is Trefoil Island, of rich
and valuable quality.

The western coast is poor and barren in the
extreme, and possesses one monotonous character
of sandy heaths and low swampy lands, extending down to the Arthur, and along the coast to
the Picman River. These rivers are deep and
navigable, but dangerous of entrance, from the
tremendous rolling surf ever prevailing along the
western coast.

Returning from Woolnorth, where there are
some three or four families only, we cross the
isthmus into Circular Head, and by a good road
along the East Bay enter the pretty and rising
town of Stanley. Here a good and comfortable
hotel rewards the weary traveller, after all the
adventures and hardships of his wanderings in the
bush. Mr. Whitebread's establishment is a fine

large stone-built house, with many good and well-furnished rooms, and every attention is paid to his guests. There are three other inns in the town. There is a neat stone-built church, and about eight hundred inhabitants in the village and its vicinity.

Stanley is very prettily situated in the valley, facing a safe and commodious bay, in the centre of which there is a very curious abutment, from which the region takes its name. At first it appears a large rock; but on nearer approach you find it a regular promontory, with a high bluff border facing the sea, and almost perpendicular. It is about four hundred feet above the level of the sea, and on the top are several acres of good land covered with timber. A narrow neck of land from the inner side leads up to the good land above, and from it you have a charming view of the town, and the very pretty residence of the Company's chief agent, Mr. James Gibson.

High Field, as it is called, is about a mile from Stanley, on the high lands behind the township. The house is a good and substantial one, and the stranger is sure to find there a hearty welcome. The grounds are very tastefully laid out, and a magnificent park, quite in the English style, spreads far out before you; it is kept in good order, and well stocked with herds of deer. In the park may also be seen the emu, a bird once common on this coast, but now rarely to be met with. There are about two thousand acres of cultivated land in the block. Several small vessels trade between Stanley and Launceston, and a steamer is now being started to trade here, and at all the townships along the northern coast, westward of George Town.

And now, kind and courteous reader, my task is over, and I must say "farewell." If I have awakened some degree of interest, and gained a friend for Tasmania, the object of this book is accomplished. Though in many respects it may be found defective, yet I trust much to the indulgent forbearance of that public for whose benefit it has been compiled. To those friends whose assistance I now gratefully acknowledge, I am indebted for some of the most valuable information. In a passing sketch, such as I have undertaken, it was not possible to give full details of very many matters connected with the colony; neither was I able, during my short sojourn, to visit many places of interest worthy of note. If, however, the present work is received kindly, it will encourage me again to come before the public; and others also will probably enter the field, and follow in the track.

Each year, changes of considerable magnitude will, beyond all doubt, take place in Tasmania;

and what we see to-day will assume a different appearance, and require a different description, to-morrow. The forest-clad township of this year may become a well-inhabited town the next; steamers will glide on waters not now even known; and roads—perchance railroads—will, ere many years, traverse the now impervious bush or the mountain steep.

APPENDIX.

[A.]

CHRIST'S COLLEGE—ANNUAL COMMEMORATION.

THE Seventh Annual Commemoration of the foundation of this Institution was held on Thursday, the 15th ultimo. The day was very fine, and the intense heat of the sun was tempered throughout the day by a cool and steady breeze. In addition to the ordinary circumstances of this ceremony, there was on this occasion one of peculiar interest—we mean the resignation of the late Warden and the induction of his successor. This may have been partly a reason why so large a company assembled at the College, a company more numerous than has been witnessed since its opening. About half-past ten the Bishop, who was the earliest arrival, was seen approaching, and his carriage was speedily followed by a long train of vehicles and horsemen— nor was it until long past eleven that the last detachment of visitors had arrived. Amongst the numerous assemblage which enlivened and embellished the College precincts, we discovered many who, in various capacities, had been themselves inhabitants within its walls; and it was highly gratifying to observe the obvious interest which they took in all matters connected with their former *alma mater*. Shortly after eleven, the proceedings of the day commenced with the usual morning service in the chapel, at which the late Warden said prayers, and the lessons were read by the Divinity Fellow in waiting for the week (Mr. Adams). Those who are admirers of sacred music had a great treat in the performance on the organ by the Rev. W. A. Brooke, whose accompaniments to the chanting of the service were of a very superior description, adding very much to the impressiveness of that solemn and beautiful ritual. It was immediately after the conclusion of this service that the distinguished ceremony of the day occurred, to which we have before alluded: this consisted in the late Warden, Rev. S. B. Windsor, M.A., Oxon, resigning his office into the hands of the Bishop as Visitor, and afterwards presenting to his Lordship the Rev. P. V. M. Filleul, M.A., Oxon, to be his successor in the Wardenship. Mr. Filleul being duly inducted, next presented to the Bishop the Rev. W. A. Brooke, B.A., Cambridge, for appointment to the office of Sub-Warden, with whose induction, after the usual forms, the chapel service for the day terminated.

The party then adjourned to the upper school-room, in which the secular part of the proceedings was to be transacted. Here, as soon as the Bishop and assemblage had taken their places, the late Warden proceeded to deliver his usual Latin speech, which, as being on this occasion his farewell oration before the College, he pronounced in a voice often broken by emotion.

Archdeacon Davies then rose, and furnished, as is his wont, an account of the receipts and expenditure of the last year. He first produced the household accounts, which reflected great credit on the Rev. C. Garnsey, the new bursar. He explained that during the first six months the expenditure exceeded the income more than £300, in consequence of the great rise in the cost of all articles of domestic supply; an appeal was then made to the parents and guardians of the pupils for an increased payment of 50 per cent. on the former charges, which was universally and readily responded to. He next produced Mr. Wedge's account of permanent improvements on the College estate, which must be effected to the amount of £200 annually. Four hundred and sixty-four rods of fencing had been erected during the past year, and there are now ready for carting from the forest seven thousand posts and rails, which, when erected, may be valued at £300. It is proposed during the next year, to erect a brick cottage on one of the farms, the tenant paying a certain portion of the expenses; and the draining of the large lagoon will, it is hoped, be completed, as the landed proprietors, who are equally interested with the College authorities, have consented to share the expense. This will give an addition of two hundred acres of valuable land to the College estate. The next paper he laid on the table was the probable value of the College estates at the present time:—

	£	s.	
3,400 acres at Bishopsbourne, at £10 per acre......................	34,000	0	0
400 acres at New Town, at £5 per acre	2,000	0	0
120 acres at New Norfolk, at £5 per acre	1,200	0	0
50 acres at the Huon, at £5 per acre	250	0	0
	37,450	0	0
From which is to be deducted the sum of	6,000	0	0*
Leaving a balance in favour of the College of	£31,450	0	0

* Money lent from the Missionary Fund.

He then handed to the Visitor the Balance Sheet for the past year :—

RECEIPTS.

	£	s.	d.
Balance from 1852	21	5	0
Rents—Bishopsbourne	1,145	0	0
Acanthe Farm	40	0	0
Huon Farm	27	10	0
From Pupils	1,675	10	9
Sale of Produce	50	0	0
Proceeds on draft for £1,000 S. P. C. K.	970	0	0
Society for the Propagation of the Gospel	200	0	0
Donations—Bishop of Tasmania £100 0			
Sir W. Denison 40 0			
Rev. W. Hesketh 5 0			
Dr. Whitfield 15 0			
	160	0	0
	£4,289	5	9

EXPENDITURE.

	£	s.	d.
Household Expenses	2,612	0	11
Improvement of College property	200	0	0
Loan to Hutchins School	300	0	0
Salaries—Warden £311 10			
Gell Fellow 100 0			
Three Divinity Fellows 90 0			
Master of Junior School 52 10			
	554	0	0
Interest to Missionary Fund	180	0	0
	3,846	0	11
To balance	443	4	10
	£4,289	5	9

The Archdeacon again rose and said, that he took this opportunity to explain that the lease of the land on which the present buildings were erected would expire in two or three years; that great complaints had been made that the College was not in some more central situation. The Trustees accordingly applied to His Excellency Sir W. Denison, for a site, similar to that granted to the Hutchins and High Schools, and suggested Tunbridge as the most central situation. The Lieutenant-Governor immediately acceded to the request, and expressed his hope to see a building erected worthy of the Institution and of the Colony. His Excellency also added that he thought "Tunbridge, as suggested by the Trustees, the best situation, from its being central, dry, and healthy; from there being capital building stone in the vicinity, and because arrangements might easily be made to convey an ample supply of water to the College." It was to this his friend, the ex-warden, referred, in speaking of new buildings on a fresh site. Ever since Sir W. Denison arrived in the colony he has been the true friend of education, and in an especial manner of this Institution. He alluded not to the willingness with which he responded to the application of the Trustees, nor his liberality in giving £40 a-year for the last six years—but the confidence he has exhibited by placing his two sons here to be educated, a step which he most certainly never would have taken, if he believed the nature of the education afforded here to be of that semi-Romish character which it has been represented to have been by persons who have never taken the trouble to inquire for themselves. He then, appealing to the ex-warden, after prefacing it with a few words of warm and friendly hope and gratulation, presented him with an Address from the Fellows and Students of the College. A similar address was afterwards presented from the parents and guardians of the pupils, and others interested in the welfare and prosperity of Christ's College.

The Lord Bishop then, as Visitor, said that it was with unmixed pleasure that he had now the satisfactory task of distributing prizes to those students who had distinguished themselves for proficiency during the preceding half-year and at the examination just concluded.

The following young gentlemen then presented themselves:—

First Prize .... Pedder.
Mathematical Prize............................... Davies.
First Prize (2nd remove) .... Arthur.
Second Prize (2nd remove) .... Mason.
First Prize (2nd division) .... Dumaresq.
Second Prize (2nd division) .... Bedford.

JUNIOR SCHOOL.

First Prize .... Gates.
Second Prize .... Denison.
French Prize .... Pitcairn.

An extra prize was given by the Warden to Mr. C. Arthur, as being the best behaved youth in the establishment, inasmuch as he was the example in his conduct and demeanour to all the others, and he did not doubt it would be their own estimate of Charles Arthur's character and conduct.

Here the proceedings closed, and the numerous party adjourned to the gardens, till a substantial and very elegant lunch invited them to the dining-hall. Everybody was pleased; and thus ended a day at the College of as much interest as has ever been created since its foundation, and by five o'clock the numerous and brilliant assemblage, which had given so animated an appearance to the College during the earlier part of the day, were all dispersed.

[B.]

A LIST OF THE PUBLIC SCHOOLS IN TASMANIA

In connexion with the Church of England receiving Aid from the Government, 31st December, 1853.

		Boys.	Girls.	Total.
1	*Brighton*, Broad Marsh, James Reddish	18	13	31
2	„ Pontville, B. Swift..................................	27	16	43
3	*Campbell Town*, Campbell Town, S. Stanton	24	11	35
4	„ Ross, James Stephens	21	10	31
5	*George Town*, George Town, Mrs. J. Fraser.................	25	18	43
6	*Hamilton*, Hamilton, Mrs. E. Roberts	9	23	32
7	*Hobarton*, Bethesda, Mrs. A. Pearsall......................	43	67	110
8	„ Campbell-street, Miss Everest	—	60	60
9	„ St. David's, T. Richards	80	63	143
10	„ St. George's, Benj. Bray...............................	77	40	117
11	„ St. James's, John Hobden	49	3	52
12	„ Goulburn Street, W. Milner.........................	74	40	114
13	„ Trinity Hill, T. E. Wilson............................	42	—	42
14	„ „ Girls, Mrs. M. Manser	—	53	53
15	„ „ Infants, Miss Dowdle..............	27	26	53
16	„ New Town, T. Cresswell	31	17	48
17	„ „ Girls, Mrs. E. Stephens	10	23	33
18	„ O'Brien's Bridge, S. Hughes........................	34	25	59
19	„ Sandy Bay, C. F. Cresswell	17	14	31
20	*Horton*, Circular Head, Mrs. Jordan	—	18	18
21	„ Forest, Charles Johnston	16	9	25
22	*Huon*, Flight's Bay, Alexander Maclean	11	1	12
23	*Launceston*, Brisbane Street, Mrs. Stainforth	20	30	50
24	„ Elizabeth Street, F. Wathen......................	67	19	86
25	„ Cameron Street, J. Richards......................	74	63	137
26	„ Frankland Street, D. Burston	33	15	48
27	*Longford*, Longford, R. S. Bird	44	—	44
28	„ „ Girls, Miss E. Thompson..............	—	20	20
29	„ Perth, Edward Anstice	25	18	43
30	*Morven*, Evandale, Mrs. Sherlock	2	5	7
31	*New Norfolk*, New Norfolk, W. Matthews	15	12	27
32	„ Dry Creek, William Perry	7	5	12
3	„ Bridgewater, W. Wilkinson	9	24	33
34	*Richmond*, Richmond, John Frost	12	—	12
35	„ Jerusalem, Miss J. Tolmey	7	5	12
36	*Sorell*, Sorell, George Peacock	20	18	38
37	„ Forcett, Frederick Holmes	16	7	23
38	„ Bream Creek, John Goodman.........................	15	8	23
39	*Swanport*, Swansea, Mrs. H. Collis	13	11	24
40	*Westbury*, Westbury, John Nottage	22	12	34
41	„ „ Girls, Mrs. S. Clements..............	3	26	29
		1039	848	1887

STATISTICS OF THE DIOCESE OF TASMANIA.

NAME OF PLACE AND CLERGYMAN.	Church room.	No. of attend-ants.	No. of Commun-icants.	Average attend-ance.	No. of Sunday Services.	Offertory and sponsor Colln.	Amount received from Com. Trust.	Amount rec. from other sources.	Pew Rents.	Bap-tisms.	Mar-riages.	Burials.
St. David's, Hobarton {Archdeacon Davies, B.A.; Rev. Robert Wilson [1]}	900	1400*	250	75	3	£723	£325†	£341	£261½	236	101	211
ARCHDEACONRY OF HOBARTON.												
St. John's, Rev. F. H. Cox, M.A.	150	170	71	35	3	100	...	416	...	61	6	...
St. George's, Rev. H. P. Fry, D.D.	720	520	90	15	3	170	230	302	67	101	305	111
Trinity, Rev. W. Brickwood [2]	450	400	60	41	4	91	175	156	65	78	44	204
Cascades, Rev. D. Galer	1000	675	...	26	4	...	...	502	...	35	...	51
Penitentiary, Rev. J. G. Medland	1000	500	90	50	2	28	...	400	...	20	...	...
New Town, Rev. T. J. Ewing	600	320	56	30	3	112	275	163	71	23	22	28
Pontville, Rev. J. Burrowes, B.A.	300	100	30	10	3	17	230	40	25	17	16	13
Huon River, Rev. R. Crooke, B.A.	75	115	...	...	...	...	...	200	...	37	17	8
Oatlands, Rev. J. L. Ison, B.A.	300	115	...	16	3	42	200	49	12	10	23	27
Green Ponds, Rev. W. Trollope, M.A.	230	100	18	12	2	31	230	10	12	21	6	16
Clarence Plains, Rev. W. W. Murray, M.A. [3]	370	80	25	13	2	8	230	16	14	19	16	17
Richmond, Rev. J. T. Gellibrand, M.A. [4]	450	140	30	12	2	28	230	25	19	21	10	25
Swansea, Rev. J. Mayson	160	40	22	5	...	1	230	73	13	21	9	11
Macquarie Plains, Rev. W. M. Hesketh, M.A.	340	150	35	26	2	19	...	260	...	20	18	7
Impression Bay, Rev. S. B. Fookes [5]	400	300	37	11	...	2	...	279	...	11	3	20
Port Arthur, Rev. J. Gurney	600	600	...	10	2	2	...	276	...	6	...	9
Kingston, Rev. E. Freeman, M.A.	40	88	26	7	2	2	230	23	...	14	22	12
Hamilton, Rev. G. Wright	390	70	15	11	3	18	230	40	8	20	12	12
Sorell, Rev. J. Norman	800	200	22	10	2	2	254	94	27	43	26	16
New Norfolk, Rev. J. B. Seaman, B.A.	350	110	30	16	3	28	200	66	14	31	17	63
O'Brien's Bridge, Rev. W. R. Bennett	120	90	13	9	2	26	...	145	8	19	8	19
Prosser's Plains, Rev. C. Dobson	124	60	10	6	2	13	230	4	...	17	4	6
Ross, Rev. G. Eastman	...	90	...	...	...	...	...	400	...	...	...	...
Broadmarsh, Rev. B. Ball	160	20	7	5	2	6	230	...	5	9	7	3
Campbell Town, Rev. W. Bedford, B.A.	700	110	47	34	2	76	310	28	67	42	29	32

Parish / Clergyman												
St. John's, Launceston, Rev. J. M. Norman	600	600		52	2	286	370	40	171	84	37	55
Trinity, Rev. J. Yarker, S.C.L.[6]	500	600	110	40	2	191	230	165	140	103	42	52
Penitentiary, Rev. G. Giles, LL.D.	260	150	40		3	150	260			8		63
Longford, {Rev. W. Tancred, M.A.	540	247		28	2	66	200	229	41	53	20	56
{Rev. D. Boyd[7]								50				
Windermere, Rev. P. Lockton, B.A.	150	50	12	5	3	6		8		12	2	5
Cullenswood, Rev. S. Parsons, M.A.	150	156	35	26	3	26	230	239	17	13	13	4
Carrick, Rev. A. Barkway	210	100	10	6	2	19		100	16	13	3	11
Bishopsbourne, §{Rev. P. V. Filleul, M.A.	150	50	8	5	2	20		300		9	4	2
{Rev. W. A. Brooke, B.A.[8]								200				
{Rev. C. F. Garnsey								100				
Lake River, Rev. T. B. Garlick	300	86	30	17	2	3	200	275	7	6	4	2
Avoca, Rev. W. Richardson, B.A.	150	65	33	15	3	10		10	7	7	9	6
Newnham, Rev. G. C. B. Smith	520	65	15	12	2	14	200	150	5	24	6	16
Evandale, Rev. A. C. Thomson[9]	160	150	22	6	3	5	200	12	30	8	3	5
George Town, Rev. J. Pereday, M.A.	230	45	13	7	2	6	300	20	10	14	3	9
White Hills, Rev. F. Brownrigg, B.A.	400	85	11	25	3	57	200		21	21	19	10
Westbury, Rev. M. Williams	550	135	35	33	3	34	230	50	27	16	7	13
Perth, Rev. A. Stackhouse, M.A.	80	230	8	5	3	2			38	3		1
Emu Bay, Rev. C. P. Pocock	370	35		15	3		230	230	20	21	2	6
Circular Head, Rev. T. N. Grigg, B.A.[10]		210										
Totals	**15119**	**10712**	**1326**	**780**	**96**	**2437**	**6889**	**7189**	**1211**	**1305**	**896**	**1226**

CHANGES IN THE ABOVE STATISTICS UP TO FEBRUARY, 1864.

[1] The Rev. Mr. Wilson has been removed to Clarence Plains, where a very pretty church has lately been consecrated, and the Rev. H. R. Dry appointed in his place. The Rev. Mr. Irwin, from Sydney, is at present doing duty for the Archdeacon, now occupied in the most praiseworthy undertaking in forming the parish of Quamby, under the patronage of Mr. Dry.

[2] The Rev. Mr. Brickwood has taken charge of Campbell Town during the absence in England of the Rev. W. Bedford, and the Rev. A. Davenport, from Norfolk Island, appointed to the incumbency of Trinity.

[3] Replaced by the Rev. Mr. Wilson (see note 1).

[4] Removed to the newly-formed parish of All Saints, in Hobarton.

[5] This chaplaincy is discontinued, and the Rev. Mr. Fookes is now the incumbent of Circular Head.

[6] Resigned, and the Rev. Francis Hales, by the unanimous wish of the congregation, appointed in his stead.

[7] Removed to Launceston.

[8] Resigned, and appointed Assistant Master of Hutchins' School.

[9] On leave, and the parish in charge of the Rev. J. Blahton.

[10] Removed.

* This column is calculated by the numbers stated to attend at the Sunday Services; thus, at St. John's, the attendance at Morning Service is 600, in the afternoon at St. John's 500. At Cullenswood—the returns show an attendance of 67 at Cullenswood, 31 at Fingal, and 57 at Falmouth: the total amount 155 is therefore inserted.

† In addition to the sums mentioned in this column as received from the Colonial Treasury, the former allowance and the temporary increase are to be added. The former is £30 per annum for Clergymen residing in the country, and £100 in the towns of Hobarton, Launceston, and George Town. The increase is fifty per cent. on existing salaries.

‡ In all money columns the fractions of a pound are omitted.

§ These Clergymen are attached to Christ's College, and receive their incomes from the endowment of that Institution.

[D.]

TASMANIAN CONTRIBUTIONS
TO THE
EXHIBITION OF INDUSTRY OF ALL NATIONS,
HELD IN LONDON, 1851.

———

MINERAL—*Ores, etc.*

Plumbago (black lead), contributed by Mr. Abraham Walker, Creekton, Norfolk Plains. Found in a shaft sunk in pursuit of indications of galena and copper ore in a seam or vein about five inches thick, traversing schistose clay, overlying old quartz and crystalline limestone in which the lodes of lead and copper are expected to be won.

Limestone with galena, by Mr. J. Milligan, from Norfolk Plains, at the foot of the western range of mountains near Quamby's Bluff, Van Diemen's Land.

Brown clay iron ore, by Mr. J. Milligan, from near Fingal, Tullochgorum estate, South Esk Valley.

Clay iron-stone, by Mr. J. Milligan, from near Fingal, in beds alternating with bituminous coal, near the Douglas River, on the East Coast, Van Diemen's Land.

Reddle, red ochre, or red chalk, by Mr. J. Milligan, from near Launceston: occurs in masses of uniform and determinate shape, imbedded in alluvium of loam and earth.

Ore of iron, *magnetic*, by Mr. J. Milligan, from Hampshire Hills, nearly pure iron, semi-crystalline, highly magnetic with polarity: occurs in masses in the line of contact between granite and basalt.

Ore of iron, by Mr. J. Milligan. Found in nodules with quartz in granite soil, near the Housetop Mountain, northwest of Van Diemen's Land: formerly used by the aborigines as a paint, being first peroxidised by roasting, and then reduced to a fine powder by grinding between two stones.

Ore of manganese, by Mr. J. Milligan, from the vicinity of the Frenchman's Cap Mountain.

Iron ore, by Mr. J. Milligan, from Long Bay: occurs in a bed about seven or eight feet thick, over sandstone, at the foot of Greenstone Hills.

Galena and iron ore (3 specimens), by Mr. R. De Little, from Tamar River, found near York Town, over limestone.

Galena, by Mr. J. Milligan, from Macquarie Harbour: occurs in a vein in mountain limestone in the channel of the Franklin River.

Red ochre, yellow ochre, and marle, (specimens of), by His Excellency Sir W. Denison, from Norfolk Island, resulting from the decomposition of a jasperous ore of iron.

Chemical Products, and Substances used in Manufactures.

Coal (2 bushels), by the Douglas River Coal Company; sample of the strong bituminous coal on the east coast of Van Diemen's Land, traceable over a large area of country, in seams varying in thickness, from a few inches to ten feet and upwards.

Salt (box of) two sorts: coarse for pickling, and table or basket salt, from Mr. R. Strachan, Bonnington, Van Diemen's Land: a fine-looking sample from which the magnesian salts are said to be thoroughly separated.

Box of soap, by Mr. Richard Cleburne, Murray Street, Hobarton; considered much superior in quality to the best English soap imported into Van Diemen's Land.

Guano, by Mr. J. Milligan, from Babel Island; brought by coasting craft from Babel Island, Bass's Straits.

Limestone, by Mr. J. Milligan, from Fingal and Break-o'-Day, valley of the South Esk River, Van Diemen's Land.

Limestone, by Sir William Denison, from Maria Island: occurs as an efflorescence in caverns in the clayey rocks.

Alum, by Mr. J. E. Bicheno, from near Bridgewater; found in caverns on the side of the Dromedary Mountain, near the Derwent.

Epsom salts (sulphate of magnesia), by Lieutenant Smith, R.N., from the Gordon River, where the formation is traceable nearly fifty miles.

Limestone, by Mr. J. Milligan, obtained near the Western Marshes, at a spot famous for very extensive caverns.

Limestone, by Mr. J. E. Bicheno, Mersey River.

Limestone, by Mr. H. Hull, from Mount Wellington Range, between Hobarton and Bridgewater.

Stones, etc., for Building, and for Personal Decoration, etc.

Hones for edged tools, from Mount Wellington and Constitution Hill, a sort of whet-slate, in common use amongst carpenters in Hobarton as an oil-stone for sharpening tools.

Marble, partially dressed, by Mr. W. Strutt, Bathurst Street, Hobarton, from Maria Island. From the great extent of the Maria Island limestone beds, and the variety of shells, encrinites, etc., enclosed, fine specimens of marble will be ultimately obtained thence.

Specimen of grey granite, by Mr. J. Milligan, from Flinder's Island, Bass's Strait, eastern side; granite prevails there on most of the islands. Also, from the east coast of Van Diemen's Land, abundant between the Scamander and George's River; a fine-grained, very hard and compact rock. And another specimen from Hampshire Hills, north-west quarter Van Diemen's Land Company's ground.

Porphyritic granite, by Mr. J. Milligan, from Wabb's Harbour, east coast of Van Diemen's Land. Garnets and schorl are met with in granite at this place.

Specimen of calcareous grit, by Sir W. Denison.

Iron-sand—a fine emery-like substance, by Mr. John Abbott; occurs in thin layers upon the sea shore at Long Bay, in D'Entrecasteaux Channel; a deposit from water passing through ironstone beds, percolating the soil, and depositing the metallic matter where it comes in contact with the salt water.

Wood opal, by Mr. J. Milligan, from Salt San Plains: occurs in fragments of various sizes, scattered upon the surface of the soil, over greenstone and sandstone.

Rock crystal (25 specimens) by Mr. J. Milligan. Found in angular pieces in the peaty soil over granite, and in rolled pieces, on the sea coast of Cape Barren and Flinder's Island, in Bass's Straits.

Beryl—aqua marine (20 specimens), by Mr. J. Milligan, varying from soft to very hard, and from blue to light green: in crystals and fragments more or less rounded and roughened, but having a brilliant lustre on the fracture.

Topaz—straw-coloured (30 specimens), by Mr. J. Milligan, from Flinder's Island and Bass's Straits, in crystals and fragments more or less worn, but possessing a high polish and great transparency: hard enough to cut glass.

Topaz—yellow (30 specimens), by Mr. J. Milligan, from the same locality. Crystals exhibit, more or less perfectly, the natural facets and angles, and possess, with a brilliant lustre, very considerable depth of tint.

Topaz—pink-coloured (30 specimens), by Mr. J. Milligan.

Cornelian, by Mr. George Kemp, from margin of Derwent, opposite Hobarton.

Jet, or lignite, by Mr. J. Milligan, from Macquarie Harbour. In the cliffs embedded with this is a fossil resin, of a rich amber colour, and agreeable perfume.

Specimen of greenstone, by Mr. J. Milligan, from Fingal, Van Diemen's Land, having dendritic forms upon it. This is a fair sample of the prevailing overlying rock of which all the roads are made and some houses and bridges are built.

VEGETABLE.—*Agricultural Produce.*

Box of apples, by Mr. James Dixon, Skelton Castle, Isis, Van Diemen's Land. More fruits are dried on the northern than the southern side of Van Diemen's Land; but the last two summers have been unfavourable, from the unusually low temperature.

Box of starch—the box made of figured Huon pine, by Mr. William Murray, Hobarton. There are now several starch manufactories in Hobarton, and the commodity is little, if at all, inferior to that from England.

Box of arrow-root, by Sir W. Denison, from Norfolk Island; has the reputation of being the finest arrow-root brought into Tasmania.

Box of maize, by Sir W. Denison, from same locality; a very fine sample.

Wheat—Farmer's Friend, a small bag weighing 63 lbs. gross; White Velvet, ditto, 116 lbs.; James's Essex, ditto, 60 lbs.; Golden Drop, ditto, 28 lbs.; White Kent, ditto, 23 lbs.; and Mother of Plenty, ditto, 42 lbs., by Sir William Denison, from Tasman's Peninsula; also White Lammas, 66 lbs., from Salt Water River, 1 bag marked G., and a bag of oats marked G., by Mr. G. Marshall, Noble Farm, Pittwater; Chidham wheat, by Sir William Denison; cask of velvet wheat, Mr. A. M'Naughten; cask White Lammas, 60 lbs. per bushel, by Mr. F. Lipscombe; cask of white Talavera, by Mr. M'Naughten; cask of wheat, by Mr. John Walker, Barrack Street

Hobarton, cask made of silver wattle, with hoops of young wattle; two casks of wheat, by Brown and Co., New Wharf: one made of Huon pine, hooped with black wattle (*Acacia Molissima*); and the other of blackwood, with hoops of black wattle.

Cask malt, by Mr. Edwin Tooth, Bagdad; cask made of blackwood staves and iron hoops. Small cask malt, by Mr. Patteson, Liverpool-street, Hobarton.

Cask pearl barley, by Mr. John Walker, Barrack Street, Hobarton; cask made of silver wattle and wattle hoops.

Cask of flour, by Mr. Henry Clayton, Wickford Steam Mills, Norfolk Plains. Cask of fine flour, by Mr. John Walker, Barrack Street, Hobarton; cask made of silver wattle, with hoops of young wattle. Three casks super-fine Van Diemen's Land flour, by Mr. M'Naughten.

Cask of biscuit, by Mr. A. M. Milligan, Launceston; sea biscuit, manu-factured in Launceston of Tasmanian flour. Cask of seaman's common biscuit, and another of ship's fine, by Mr. Brock, Macquarie Street, Hobar-ton. Mr. Brock supplies whalers and others to a large extent.

Tasmanian hops, by Mr. C. T. Smith.

Prepared groats, by Mr. Harpur, Launceston; in six tin canisters, much superior to the groats imported from England, and to be obtained for less than half the price.

Mylitta Australis, by Mr. Dunn, Davey Street. Obtained on the "Snug" estate, near North-West Bay, D'Entrecasteaux Channel, "Native Bread of Tasmania," grows under ground like the truffle in England, and, like it, has a peculiar smell; edible, having formed, in a half-roasted state, a portion of the diet of the aborigines. Has been tried with approval in soup and in puddings by Europeans. This specimen of Mr. Dunn's is unusually large, having weighed 14lbs. 2 oz. in 1846; it still weighs 10lbs. 10 oz. Another large specimen, by Mr. T. Y. Lowes, obtained near Glenorchy seventeen years ago.

Coffee, by Sir William Denison, from Norfolk Island.

Tanning Substances, Gums, Spices, and Miscellaneous.

Concentrated solution of Mimosa (wattle) bark, extracted by cold water, by Mr. Thomas Button, Launceston. Mr. Button considers that this solution is in a great measure free from colouring matter, and also from those principles which give a dark uneven character to leather, rendering it brittle, and depreciating it in the English market. Mimosa bark *(Acacia Mollisima)* ground, by Mr. Thomas Button, Launceston. Bark of the black wattle; this species of acacia is said to yield the best bark for tanning purposes.

Box of tobacco, in leaf, and box of cayenne pepper, by Sir W. Denison, from Norfolk Island. The box of cayenne pepper contains 190 lbs.; a sample of the finest quality and highest colour.

Tasmanian sassafras (bark of *Atherosperma Moschata*), by Mr. J. Milli-gan, from Oyster Cove. Small box of dried bark, used here medicinally, as a bitter and stomachic.

Gum and gum resin of the grass tree (*Xanthorrœa Australis*), by Mr. J. Milligan, from Flinder's Island. This gum resin, or balsam, is highly in-flammable, yielding on combustion a clear white flame and rich fragrant odour, said to be used in churches in place of frankincense; dyes calico a nankin colour; enters into the composition of some sealing-wax, and may be made the basis of a varnish; very abundant on many of the meagre soils of clay and sand in this and the neighbouring islands and continent.

Jams—Raspberry, currant, green and red gooseberry, and quince, by Lieutenant Smith, R.N.

Gum of *Acacia Mucronata*, by Mr. J. Milligan, from a shrubby tree on Flinder's Island, Bass's Straits.

Blood juice, by Sir W. Denison, from Norfolk Island, makes an indellible marking ink, and used as a dye for calico.

Gum kino, equal as a medicinal agent to the kino from the East Indies; manna, an exudation from the leaves and delicate succulent twigs of the white gum tree; resin of Oyster Bay pine, delicately white.

Flax; blue gum, equal to oak as a ship-building timber; stringy bark, forms, for the most part, a very large tree; black wood or light wood, a very hard, close-grained, dark, and richly-veined cabinet wood; sassafras, a soft, even, and cross-grained timber, well adapted for turnery; myrtle, a hard and very close-grained wood; musk wood, valuable for the purposes of the cabinet maker; cedar, or pencil pine of Tasmania; celery-topped pine, timber beautifully white; rosewood, or zebra-wood; he-oak; iron-wood; maple; timber of silver wattle; Huon pine, musk-wood, and myrtle-wood picture-frames; veneer of he-oak, the beef-wood of Van Diemen's Land; native cherry-tree, a small graceful tree, with lively green foliage;- honeysuckle tree, a low and often umbrageous, but stiff-looking tree, yielding a fancy wood for the cabinet maker; *Richea Pandanifolia;* pink-wood, attains an elevation of from one hundred to one hundred and fifty feet, with a good clear barrel; maple of Norfolk Island; blue gum tree; section of Norfolk Island pine; white-oak timber of Norfolk Island.

Cheese, preserved meats, honey, and one ham.

Neatsfoot, sheep's trotter, mutton-bird or sooty petrel, and shark's oil; bees'-wax of Tasmania.

Glue; swan's down; tallow; feathers of mutton bird, much used for pillows, bolsters, and mattresses; wool, the produce of sheep imported from England in 1837; *Thylacinus cyanocephalus,* the hyena or tiger of the colonists; *Ornithorynous parodoxus,* the platypus of colonists; goldbeater's skin; jaw of a sperm whale, with forty-eight teeth complete; parchment; ivory, eight teeth of sperm whale; whalebone; curled horsehair; whale-oil.

Gold-leaf; crockeryware; dripstone; marble.

Candlestick of iron-wood; snuff-box turned of iron-wood; cribbage-board, veneered on pine, inlaid with musk-wood, black-wood, oak, and pine; baskets, and model of water-pitcher, made by aborigines.

Models of canoes of aborigines; hall chair, of black-wood; small round table of Huon pine, with chess-board in centre; pier table, of black-wood; carriage-wheels; table of musk-wood; sideboard of black-wood; case containing top of star loo table of Huon pine and black-wood; ladies' work table of musk-wood; a gun-stock of black-wood; Huon pine table top; dog-wood table top; top of sofa table, inlaid with chess-board in the middle; line or small roap; best small roap; cable-laid lines; carpenters' bench screw; organ pipe of Huon pine, bored in the solid, with stops, etc.; musk-wood writing desk, inlaid with pine, black-wood, she-oak, and myrtle;

dressing-case, or work-box, of similar materials; small round table, Huon pine inlaid; thread-lace.

Model of a bridge across the Derwent at Bridgewater, constructed of Huon pine; coloured sectional elevation of the bridge and causeway at Bridgewater.

Case of leather containing different descriptions; mould candles; worsted work; roll of tweed; knitted woollen gloves; knitted shawls; portmanteau; gloves made of opossum fur; carriage rug; dressed kangaroo skins; blacking for shoes, equal to Warren's; book, printed and published in Van Diemen's Land; necklaces of shells, as worn by the aborigines; "Tasmanian Journal," 3 volumes, printed and published in Van Diemen's Land, gilt and lettered with gold leaf made in Hobarton from Californian gold.

[D 2.]

The following is an Extract from the Pamphlet containing a Detailed Account of all the Articles sent forward to the Paris Exhibition, 1855, being a List of the Contributors' Names and of their Contributions.

Abbott, John	Window-sill, freestone.
	Coal, anthracite.
	Piece of musk-wood.
	Bundle of broad palings.
	One-fourth section of blue gum-tree.
	Section of blue gum.
	Bundle of laths.
	Bundles of shingles.
	Music.
Allport, Mrs.	Chess-table with paintings, native flowers.
Belbin and Dowdell	Bundle of broad palings.
Best, H. & C.	Specimens of printing.
Bisdee, John	Package of wool.
Browne, Fielding	Norfolk Island iron-wood.
	Candlesticks of ditto.
Boyd, James	Marble.
	Two specimens of clay.
	Freestone.
	Specimens of native laurel.
	Ditto, pink-wood.
	Ditto, she-oak.
	Ditto, native cherry.
	Ditto, musk-wood.
	Ditto, myrtle.
	Ditto, booby-alla.
	Ditto, musk-wood.
	Ditto, bursaria.

Boyd, James............ .... Specimens of black-wood.
                                  Section of she-oak.
                                  Bundle of split wattle.
                                  Whip-handles.
                                  Bundle of green willows.
                                  Ditto, peeled.
                                  Specimen of pittosporum.
                                  Bundle of shingles.
                                  Kangaroo leather.
                                  Ditto, skins (2 varieties).
                                  Wombat ditto (2 varieties).
                                  Wattle bark.
                                  Sassafras ditto.
                                  Door scraper, iron.
                                  Barrow wheel, ditto.
                                  Jack crane, brass.
                                  Iron stand, ditto.
                                  Flowerpots and stands.
                                  Paving-tiles.
                                  Bricks.
                                  Hat of lightwood.
                                  Pair of shoes.
Burgess, Mrs. ....   Needlework (3 specimens).
Calder, J. E................ ....   Geological specimens (11 collections).
                                  Map of Tasmania.
Champ, Mrs. ....   Algæ Tasmanian.
Champ, W. T. N. ....   Seaweed, Slopen Island.
Chase, Mrs. ....   Plate, silver, first piece made in Van
                                      Diemen's Land.
Clifford, Samuel .... Case of Tasmanian birds.
                                  Writing-desk.
Cox, Francis...... .... Native alum.
                                  Collection of pebbles.
                                  Hippocampus, Seahorse.
                                  Phyllopteryx (var.)
                                  Cabinet of Tasmanian insects.
Crook, William .... Writing-desk.
Davies, Rowland.....................: Musk-rat skin.
D'Emden, L............................ Printing, specimens of.
Denison, Sir W. ....   Specimens of Tasmanian woods (2 cols.)
                                  Fern-tree, longitudinal section of.
                                  Ditto, section transverse.
                                  Coffee.
                                  Yellow-wood bark.
                                  Cherry-tree bark.
                                  Dripstones.
                                  Arrowroot.
                                  Bloodjuice.
                                  Cayenne pepper.
                                  Woollen tweeds.

Denison, Sir W.	New Zealand flax.
	Wooden tray.
	Billiard cues.
Dickenson & Hewatt.........	Merino wool.
	Platypus skin.
	Kangaroo leather.
	Wattle bark.
Dobson, F. S.	Specimens of Tasmanian woods.
	Manna.
	Pair of candlesticks, iron-wood.
Douglas River Coal Company ...	Coal.
Dry, Richard	Wheat.
Elliston, William Gore............	Chess-table.
Executive Committee	Marble.
	Dog-wood slab.
	Honeysuckle section.
	Black-wood plank.
	Loo-tables (two).
	Lady's work-tables (two).
	Carved work.
	Writing-desk.
	Lady's trinket box.
	Ditto work-box.
	Vase, dog-wood.
	Pair of candlesticks, Huon pine.
	Vases.
	Goblet, Norfolk Island pine.
	Frame of dog-wood.
	Gun-stocks.
	Pair of candlesticks, Norfolk Island pine.
	Book-case.
	Painting, View of Hobarton.
	Brushes.
Fereday, Rev. J......................	Specimen of pencil-wood.
	Ditto, zieria.
	Ditto, banksia.
	Ditto, iron-wood.
	Ditto, rock-oak.
	Scented wood of Tasmania.
	Section of booby alla.
	Specimen of turnery.
	„ „ alyxia.
	Algæ, Tasmanian, collection of.
	Carpenter's hand screw, cherry-tree.
	Candlestick, peppermint.
	„ musk.
Fogg, Miss S. A.	Drawings, water-colour.
Gardner, W. A.	Rug, Tasmanian furs.
Gibson, David	Wheat.
Goldsmith, Captain	Blue gum plank.

Gourlay, Captain	Fern-tree, pith of.
Grant, James	Gold, Tasmanian.
Hawkins, Captain J. S.............	Table, musk.
Hawkes, W. K.	Caterpillar plant.
Hall, C. W.	Specimens of woods.
	Ditto, sassafras.
	Ditto, white-wood.
	Printers' planers, etc.
	Sassafras bark.
	Sassafras leaves.
Haller, Mrs.	Fossil, bivalve shell.
	Lock of hair, aboriginal chief.
Hedberg, O. H.	Whale oil, black.
Henslowe, F. H.	Music.
Hood, R. L.	Woods, collection of specimens of.
	Picture-frames.
	Gold leaf, dentist's (2 specimens).
Hood, R. V.	Gun-stock, black-wood.
Hopkins, Henry	Wool (2 specimens).
Hughes, Mrs.	Skull and tusks, walrus.
	Teeth, sperm whale.
Hull, H. M.	Coal (2 specimens).
	Iron sand.
	Coal.
	Statistical tables.
Jennings, T. D.	Churn.
Kermode, R. Q.	Wool.
Kilburn, D. T...............	Calotype views, series of.
Lipscombe, F.	Jams and jellies.
Lipscombe, E.	Wines.
Lloyd, C. G. H.	Birds' skins.
	Gum, black wattle.
Lord, James.....	Stock whip.
Lowes, T. Y...............	Native bread.
	Wheat (seed).
M'Naughtan, Alexander	Musk-wood.
	Loo-table.
	Small round table.
	Writing-desk.
May, J. M...............	Loo-table.
Makeig, G. A.	Goblet and cup, Norfolk Island pine.
Morrison, Askin	Tusks of walrus.
Milligan, Joseph	Coal, bituminous.
	Geological specimens (2 collections).
	Fossil wood, etc.
	Pink-wood, she-oak, honeysuckle.
	Norfolk Island pine knot.
	Myrtle planks (two).
	Celery-topped pine (2 specimens).
	Oyster Bay pine.

Milligan, Joseph	Musk-wood plank.
	Native cherry ditto.
	Black-wood ditto.
	Iron-wood ditto.
	Section of Oyster Bay pine.
	Huon pine.
	Black-wood.
	Oyster Bay pine, slab.
	Waddies, aboriginal.
	Spears, ditto.
	Cattamarans model.
	Baskets, aboriginal.
	Resins.
	Guano.
	Shells, Tasmanian, collection of.
	Rug, opossum.
	Glue.
	Honey.
	Gum, grass-tree.
	Bees'-wax.
	Capsicum pods.
	Kino.
	Mutton bird oil.
	Gems, Tasmanian.
	Walking-stick.
	Muff, opossum.
	Swansdown.
Moses, Samuel......................	Sperm oil.
Murray, William	Candles, starch, vinegar.
Nicholas, Alfred	Dysodile.
	Frames, fancy woods.
Packer, Jun., F. A..................	Music.
Pescodd & Sim......................	Biscuits.
Pitt, William	Walking-stick.
Powell, William	Bench screw.
Proctor, William....................	She-oak plank.
Propsting, George	Algæ.
Ransome, Thomas	Chain of Huon pine, and box.
Rodd	Fossil-wood.
	Cranium, aborigine of Tasmania.
Rolwegan, George	Seeds of Norfolk Island pine.
	History of Tasmania.
Rout, William......................	Myrtle-wood and dog-wood.
	Musk-wood.
	Rug, opossum.
	White line.
	Huon pine table.
	Music-stand.
Seal, Charles	Platypus skins.
	Whalebone.

Seal, Charles	Sperm oil.
	Sunfish oil.
Seal, Mrs.	Teeth, sperm whale.
	Head matter.
Smith, Miss Julia	Music.
Smith, Arthur	Fossil-wood.
Stieglitz, F. L.	Coal.
	Rug, opossum.
	Portraits, aborigines.
Stieglitz, Mrs.	Gloves, opossum.
Stokell, W.	Musk duck.
Stoney, Capt. H. B.	Year in Tasmania.
	Music.
	Watchstand and box.
	Draughtsmen and model temple.
Strutt, George	Lady's work-table.
Strutt, William	Marble.
Stuart, A. T.	Wheat.
Tasmania, Lord Bishop of	Knot of Huon pine,—slice of ditto.
Turnbull, James	Hops.
Walker & Son	Wheat and flour.
Watchorn & Perkins	Candles and tallow.
Wilkinson, John	Fossil-wood.
Wilkinson, Mrs.	Muff and boa.
Wiseman, J.	Whips.
Wolff, C.	Huon pine slab.
	Ditto, honeysuckle.
	Ditto, myrtle-wood.
	Ditto, musk-wood.
	Black-wood.
	She-oak.
	Musk-wood.
	Huon pine planks.
	Table, myrtle.
Woolley, J. W.	Loo-table, myrtle.
Wright, Isaac	Oats.

[E]

ANNUAL RETURN OF SICK AND WOUNDED

In H.M. General Hospital, Hobarton, from 1st January to 31st December, 1853.

DISEASES.	Remained last.	Admitted during the period.	Total treated.	Discharged during the period.	Died ditto.	Remaining.
Febris Cont. Communis ...	4	55	59	157	...	2
„ Typhus	...	3	3	1	1	1
Scarlatina	...	13	13	11	1	1
Asthma	1	7	8	4	3	1
Catarrhus, Ac.	11	117	128	121	5	2
„ Chron.	5	24	29	26	1	2
Bronchitis	7	27	34	26	7	1
Pneumonia	7	34	41	24	15	2
Pleuritis...	1	15	16	11	3	2
Hæmoptysis	...	2	2	2	...	...
Phthisis Pulmon.	2	39	41	7	32	2
Hepatitis	1	15	16	13	2	1
Icterus	...	3	3	...	1	2
Obstipatio	...	15	15	15	...	..
Constipatio	...	2	2	2	...	...
Diarrhœa	2	44	46	38	7	1
Dysenteria	2	18	20	9	9	2
Dyspepsia	4	38	42	41	1	...
Colica	...	19	19	18	...	1
Cholera	...	2	2	2	...	...
Hæmatemesis	...	3	3	2	1	...
Cephalagia...	2	9	11	11	...	...
Apoplexia	...	8	8	4	4	...
Paralysis	2	35	37	21	12	4
Amentia...	1	15	16	16	...	...
Mania	1	19	20	18	2	...
Epilepsia	3	13	16	14	1	1
Trismus	...	1	1	...	1	...
Delirium Tremens...	...	21	21	12	6	3
Hemiphegia	...	2	2	2	...	...
Concussio Cerebri...	...	2	2	2	...	...
Tetanus	...	1	1	...	1	...
Anasarca	...	4	4	3	1	...
Ascites	1	7	8	2	5	1
Podagra...	...	1	1	...	...	1
Rheumatismus	16	101	117	108	2	7
Lumbago	...	4	4	4	...	...
Arthritis	1	1	2	2	...	...
Sciatica	1	1	2	2	...	...
Syphilis	8	46	54	50	...	4
Bubo	...	5	5	5	...	...
Condylomata	...	1	1	1	...	...

DISEASES.	Remained last.	Admitted during the period.	Total treated.	Discharged during the period.	Died ditto.	Remaining.
Gonorrhœa	1	9	10	9	...	1
Hernia Humoralis	1	10	11	11	...	...
Strictura Urethræ...	1	5	6	6	...	...
Paraphymosis	...	1	1	1	...	...
Phlegmon et Abescessus ...	9	85	94	88	1	5
Ulcus	9	82	91	75	2	14
Paronychia	...	4	4	3	...	1
Fractura	5	31	36	32	2	2
Vulnus Incis	1	20	21	17	3	1
„ Contus. ..., ...	3	7	10	8	...	2
„ Sclopit. (gun shot) ...	3	8	11	9	1	1
Contusio	4	38	42	38	1	3
Subluxatio	5	13	18	18	...	...
Luxatio	2	7	9	9	...	...
Ambustio	1	22	23	17	5	1
Cynanche Tonsillaris ...	2	14	16	16	...	...
„ Trachealis ...	...	2	2	2	...	...
Fistula in Perine	2	...	2	2	...	...
Erysipilas	...	8	8	7	1	...
Hæmorhois	...	3	3	3	...	...
Scrophula	1	8	9	7	1	1
Morbus Coxarius	2	5	7	5	2	...
„ Cordis	1	18	19	13	4	2
„ Spinalis	...	2	2	1	1	...
Scorbutus	1	4	4	3	1	...
Tumor	...	3	4	2	...	2
Amputatio	...	5	5	4	1	...
Caries...	...	3	3	3	...	...
Periostitis	...	1	1	1	...	...
Synovitis	...	1	1	1	...	...
Anthrax...	...	1	1	...	1	...
Odontalgia...	...	3	3	3	...	...
Pleurodynia	...	3	3	3	...	...
Pericarditis	1	1	2	1	1	...
Hydrarthrus	...	1	1	1	...	...
Hydrocele	...	3	3	3	...	...
Hernia Inguin	1	1	2	2	...	...
Nephritis	...	1	1	...	1	...
Necrosis...	...	2	2	2	...	...
Dysuria	...	5	5	5	...	...
Debilitas	...	20	20	18	2	...
Epistaxis	...	3	3	3	...	...
Aneurisma	...	1	1	...	1	...
Puncturæ	...	1	1	1	...	...
Œdema	...	2	2	2	...	...
Venucæ	1	...	1	1	...	...
Sphacelus	...	3	3	...	1	2
Observatio	3	11	14	14	...	...
Morbi Cutis	...	11	11	11	...	...
„ Oculorum	32	182	214	201	..	13

DISEASES.	Remained last.	Admitted during the period.	Total treated.	Discharged during the period.	Died ditto.	Remaining.
Peritonitis	...	1	1	...	1	...
Ebrietas	...	1	1	1	...	...
Hysteria...	...	1	1	1	...	...
Amenorrhœa	1	1	2	2	...	...
Leucorrhœa	...	1	1	1	...	...
Menorrhagia	1	3	4	4	...	...
Eneuresis	...	1	1	1	...	...
Abortio	...	2	2	2	...	...
Partus	..	1	1	1	...	...
Morbus Uteri	1	...	1	...	1	...
Carcinoma (Cancer)	2	3	5	2	3	...
Urticaria	...	1	1	1	...	...
Neuralgia	...	2	2	2	...	...
Total	181	1483	1664	1407	162	95

[F.]

MILITARY SETTLERS.

Agreeably to a notice in our paper, a meeting of gentlemen was held last night, at Webb's, Murray Street, to take into consideration the necessity of entering into some scheme so as to induce the large number of soldiers of the 99th regiment that may be likely to obtain their discharge, previous to the return of that regiment to England, to remain in this colony.

Thomas D. Chapman, Esq., Member for the City, being unanimously called to the chair, requested Captain Stoney, the Acting Secretary to the meeting, to state what the plan was he had in view relative to the formation of the town of Wyvenhoe.

Captain Stoney stated that, being aware of the likelihood of the speedy return to England of the regiment, and knowing the custom of the service in such cases to grant discharges to a large portion of the men, he had formed the plan of creating from them a community likely to form a highly respectable town in the colony. For this purpose he had made several trips through the country, seeking an eligible situation; and finally having, during the last month, explored the northern coast, he had carefully inspected the Government reserve township of Wyvenhoe, on the Emu, as affording peculiar advantages not met with elsewhere—such as the fertility of the soil, well watered and richly wooded with the most valuable timber—the salubrity of its climate and its location, so favourable for a produce market, both in reference to Launceston and Port Philip. He had, on his return a few days back, waited on the Governor, and stated to him his intentions. His Excellency having kindly entered into his scheme, had directed him to lay before him in Council such propositions as he deemed requisite for the formation of the town; but as no answer has yet been received relative to them, he would merely explain their purport, as being requests to secure a charter, small building allotments, and other privileges to the settlers. His object being to settle there himself, he would thus be enabled—from the tract of land he had applied for, and twenty suburban allotments, for which he had sent in application for purchase—to afford occupation and labour to the great mass of the settlers. That he had written to the inhabitants of the neighbouring town of Birnie, situated also in Emu Bay, to guarantee accommodation for at least one month after their arrival, and every other assistance in their power; but that, as such an undertaking was one of great difficulty, and likely to involve a considerable outlay, he had thrown himself upon the generosity of the public at large for their co-operation and assistance; that looking upon these men as a band of emigrants already on their shores, they would not allow them to leave for the neighbouring colony, which they were certain to a man to do unless some inducement was held out to retain them.

The Lord Bishop of Tasmania stated that he looked upon the matter with the greatest possible interest—that though eleven years' experience in the colony had shown to him that the disbanded soldier was not the best labourer, still it was hardly fair to look upon these men in the same light as the veteran pensioner; it was worthy, therefore, of much consideration, and a matter of much importance to the colony to locate those men. He looked upon it as two hundred families being about to be located under the supervision of one of their own officers in a situation which, from having visited, he could say, stood unrivalled in point of locality: fertility of soil, well wooded and watered, and without exception the most beautiful climate in the world, were advantages not to be overlooked. But still, without wishing to check or discourage the undertaking, he could not refrain from stating that he saw very many difficulties on the first outset,—such as the requisites for locating, the expenditure for provisions, comforts, etc., and the small lot of ground,—which seemed to him entirely inadequate as sufficient inducement to a settler. However, he was willing to grapple with those difficulties, and for himself individually would support the measure to the utmost of his interest and ability; that, however, he would propose that, previous to holding out inducements to those settlers, a written guarantee should be given by the neighbouring gentlemen for a certain and remunerative employment for these men. Nor would he leave anything undone, or that in after time any of the settlers could reproach him for holding out inducements which they were not able to perform. He would also remark that there were other advantages in the locality chosen by Captain Stoney, a flourishing town of three hundred inhabitants being in its immediate neighbourhood, with a resident Doctor, a Clergymen of much zeal and ability, and a school established, of which latter he would guarantee his services for the new colony.

The Vicar-General stated that he was ready to co-operate with and coincide in the views of His Lordship, and was prepared to find a pastor for his flock on the formation of the colony.

The Chairman, in addressing the meeting, stated that he concurred fully with His Lordship, and that he also did not consider that the inducements held out by Captain Stoney were sufficient to induce the men to become settlers; that, however, he considered it the duty of the community at large, and of the Government in particular, to hold out more inducements than those proposed.

It was then proposed by the Lord Bishop of Tasmania, and seconded by the Vicar-General, that this meeting, feeling the necessity of making some exertion to retain in the colony the soldiers of the 99th Regiment, now about to obtain their discharge, do request the Government to deal with them in every respect as with the pensioners sent from England.

Secondly,—It was proposed by J. D. Kilburn, Esq., and seconded by Charles Akers, Esq.,

That this meeting do now adjourn, to be convened again at an early day by Captain Stoney, after an answer has been received by the Colonial Secretary.

[G.]

LIST OF THE BIRDS OF TASMANIA.

BY THE REV. T. J. EWING, OF NEW TOWN.

RAPTORES.

1 Fam. FALCONIDÆ.

1. *Aquila*, Mœhring. *audax*, Latham. *A. fucosa*, Gould. Wedge-tailed eagle. Eagle-hawk of the colony.
2. *Pontœtus*, Kaup. *leucogaster*, Latham. *Ichthyætus leucogaster*, Gould. White-bellied sea-eagle.
3. *Pandion*, Savigny. *P. leucocephalus*, Gould. White-headed osprey. Fish-hawk of the colony.
4. *Falco*, Linnæus. *F. melanogenys*, Gould. Black-cheeked falcon. Blue hawk of New South Wales.
5. *Hypotriorchis*, Boie. *frontatus*, Gould. *Falco frontatus*, Gould. White-fronted falcon. Little falcon of the colony.
6. *Ieracidea*, Gould. *berigora*, Vigors and Horsf.
       ,,   *berigora*, Gould. Brown hawk.
7. *Astur*, Lacepede. *albus*, Shaw.
       ,,   *Novæ Hollandiæ*, Gould. White goshawk. White hawk of the colony.
8. *Accipiter*, Brisson. *approximans*, Vigors and Horsf. *Astur approximans*, Gould. Australian goshawk.
9. *Accipiter* Brisson. *torquatus*, Cuvier.
       ,,   *torquatus*, Gould. Collared sparrow-hawk. Sparrow-hawk of the colony.
10. *Circus*, Lacepede. *assimilis*, Jardine and Selby.
        ,,   *assimilis*, Gould. Allied harrier. Swamp hawk of the colony.

2 Fam. STRIGIDÆ.

11. *Strix*, Linnæus. *castanops*, Gould.
  „ *castanops*, Gould. Chestnut-faced owl.
12. „ Linnæus. *S. delicatulus*, Gould. Delicate owl.
13. *Athene*, Boie, *boobook*, Latham. *A. boobook*. Gould. Boobook, or
    brown owl of the colony.
14. „ *maculata*, Vigors and Horsf.
  „   „ Gould. Spotted owl.

INCESSORES.

FISSIROSTRES. 3 Fam. CAPRIMULGIDÆ.

15. *Ægotheles*, Vigors and Horsf. *Novæ Hollandiæ*, Latham.
  „ *Novæ Hollandiæ*, Gould. Owlet night jar.
16. *Podargus*, Cuvier. *cinereus*, Vieillot.
  „ *Cuvieri*, Gould. More-pork of the colony.

4 Fam. HIRUNDINIDÆ.

17. *Acanthylis*, Boie. *caudacuta*, Latham.
  „ *caudacuta*, Gould. Australian spine-tailed swallow.
18. *Hirundo*, Linnæus. *H. neoxena*, Gould. Welcome-swallow.
19. „ Linnæus. *nigricans*, Vieillot. *Chelidon arborea*, Gould.
  Free-martin.

5 Fam. ALCEDENIDÆ.

20. *Alcyone*, Swainson. *azurea*, Latham.
  „ *diemenensis*, Gould. King-fisher of Tasmania.

TENUIROSTRES. 6 Fam. MELIPHAGIDÆ.

21. *Meliphaga*, Lewin. *Novæ Hollandiæ*, Vigors and Horsf.
  „ Lewin. *Novæ Hollandiæ*, Gould. New Holland honey-
   eater.
22. *Meliphaga*, Lewin. *Australasiana*, Shaw.
  „ *Australasiana*, Gould. Tasmanian honey-eater.
23. *Glyciphila*, Swainson. *melanops*, Latham. *G. fulvifrons*, Gould.
  Fulvous fronted honey-eater.
24. *Ptilotis*. Swainson. *P. flavigula*, Gould. Yellow-throated honey-eater.
25. *Anthochæra*, Vigors and Horsf. *inauris*, Gould.
  „ *inauris*, Gould. Wattled honey-eater. Wattle-bird of
   Tasmania.
26. *Anthochæra*, Vigors and Horsf. *mellivora*, Latham.
  „ *mellivora*, Gould. Brush wattle-bird.
27. *Acanthorhynchus dubius*, Gould. Slender-billed spine-bill.
28. *Melithreptus*, Vieillot. *agilis*, Latham.
  „ *melanocephalus*, Gould. Black-headed honey-eater.
29. *Melithreptus*, Vieillot. *virescens*, Wagler.
  „ *validirostris*, Gould. Strong-billed honey-eater.
30. *Myzanthe*, Vigors and Horsf. *garrula*, Latham.
  „ *garrula*, Gould. Garrulous honey-eater. Miner of Tasmania.

DENTIROSTRES. 7 Fam. LUSCINIDÆ.

81. *Malurus*, Vieillot. *M. longicaudus*, Gould. Blue-headed wren of Tasmania.
82. *Stipiturus*, Lesson. *malachurus*, Latham.
   „ *malachurus*, Gould. Emu wren of Tasmania.
83. *Sphenœacus gramineus*, Gould. Grass-loving sphenœacus.
84. *Calamanthus*, Gould. *fuliginosus*, Vigors and Horsf.
   „ *fuliginosus*, Gould. Striated reed-lark.
85. *Anthus*, Bechstein, *Australis*. Vigors and Horsf.
   „ *Australis*, Gould. Australian pipit.
86. *Sericornis humilis*, Gould. Sombre-coloured sericornis.
87. *Acanthiza*, Vigors and Horsf. *A. Diemenensis*, Gould. Tasmanian Acanthiza. Brown-tail of the colony.
88. „ Vigors and Horsf. *A. Ewingii*, Gould. Ewing's acanthiza.
89. „ Vigors and Horsf. *chrysorrœa*, Qu. and Gai. *chrysorrhœa*, Gould. Yellow-tailed acanthiza. Yellow-tail of the colony.
40. *Zosterops*, Vigors and Horsf. *lateralis*, Latham.
   „ *dorsalis*, Gould. Grey-backed Zosterops. White-eye of the colony.
41. *Epthianura*, Gould. Albifrons, Jardine and Selby.
   „ *albifrons*, Gould. White-fronted epthianura.
42. *Petroica*, Swainson. *rhodinogaster*, Drapier. *Erythrodryas rhodinogaster*, Gould. Pink-breasted wood-robin.
43. „ Swainson. *multicolor*, Gmelin. *multicolor*, Gould. Scarlet-breasted robin.
44. „ Swainson. *phœnicia*, Gould. Flame-breasted robin.
45. „ Swainson. *fusca*, Gould. Dusky robin.

INSESSORES.

DENTIROSTRES. 8 Fam. MUSCICAPIDÆ.

46. *Myiagra*, Vigors and Horsf. *M. nitada*, Gould. Shining-flycatcher "Satin sparrow" of Tasmania.
47. *Rhipidura*, Vigors and Horsf. *R. albiscapa*, Gould. White-shafted fantail.

9 Fam. TURDIDÆ.

48. *Oreocincla lanulata*, Gould. Mountain thrush.
49. *Cinclosoma punctatum*, Vigors and Horsf.
   „ „ Gould. Spotted ground thrush.

11 Fam. LANIIDÆ.

50. *Colluricincla*, Vigors and Horsf. *rectirostris*, Jardine and Selby.
   „ *Selbii*, Gould. Whistling Dick of the colonists.
51. *Cracticus*, Vieillot. *C. cinereus*, Gould.

CONIROSTRES. 12 Fam. CORVIDÆ.

52. *Gymnorhina*, G. R. Gray. *C. organicum*, Gould. Tasmanian crow-shrike.

53. *Strepera*, Lesson. *S. arguta*, Gould. Hill crow-shrike.
54. ,, Lesson. *fuliginosa*, Gould. Black magpie of the colony.
55. *Corvus*, Linnæus. *Australis*, Latham.
,, *coronoides*, Gould. White-eyed crow.

13 Fam. FRINGILLIDÆ.

56. *Estrelda*, Swainson. *bella*, Latham.
,, *bella*, Gould. Fire-tail finch. "Fire-tail" of Tasmania.

DENTIROSTRES. 10 Fam. AMPELIDÆ.

57. *Graucalus*, Vigors and Horsf. *melanops*, Latham.
,, *parvirostris*, Gould. "Blue Pigeon" of the colony.
58. *Pachycephala*, Swainson. *olivacea*, Vigors and Horsf.
,, *olivacea*, Gould. Olivaceous thick-head.
59. ,, Swainson. *glaucura*, Gould. Grey-tailed thick-head.
60. *Pardalotus*, Vieillot. *P. affinis*, Gould. Allied pardalote.
61. ,, Vieillot. *punctatus*, Latham.
,, Vieillot. *punctatus*, Gould. Spotted pardalote. "Diamond bird" of colonists.
62. ,, Vieillot. *quadragintus*, Gould. "Forty-spot" of Tasmania
63. *Artamus*, Vieillot. *sordidus*, Latham.
,, *sordidus*, Gould. Wood swallow.

SCANSORES. 14 Fam. PSITTACIDÆ.

64. *Cacatua*, Brisson. *galerita*, Latham.
,, *galerita*, Gould. Crested cockatoo. White cockatoo of Tasmania.
65. *Callocephalon*, Lesson. *galleatum*, Latham.
,, *galleatum*, Gould. Grey cockatoo.
66. *Calyptorhyncus*, Vigors. *C. xanthonotus*, Gould. Black cockatoo.
67. *Platycercus*, Vigors and Horsf. *eximius*, Shaw.
,, *eximius*, Gould. Ross-hill parrakeet.
68. ,, Vigors and Horsf. *caledonicus*, Gmelin.
,, *flaviventris*, Gould. Yellow-bellied parrakeet.
69. *Euphema*, Wagler. *chrysostome*, Kuhl.
,, *chrysostome*, Gould. Blue-banded grass parrakeet.
70. ,, Wagler. *aurantia*, Gould. Orange-bellied grass parrakeet.
71. *Lathamus*, Lesson. *discolor*, Shaw.
,, *discolor*, Gould. Swift lorikeet. "Swift parrakeet" of Tasmania.
72. *Pezoporus*, Illiger. *formosus*, Latham.
,, *formosus*, Gould. Ground parrakeet.
73. *Trichoglossus*, Vigors and Horsf. *Swainsonii*, Jardine and Selby.
,, *Swainsonii*, Gould. Swainson's lorikeet. Blue-bellied parrakeet.
74. ,, Vigors and Horsf. *Australis*, Latham.
,, *concinnus*, Gould. Musk parrakeet.
75. ,, Vigors and Horsf. *pusillus*, Shaw.
,, *pusillus*, Gould. Small parrakeet.

15 Fam. CUCULIDÆ.

76. *Chrysococcyx*, Boie. *lucidus*, ———
     „   *lucidus*, Gould. Shining cuckoo.
77. *Cuculus*, Linnæus. *flabelliformis*, Latham.
     „   Linnæus. *cineraceus*, Gould. Ash-coloured, or lesser cuckoo.
78.   „   Linnæus. *inornatus*, Vigors and Horsf.
     „   Linnæus. *inornatus*, Gould. Greater cuckoo.

RASORES.

16 Fam. COLUMBIDÆ.

79. *Lopholaimus*, G. R. Gray. *L. antarcticus*, Gould. Top-knot pigeon of New South Wales.
80. *Phaps*, Selby. *chalcoptera*, Latham. *Peristera chalcoptera*, Gould. Bronze-winged pigeon.
81.   „   Selby. *elegans*, Temminck.
     „   Selby. *elegans*, Gould. Brush bronze-winged pigeon.

17 Fam. TETRAONIDÆ.

82. *Coturnix*, Mœhring. *C. Pectoralis*, Gould. Stubble-quail of Tasmania·
83. *Synoicus*, Gould. *Australis*, Latham.
     „   *Australis*, Gould. Australian partridge. Brown quail.
84.   „   *diemenensis*, Gould. Greater brown quail.
85. *Turnix*, Bonnaterre. *varia*, Latham. *Hemipodius varius*, Gould. Painted quail.

18 Fam. STRUTHONIDÆ.

86. *Dromaius*, Vieillot. *Novæ Hollandiæ*, Latham.
     „   *Novæ Hollandiæ*, Gould. Emu.

GRALLATORES.

19 Fam. CHARADRIDÆ.

87. *Hæmatopus*, Linnæus. *H. fuliginosus*, Gould. Sooty oyster-catcher.
88.   „   Linnæus. *longirostris*, Vieillot.
     „   Linnæus. *longirostris*, Gould. White-breasted oyster-catcher.
89. *Lobivanellus*, Strickland. *lobatus*, Latham.
     „   *lobatus*, Gould. Wattled pewit.
90. *Sarciophorus*, Strickland. *tricolor*, Vieillot.
     „   *pectoralis*, Gould. Black-breasted pewit.
91. *Charadrius*, Linnæus. *xanthocheilus*, Wagler.
     „   *xanthocheilus*, Gould. Golden plover of Australia.
92. *Hiaticula*, G. R. Gray. *bicincta*, Jardine and Selby.
     „   *bicincta*, Gould. Double-banded dottrel.
93.   „   G. R. Gray. *monacha*, Geoffroy.
     „   *monacha*, Gould. Hooded dottrel.
94.   „   G. R. Gray. *ruficapilla*, Temminck.
     „   *ruficapilla*, Gould. Red-capped dottrel. Sandlark. Red-necked plover.

20 Fam. SCOLOPACIDÆ.

95. *Himantopus*, Brisson. *leucocephalus*.
  „ *leucocephalus*, Gould. White-headed stilt.
96. *Recurvirostra*, Linnæus. *rubricollis*, Temminck.
  „ *rubricollis*, Gould. Red necked avocet.
97. *Cladorhynchus*, G. R. Gray. *pectoralis*, Dubois.
  „ *pectoralis*, Gould. Banded stilt.
98. *Limosa*, Brisson. *L. uropygialis*, Gould. Barred-rumped godwit.
99. *Schœniclus*, ————. *Australis*, Jardine and Selby.
  „ *Australis*, Gould. Australian tringa.
100. „ ————. *albescens*, Temminck.
  „ *albescens*, Gould. Land snipe. Little sand-piper.
101. „ ————. *subarquata*, ————.
  „ *subarquata*, Gould. Curlew. Sand-piper.
102. *Glottis*, Nilson. *glottoides*, Vigors.
  „ *glottoides*, Gould. Australian greenshank.
103. *Strepsilas*, Illiger. *interpres*, Linnæus.
  „ *interpres*, Gould. Turnstone.
104. *Scolopax*, Linnæus. *Australis*, Latham.
  „ *Australis*, Gould. Australian snipe.
105. *Numenius*, Mœhring. *N. Australis*, Gould. Australian curlew.
106. „ Mœhring. *N. uropygialis*, Gould. Australian whimbrel.

21 Fam. ARDEIDÆ.

107. *Ardea*, Linnæus. *Novæ Hollandiæ*, Latham.
  „ *Novæ Hollandiæ*, Gould. White-fronted heron. Blue crane of the colonists.
108. *Herodias*, Boie. *H. syrmatophorus*, Gould. Australian egret.
109. *Nycticorax*, Stephens. *Caledonicus*, Latham.
  „ *Caledonicus*, Gould. Nankin night-heron. Nankin-bird of the colonists.
110. *Botaurus*, Stephens. *B. Australis*, Gould. Australian bittern.

22 Fam. RALLIDÆ.

111. *Porphyrio*, Brisson. *melanotus*, Temminck.
  „ *melanotus*, Gould. Black-backed porphyrio. Black-backed gallinule.
112. *Tribonyx*, Dubois. *mortieri*, Dubois.
  „ *mortieri*, Gould. Native hen of the colonists,
113. *Fulica*, Linnæus. *F. Australis*, Gould. Australian coot.
114. *Rallus*, Linnæus. *pectoralis*, Cuvier.
  „ *pectoralis*, Gould. Land-rail of the colony.
115. „ Linnæus. *Lewinii*, Swainson.
  „ *Lewinii*, Gould. Lewin's water-rail.
116. *Ortygometra*, Linnæus. *immaculata*, Swainson. *Porzana immaculata*, Gould. Spotless gallinule. Little swamp-hen of the colonists.
117. „ Linnæus. *O. fluminea*, Gould. Spotted water-crake.
118. „ Linnæus. *O. palustris*, Gould. Water-crake.

NATATORES.

23 Fam. ANATIDÆ.

119. *Cereopsis*, Latham. *Novæ Hollandiæ*, Latham.
      " *Hollandiæ*, Gould. Cape Barren goose.
120. *Cygnus*, Linnæus. *atratus*, Latham.
      " *atratus*, Gould. Black swan.
121. *Casarca*, Bonaparte. *tadornoides*, Jardine and Selby.
      " *tadornoides*, Gould. Chestnut-coloured shieldrake. Mountain duck.
122. *Anas*, Linnæus. *superciliosa*, Gmelin.
      " *superciliosa*, Gould. Australian wild duck. Black duck.
123. *Mareca*, Stephens. *punctata*, Cuvier. *Anas punctata*, Gould. Chestnut-breasted duck.
124. *Spatula*, Boie. *rhyncotis*, Latham.
      " *rhyncotis*, Gould. Australian shoveller. Shovel-nosed duck of Tasmania.
125. *Malacorhynchus*, Swainson. *membranaceus*, Latham.
                   membranaceus, Gould. Pink-eyed duck.
126. *Biziura*, Leach. *lobata*, Shaw.
      " *lobata*, Gould. Musk duck.
127. *Nyroca*, Leach. *N. Australis*, Gould. White-eyed duck.

24 Fam. LARIDÆ.

128. *Larus*, Linnæus. *Pacificus*, Latham.
      " *Pacificus*, Gould. Pacific gull. Large gull of the colonists.
129. *Xema*, Leach. *Novæ Hollandiæ*, Stephens.
      " *Jamesonii*, Gould. Little gull of the colony.
130. *Stercorareus*, Brisson. *antarcticus*, Lesson. *Lestris catarractes*, Gould. Skua gull.
131. *Sylochelidon*, Brehm. *S. strenuus*, Gould. Powerful tern.
132. *Thalasseus*, Boie. *T. poliocercus*, Gould. Bass's Strait's tern.
133. *Gelochelidon*, Brehm. *G. macrotarsus*, Gould.
134. *Sterna*, Linnæus. *S. melanorhynca* and *velox*, Gould. Black-billed tern.
135. *Sternula*, Boie. *S. Nereis*, Gould. Australian little tern.

25 Fam. PROCELLARIDÆ.

136. *Diomedea*, Linnæus. *exulans*, Linnæus.
      " *exulans*, Gould. Wandering albatross.
137.   " Linnæus. *D. cauta*, Gould. Cautious albatross.
138.   " Linnæus. *D. culminata*, Gould. Culminated albatross.
139.   " Linnæus. *chlororhychus*, Latham.
      " *chlororhychus*, Gould. Yellow-billed albatross.
140.   " Linnæus. *melanophrys*, Temminck.
      " *melanophrys*, Gould. Black-eyebrowed albatross.
141.   " Linnæus. *fuliginosa*, Gmelin.
      " *fuliginosa*, Gould. Sooty albatross.
142. *Procellaria*, Linnæus. *gigantea*, Gmelin.
      " *gigantea*, Gould. Giant petrel.

143. *Procellaria*, Linnæus. *P. conspicillata*, Gould. Spectacled petrel.
144. „ Linnæus. *hasitata*, Kuhl.
 „ *hasitata*, Gould. Great grey petrel.
145. „ Linnæus. *P. Solandri*, Gould. Solander's petrel.
146. „ Linnæus. *glacialoides*, A. Smith.
 „ *glacialoides*, Gould. Silvery grey petrel.
147. „ Linnæus. *Lessonii*, Garnot.
 „ *Lessonii*, Gould. White-headed petrel.
148. „ Linnæus. *Cookii*, G. R. Gray.
 „ *cookii*, Gould. Cook's petrel.
149. „ Linnæus. *cærulea*, Gmelin.
 „ *cærulea*, Gould. Blue petrel.
150. „ Linnæus. *capensis*, Linnæus.
 „ *Daption capensis*, Gould. Cape petrel. Cape pigeon.
151. *Prion*, Lacepède. *turtur*, Banks.
 „ *turtur*, Gould. Dove-like prion.
152. „ Lacepède. *vittatus*, Forster.
 „ *vittatus*, Gould. Broad-billed prion.
153. „ Lacepède. *Banksii*, A. Smith.
 „ *Banksii*, Gould.
154. *Puffinus*, Brisson. *brevicaudus*, Brande.
 „ *brevicaudus*, Gould. Short-tailed petrel.
155. *Pelecanoides*, Lacepède. *urinatrix*, Gmelin. *Puffinuria urinatrix*,
 Gould. Diving petrel.
156. *Thalassidroma*, Vigors. *T. melanogaster*, Gould. Black-bellied storm
 petrel.
157. „ Vigors. *T. leucogaster*, Gould. White-bellied storm
 petrel.
158. „ Vigors. *T. nereis*, Gould. Grey-backed storm petrel.
159. „ Vigors. *T. Wilsonii*. Bonaparte.
 „ *Wilsonii*, Gould. Wilson's storm petrel.

26 Fam. PELICANIDÆ.

160. *Phalacrocorax*, Brisson. *P. carboides*, Gould. Australian cormorant
 Black shag.
161. „ Brisson. *P. leucogaster*, Gould. White-breasted cormorant.
162. „ *melanoleucus*, Vieillot.
 „ *melanoleucus*, Gould. Pied cormorant.
163. *Pelecanus*, Linnæus. *conspicillatus*, Temminck.
 „ *conspicillatus*, Gould. Australian pelican.
164. *Sula*, Brisson. *Terrator*, Banks.
 „ *Australis*, Gould. Australian gannet.

27 Fam. COLYMBIDÆ.

165. *Podiceps*, Latham. *P. Australis*, Gould. Australian tippet grebe.
 Diver of colonists.
166. „ Latham. *poliocephalus*, Jardine and Selby.
 „ *poliocephalus*, Gould. Hoary-headed grebe. Dab chick.

28 Fam. ALCIDÆ.

167. *Eudyptes,* ———. *chrysocome,* Forster.
    „   *chrysocome,* Gould. Crested penguin.
168. *Spheniscus,* Brisson. *minor,* Forster.
    „   *minor,* Gould. Little penguin.
169.   „   Brisson. *S. undina,* Gould. Fairy penguin.

RECAPITULATION.

	FAM.	GENERA.	SPECIES.
RAPTORES	2	11	14
Fissirostres	3	5	6
Tenuirostres	1	7	10
INSESSORES—Dentirostres	5	20	28
Conirostres	2	4	5
Scansores	2	10	15
RASORES	3	6	8
GRALLATORES	4	22	32
NATATORES	6	29	51
Total	28	114	169

FOURTEEN DAY USE

RETURN TO DESK FROM WHICH BORROWED

This book is due on the last date stamped below, or
on the date to which renewed.
Renewed books are subject to immediate recall.

29Mar55	
MAR 2 9 1955 LU	
31May'64SB	
REC'D LD	
MAY 28'64 -12 M	
DeL RECEIVED	
DEC 13 '66 -8 AM	
LOAN DEPT.	